A Word About Recipe Donors

In this age of 17,000-mile-an-hour satellites, many wonderful people in the California wine industry still take time to put together taste treats that would have brought ecstasy to Epicurus himself— the founder of the Epicurean movement.

To bring you recipes that would qualify as Epicurean, we appealed to the winemakers of California, their wives and those associated with them in wine production, promotion, sales and research.

We asked them to send in those recipes for wine cookery that they, their families and friends found so delightful as to be worthy of preparation over and over again.

The experience and discriminating taste of flavor-conscious cooks will be detected in both the simple and complicated recipes that make up this unusual Epicurean collection to which they contributed.

They also shared with us one or more specific choices of wines to accompany each main dish as a table beverage. Following their selections will prove what every vintner knows—that wine-cooked foods accompanied by compatible and complementary vinous beverages can change an ordinary dinner into a banquet and an ordinary banquet into a feast.

We know from our previous books, *Favorite Recipes of California Winemakers* and *Adventures in Wine Cookery by California Winemakers* that our contributors receive many complimentary letters from those who read and use their recipes.

To the warm, friendly appreciation that most likely will be forthcoming from readers, let us add our sincere thanks to California winemakers, their friends and associates for sending us the recipes that made this book possible.

Donna Bottrell
THE WINE APPRECIATION GUILD
1377 Ninth Avenue
San Francisco, California 94122

Other books published by
THE WINE APPRECIATION GUILD

Favorite Recipes of California Winemakers
Adventures in Wine Cookery by California Winemakers
Gourmet Wine Cookery the Easy Way
Wine Cookbook of Dinner Menues
Easy Recipes of California Winemakers

Epicurean Recipes
of California Winemakers

by Wine Advisory Board

EDITOR: David R. Wilcox
FOOD EDITOR: Marjorie L. Lumm
BOOK DESIGN AND ILLUSTRATIONS: Nancy J. Kennedy
COVER ART: Francis Redman
FOOD CONSULTANT: Dorothy Canet

Copyright © 1978 The Wine Appreciation Guild
San Francisco California
ALL RIGHTS RESERVED
ISBN 0-932664-00-8
Printed in U.S.A.
Library of Congress Card No. 79-89806

Wine and Food for Epicures
...a matter of taste

by Marjorie L. Lumm

There are a number of definitions of "Epicurean." We like the one which says "... suited to an Epicure," along with the definition of an Epicure as "... one with discriminating tastes in food and wine." This is the sense in which Epicurean is used in this book.

The word Epicurean came from Epicurus, a Greek philosopher who lived and taught in the vicinity of Athens in the third century, B.C. The school he established was set in a garden. There he lived with his pupils. The society which he gathered around him included women as well as men, a circumstance which occasioned some scandalous legends.

History records his unsurpassed kindness to all, and the simplicity which characterized the regimen of his school.

The philosophic outlook of Epicurus was fundamentally ethical. Even his interest in physics was to obtain a theory of life which "shall insure quietude of mind and a steadfast faith." He taught that a right conception of pleasure itself induces to right living, because it is not possible to live pleasantly without living wisely and well and righteously.

Thus the appreciation of foods and wines which we term "Epicurean" and regard as very much a part of today's scene, is actually as old as written history. Since the days of Epicurus, Epicurean wining and dining has fallen and risen often through many cultural changes—climbing when times were good, when man had leisure and means, and falling when there were wars or hardships. In the past this art has oftentimes been limited to the few who had the means and the time to devote to it.

Now our affluent society is fostering a more extensive interest in foods and wine than at any other period of history. A much larger segment of the population of America now has the interest and the time to practice the art of good living. The enjoyment of food and wine need be limited only by our knowledge and our taste.

"Epicurean" connotes validity—the honest use of honest products, and a feeling for the harmony of wines and foods. These are cultivated tastes. This is knowledge pleasantly come by through experience. The recipes in this book and the suggestions for matching them with wines are guides to enjoyment and the good life.

Modern agriculture and our fast distribution systems make the finest products of the world easily available to us in one convenient form or another. It takes the discernment of an Epicure more than a generous purse to choose the freshest vegetables, the quality and cut of meat best suited to the occasion, and the wines to complement them.

The practice of the art of good living means giving the same attention to our daily food and drink that we would give to a company meal. Selecting the foods and wines is the first step. Preparing them for the table is the next. Both are equally important. Both benefit from experience. Sometimes the best combination of ingredients, the most skillful method of putting them together, the most suitable equipment and cooking methods come after doing a recipe several times. And once the food is perfect, there is the art of presenting it most attractively.

From start to finish, it's a fascinating process, with continuing opportunities for change and improvement.

Table of Contents

A Word About Recipe Donors	2
Wine and Food for Epicures... A matter of taste	4
The ABC's of Vintage Years	6
How to Read a Wine Label	7
California Wines (chart)	8
Wine Accessories	10
Wine as a Food	12

Recipes

Main Dishes	13
Meats	15
Poultry	33
Fish and Shellfish	45
Specialty Main Dishes	55
Accompaniments to Main Dishes	59
Vegetables	61
Soups and Salads	67
Hors d'Oeuvres and Beverages	71
Hors d'Oeuvres	73
Beverages	79
Desserts	81
A Cellar in Your Home	92
Kitchen Notes	94
Index of Recipes in this book by Category	95
Alphabetical Index of Recipes in This Book	96
Comprehensive Index of All Recipes in the Series of Six Wine Advisory Board Cookbooks	97

The ABC's of VINTAGE YEARS

The question comes up now and then: Does California have vintage years, or doesn't it? The answer, as all good answers must be, is yes and no.

A grapevine is a fussy plant. It reacts to minor changes in its environment. Each new season, in California or anywhere else, each vine produces a different grape than it did the year before. And, since a wine depends in large part on the grapes that go into it, there are inevitable differences in the wines from each year to the next.

The thing about California is that its winemakers expect a vintage every year—year in and year out. They differ from their European counterparts in this. Some years (1968, for one) European vintners endure vintages they would just as soon forget. It is this which has aroused the mystique of the vintage.

In its broadest definition, a vintage year is one which produces ripe grapes. There is an absolute relationship between the amount of natural sugar in the grape and the level of alcohol that fermentation will produce from it. A wine too low in alcohol, from a "poor" vintage, will not amount to much. This calamity does not befall California's vintners. When it happens to other vintners, they are apt to add non-grape sugar during fermentation to increase the alcohol to a normal level.

In narrow definitions, vintage years depend on more subtle details in the grape's development—color intensity, sugar-acid ratios, and other technical considerations. These minor variations produce varying characteristics. The Cabernet Sauvignon from a cool year, say, is likely to produce a powerful, long-lived wine that takes some time to reach its best. The same grape in a warmer year will yield a wine that will be soft and agreeable much sooner after the harvest.

The winemaker can choose between two basic alternatives in these aspects of a vintage year. He can elect to make a "vintage" wine—which in California means it is made entirely from the grapes of a single harvest and labelled as being of that year. Or he can blend in some wines of two or three years earlier to smooth out differences and so offer wine that is much the same year after year, no matter how capricious the summer sun. Happily, there are different winemakers who choose to do each (and sometimes both). This offers the Epicure a greater range of wines to choose among, and assures him of wines ready for drinking now, and after five or more years of patient waiting.

Vintages apply almost exclusively to table wines. Dessert wines—with the rare exception of some Ports and sparkling wines—usually are blended from several different vintages in order to have both new and aged flavors contribute to the character of these elixirs.

How to Read a Wine Label

One of the joys in creating an Epicurean meal is selecting the wines. This takes some time and thought, just as menu-planning does. But perfect pairings of wines and foods are basic to truly memorable meals.

Wine selection is easier when the art of label-reading is well in hand. This is uncomplicated business in the case of California wines.

All California wine labels state the origin of the bottle contents prominently. The word "California" itself tells a lot about the wine. It automatically guarantees that every drop in the bottle was made from the juice of pure, fresh grapes grown and fermented in California. No water added. No sugar. No other non-grape substance of any kind.

The only exceptions are sparkling and special natural flavored wines, including Vermouth. A bit of sugar or sugar-syrup may be added to promote second fermentation (the one which puts the bubbles in sparkling wines) and to control the sweetness. With flavored wines, sugar may be added, as well as citrus, coffee, or other special natural essences that give the wine its particular character. Otherwise, only the grapes themselves provide the sweetness and alcohol present in California wines.

As for more definitive vineyard locations, a California bottle naming "Fair Valley" on the label must contain at least 75% of wine grown in that valley. In the same way, at least 75% of a wine labeled "Mountain" red or white must come from grapes grown in mountainous regions or on hillsides.

The winery name on a California label may be preceded by the words "Produced and Bottled By" or "Made and Bottled By." "Produced" means that at least 75% of the wine was crushed, fermented, and finished by the bottler. "Made" means that generally 10% of the wine was made by the bottler. In either case, the vintner considered the wine worthy of his name and representative of his skill.

If a California wine has a varietal name—Cabernet Sauvignon, Pinot Blanc, etc.—at least 51% of the wine must be made from the grape variety named on the label. (The figure is usually much higher, frequently 100% of the variety.) The wine must also display the predominant taste, aroma, and characteristics of that grape variety.

A generic designation like Claret, Burgundy, Sherry, Rhine wine, Chablis, Sauterne, Chianti, or Rosé is more general. This kind of labeling describes a California wine type in broad terms varying from vintner to vintner.

Some California labels show vintage dates. When this happens, all of the grapes used in the wine were harvested and crushed during the year named.

Alcoholic content is also shown on California wine labels in percentage by volume. In appetizer and dessert wines, the alcoholic content ranges from 19.5 to 21 percent; except Vermouths and special natural wines may be lower. Table wines contain an alcoholic content varying from 10% to 14% by volume—the percentage is always shown on the label.

CALIFORNIA TABLE
(Also known...

GENERICS

Generics are named for districts which originally produced wines with similar characteristics.

WHITE WINES

Most preferred chilled with fish, shellfish, poultry. Usual serving—4 ounces.
Light, medium dry white wines, ranging in color from pale golden to slightly green-gold.

Rhine Wine   **White Chianti**

Rich, distinctive whites with full flavor and a pale or light gold color. These wines are dry, often fruity.

Chablis   **Dry Sauterne**   **Mountain White**

Medium sweet to quite sweet wines. Especially good with desserts, fruits, fruit salad, and other sweet foods.

Haut Sauterne   **Sweet Sauterne**
Light Muscat   **"Chateau" White Wines**

ROSÉ WINES

Most preferred chilled with ham, pork, veal, lamb, poultry. Usual serving—4 ounces.
These wines are light and fruity, usually medium-dry. They're ideal picnic and luncheon wines.

Vin Rosé   **Rosé**

STORING WINE. Air and light are wine's enemies. Good home storage conditions for wine are found in closets, drawers, cupboards, and cellars where it is cool and dark. Lay corked bottles on their sides to keep the corks moist and tight. Screw cap bottles can be safely stored upright.

RED WINES

Most preferred at cool room temperature with steaks, roasts, game, spaghetti, cheeses, stews, casseroles. Usual serving—4 ounces.
Dry wines, from light red to deep ruby in color, often pleasantly tart, with medium to full body.

Burgundy   **Claret**
Chianti   **Mountain Red**

Mellow reds, of medium body with just a touch of sweetness and a pleasing, hearty flavor.

Barberone   **Vino-Rosso**

PROPRIETARIES: Other red, white, and rosé dinner wines are labeled with special names selected by the winemaker. These proprietary names may be coined or descriptive words, sometimes indicating the region in which the wine was produced. Proprietary wines parallel Generics in range and use.

APPETIZER WINES

Aperitif or appetizer wines are usually dry and are drunk before meals or with the soup course. Chill them, or serve at room temperature, or pour over ice. Usual serving—3 ounces.

Sherry   **Vermouth**
  Cocktail   Dry
  Dry   Sweet
  Medium Dry

DESSERT WINES

Pour dessert wines after dinner, either with dessert or later. They are all sweet, rich wines that are particularly good with fruit, nuts, cheese, plain cake, cookies. Dessert wines are usually served at room temperature. Usual serving—3 ounces.

Port   **Angelica**
  Ruby   **Cream Sherry**
  Tawny   **Madeira**
  Tinta   **Marsala**
  White   **Tokay**

Muscatel
  Black Muscat
  Muscat Frontignan
  Muscatel (gold or red)

Sweet Sauterne and Sweet Semillon are also often served as dessert wines.

WINES

WINES
(inner wines.)

VARIETALS
Varietals are named for the grapes from which they are made.

WHITE WINES

Most preferred chilled with fish, shellfish, poultry. Usual serving—4 ounces.
Light crisp white wines, pale golden or slightly green-gold in color. Most are pleasantly dry. Some may have a hint of sweetness.*

- *Emerald Riesling
- *Gewurztraminer
- *Green Hungarian
- Grey Riesling
- Johannisberg Riesling (White Riesling)
- Sylvaner
- Traminer

Rich, fuller-flavored wines. These are usually dry wines, pale to light golden in color. Some may have a hint of sweetness.*

- Chardonnay (Pinot Chardonnay)
- Pinot Blanc
- *Chenin Blanc (White Pinot)
- Sauvignon Blanc
- Dry Semillon

Medium to pronounced sweetness in these wines. They may be enjoyed most with dessert, fruit, fruit salad, and other sweet foods.

- Malvasia Bianca
- Muscat Bordelaise
- Muscat Canelli
- Sweet Semillon

ROSÉ WINES

Most preferred chilled with ham, pork, veal, lamb, poultry. Usual serving—4 ounces.
These are light, fruity wines, sometimes dry, sometimes slightly sweet,* with a cheerful pink color, ranging in tone from deep rose to a pale, orange-tinged hue.

- Cabernet Rosé
- Grignolino Rosé
- Gamay Rosé
- Zinfandel Rosé
- *Grenache Rosé

SERVING WINE. Most people enjoy white and rosé wines chilled to about 45-55 degrees. An hour in the refrigerator will do it handily.

RED WINES

Most preferred at cool room temperature with steaks, roasts, game, spaghetti, cheeses, stews, casseroles. Usual serving—4 ounces.
Fresh, fruity red wines, dry and aromatic, light to medium in body.

- Cabernet
- Grignolino
- Pinot St. George (Red Pinot)
- Gamay
- Gamay Beaujolais
- Ruby Cabernet
- Zinfandel

Rich, red wines with distinctive flavor and appealing ruby color, medium to full in body.

- Barbara
- Charbono
- Cabernet Sauvignon
- Pinot Noir
- Petite Sirah

SERVING WINE. Many wine drinkers agree that red wines benefit from a little "breathing time," and open them about an hour before dinner and leave the closure off. You may be pleased by the changes in aroma and flavor this short exposure gives the wine.

SPARKLING WINES

These festive wines are appropriate anytime, along with food or by themselves. They range from extremely dry to quite sweet, from pale gold to deep red. Sparkling wines are best when thoroughly chilled. Usual serving—3-4 ounces.

Champagne
- Natural—very dry
- Brut—dry
- Extra Dry — with just a hint of sweetness
- Dry — medium sweet
- Sec — noticeably sweet
- Demi-Sec — very sweet

Rosé
- Pink Champagne
- Crackling Rosé

Red
- Sparkling Burgundy

Muscat
- Sparkling Muscat

SERVING WINE. Traditionally, wine is served in clear, stemmed glasses, filled about half way. This leaves room for the aroma to gather above the wine. Winemakers recommend a tulip-shaped glass with an 8-9 ounce capacity as being suitable for any wine.

SPECIAL NATURAL WINES

These wines are pure, grape wines flavored with fruit juices or essences. Citrus flavors are especially popular, also mint, coffee, chocolate, and herbs. The wines are given descriptive or colorful names by the winemaker. They may be enjoyed before meals, with dessert, after dinner, or as between meal refreshments. Usual serving—3 ounces.

WINE ACCESSORIES

Many people who enjoy wine like to collect a selection of serving accouterments. Quite an array of glassware, coasters, corkscrews, and other equipment is available at a wide range of prices, making it possible for anyone interested to expand the household supply of wine gear.

Glasses are probably the most important wine items—aside from the bottles themselves. A clear, thin glass, designed especially to present wine attractively, compounds the pleasures of the beverage. Although wine cheers a table even when served in jelly glasses.

The wine growers of California agree that wine glasses should be plain and clear—the better to see the color of the wine. They should also be roomy, to allow for generous servings of wine, and tulip shaped, so the good wine aroma is captured in the glass above the wine. Wine growers also recommend glasses with stems. A stem acts as a sort of handle, keeping warm fingers away from chilled wine.

A single style glass will work well for all wines, if it is the 8–9 ounce, tulip-shaped, all-purpose wineglass recommended by both wine growers and connoisseurs. Or, a whole range of special glasses, a different one for each type of wine, may be collected. Hostesses who prefer the array may set the table with conical or elongated-tulip Sherry glasses, round-bowled hock glasses, classic red and white Burgundy glasses, Claret glasses, saucer-shaped or tulip Champagne glasses, in any combination that fits the meal and wine list. There is no question about the aura of elegance surrounding a table laden with shining crystal wine-glasses, each place set with a separate glowing vessel for every wine presented during the meal. But the simpler solution of a single all-purpose glass is perfectly proper and commands less table space.

Outsized glasses are the special pleasure of wine lovers. These Burgundy balloons or enormous Bordeaux glasses allow the connoisseur to swirl his wine enthusiastically without spilling a drop. Capacity is two or three times the usual 8–9 ounce all-purpose wine glass. These glasses seem to emphasize the presence of wine and dramatize a table setting.

Dinner tables are also enhanced by wine coasters. Many are made of silver or are silver-plated. Others are crockery, wood, pewter, straw, or what-have-you. They come in sizes just right for ordinary 4/5 quart bottles, or larger to accommodate magnum or Champagne bottles. These devices serve a practical purpose, as well as a decorative one. They protect the table linen.

Another item which serves this same end is the drip-stopper. It's usually made of silver and fits snugly in the top of the wine bottle. The drip-stopper assures neat pouring, even by novices.

Wine coolers may add to the enjoyment of chilled wines. A silver bucket, beaded with moisture and exhibiting a chilled bottle, lends a special authority to the wine and a festive note to the table. Practically speaking, a cooler assures a host of pouring white or sparkling wines at a desirable serving temperature throughout the whole meal.

An effective, easy-to-use corkscrew is one of the most important pieces of equipment a wine lover can own. Although many wines come in screwcap bottles, eliminating the need for corkscrews entirely, a corkscrew is still a necessary tool for removing the barrier between many wines and the people who want to drink them. There are almost limitless shapes and sizes of corkscrews. But the thing to pay attention to when selecting one is the length and turn of the screw. The helix (screw portion) should be long enough to penetrate all the way through any cork likely to be used in a wine bottle. 2¼ inches should do it. And the coil should follow the path set by the point exactly. A leverage device of some kind is a great advantage on a corkscrew.

An alternative to the classic corkscrew is a hand-pump cork remover. This little instrument features a needle attached to a plunger-type pump. It's easy to use. Just insert the needle in the cork, pump the plunger two or three times, and out pops the cork. A similar cork remover using Freon gas with a very slight touch does the same job with less effort. But careful! A heavy touch can cause trouble.

Carafes and decanters are other wine items which bring pleasure to the table. These containers are generally graceful in shape, attractive in design. They may be simple or elaborate. Carafes come without lids and are useful for holding meal-size quantities of wine poured from gallon or half gallon jugs. Most decanters have stoppers and are the traditional sideboard containers for displaying the family Port or Sherry. They are also meant to hold old, sediment-filled wine which must be decanted, or poured from the original bottle into another clean receptacle, leaving the sediment behind. When this purpose is to be served, a decanter with a wide mouth eases the delicate job of pouring without disturbing sediment.

Some special wine equipment is meant for outdoor use. The bota is one such item. It is a hide bag, Spanish in origin. The bota is the skier's and hiker's friend. It is lightweight and unbreakable, ideal for carrying wine along on outdoor sojourns.

Another outdoor item is the plastic wine glass. Because it doesn't shatter, this kind of glass is perfect for poolside use. It is also inexpensive. Large parties indoors or out may be more pleasant for the hostess who uses these throw-away plastic glasses instead of regular wine glasses.

Most of these accompaniments to wine drinking can be found at wine shops or winery tasting rooms. If a desirable item is not available in your area, or for information on any wine connected item or book, write to The Wine Appreciation Guild 1377 Ninth Avenue, San Francisco 94122.

Wine As a Food

By SALVATORE P. LUCIA, M.D.

Professor Emeritus of Medicine, University of California School of Medicine

Wine was a safe and healthful beverage from the very beginning of early civilizations. It provided calories and vitamins before the science of nutrition was established, and at a time when food was neither plentiful nor always of good quality. During those times when life was physically strenuous, wine offered the tranquility and relaxation necessary to bind societies of men together, as well as to lessen tensions and relieve pain.

Health Laden Elixir

In time, the dietary alcoholic beverage, wine, came to be esteemed in its own right as a health-laden elixir, bringing to man bounties which only now are being specifically identified and given a scientific verification. As a food, wine plays, in addition, an important role in present day nutrition. Wine contains many of the elements essential for quick energy and body maintenance, support, and repair. The energy element is derived largely from alcohol, a simple carbohydrate—the necessary substratum without which, wine would not be wine. This is balanced by organic and inorganic acids, other carbohydrates, vitamins, and a myriad of diverse congeners present in wine in varying proportion, depending upon the climate and soil of the vineyards, the variety of grapes, the degree of maturity of the grapes at harvest, the processes used in fermentation, aging and all the other operations well known to the maker of wine.

In addition to the alcohol, other sources of calories in wine are the simple sugars, principally levulose and dextrose, which occur in amounts of 0.25% to 10%, depending upon the type of wine. It has been shown that levulose acts in the maintenance and repair of the liver and as an intermediary substance in metabolism. Dextrose is considered the most important single factor in the prevention of fatty infiltration of the liver, a condition which predisposes this organ to cirrhosis.

B Vitamins

The vitamins in grapes are used primarily as accessory growth factors for micro-organisms although some of them are present in sufficient amount to be of importance in human nutrition. The B vitamins are represented fairly well in the grape, its musts and wines. In wines that were tested for B vitamins, Agnes Fay Morgan demonstrated that while low in thiamine content they provided 13 to 18% of the daily minimum requirement of riboflavin, 52 to 94% of pyridoxine, 5 to 14% of niacin, and 2 to 5% of pantothenic acid. Sweet red wines shelter much more of the thiamine, all of the riboflavin and niacin, 3/4 of the vitamin B_6 and 1/3 of the pantothenic acid present in the natural grape. The reasons for this better showing by sweet red wines may be due to the inclusion of the skins and seeds of the grapes during fermentation; the shorter fermentation period, as attested by the high sugar content of the wine; and to the shielding of the riboflavin from the destructive action of light by the heavy pigments in the wine. The presence of B vitamins in wine significantly distinguishes it from distilled liquors and even from beer. Not only original endowment of the grape, but the additions and subtractions produced in the fermented juice by the yeasts, must be taken into account in assessing the quality content of B vitamins in wines.

Tonic Action

Experiments have also revealed that wine has a remarkable vitamin P potency, a factor which may strengthen capillary resistance. Owing to the importance of the capillaries in the nutrition of tissues, the "tonic" action of wines can and should be attributed in considerable measure to their content of vitamin P.

As for minerals, wines contain in some degree all thirteen of the major mineral elements considered necessary for the maintenance of human life, i.e., calcium, phosphorous, magnesium, sodium, potassium, chlorine, sulphur, iron, copper, manganese, zinc, iodine, and cobalt.

Port wine has long been recommended in the treatment of iron-deficiency anemia, and for good reason, for it contains an average of 3.5 mg. of iron per liter—the daily requirement of elemental iron being 5.5 mg., according to the latest scientific findings. Other wines are richer still in iron, with an average of 4.7 mg. per liter for the dry white table wines and 6.0 mg. for the dry red table wines.

Wine in Cooking

Wine is a most versatile flavoring agent and adds "a gourmet touch" to any dish from appetizer to dessert. Wines packaged in gallon and half-gallon jugs are quite satisfactory for cooking as well as those in fifths and other bottle sizes.

Foods cooked with wine have the flavor of the wine without any residue of alcohol, because alcohol evaportes long before the cooking temperature of food is reached.

The plans for most Epicurean meals start with the main dish. So here, grouped for easy perusal, are recipes for wine-flavored meats, poultry and fish — any one of which may be the center of interest in an outstanding menu. The contributors of many of these recipes have listed the accompaniments they've found most compatible. A further menu planning aid is the suggestion of a California wine that complements each main dish.

Among the fish recipes are several that may serve as a separate fish course to precede the main course. When a multi-course menu will include two or more wines, tradition suggests that the wines for the first courses will be lighter in color, body and flavor than those that follow. The most robust wine of the meal — whether it be red or white — accompanies the main course.

MAIN DISHES

Meats

Beef Ragout

(6 TO 8 SERVINGS)

Mrs. Edmund Accomazzo, Cucamonga Winery, Cucamonga
Editor's note: This stew is excellently seasoned. Though the meat is not browned in advance, the long cooking gives it good color and flavor.

- 3 pounds boneless beef chuck, cut into 1-inch cubes
- Flour
- 1 (10½-oz.) can condensed consomme
- ½ cup California Dry Sherry
- 2 small onions, thinly sliced
- ½ teaspoon curry powder
- ¼ teaspoon dried basil leaves
- 1 whole clove
- 1 bay leaf
- Dash of garlic salt
- Dash freshly ground black pepper
- ½ strip bacon
- 1 coarse stalk celery
- 12 to 15 whole baby carrots, scraped and sliced
- 1 mint leaf or pinch of dried mint
- 4 small tomatoes, peeled and cubed
- ½ pound sliced fresh mushrooms or
- 1 (6-oz.) can slice mushrooms, drained
- 2 tablespoons flour
- 1 (8 oz.) can tomato puree
- ½ cup finely chopped celery
- ½ cup finely chopped parsley

Roll beef pieces in flour to coat evenly. Place meat, consomme, Sherry onions, curry powder, basil leaves, clove, bay leaf, garlic salt and pepper in an ovenproof Dutch oven. Place over moderate heat (about 250°) and heat until mixture begins to boil. Add the bacon and celery stalk. Cover Dutch oven and place in a preheated 350° oven. Bake about 2 hours, or until meat is fork-tender. While meat is cooking, place carrots and mint leaf in a saucepan. Add about 1 cup water. Place over moderately low heat and cook 10 to 15 minutes or until tender. Drain. When meat is fork-tender, take Dutch oven out of oven and remove bacon and celery stalk Place oven over moderate heat. Add tomatoes and mushrooms; sprinkle the 2 tablespoons flour over mixture and stir to blend. Simmer, covered, 10 to 15 minutes. Add cooked carrots, tomato puree, the chopped celery and parsley and stir to blend. Season to taste with salt and pepper.

Editor's Note: Any **CALIFORNIA RED TABLE WINE** *would go well with this dish.*

Braised, Stuffed Flank Steak

(3 TO 4 SERVINGS)

Mrs. Aldo Nerelli, Pesenti Winery, Templeton
Editor's note: Dry red wine both flavors and tenderizes this stuffed flank steak

1 to 1½ pound flank steak
¼ cup minced onion
1 tablespoon butter
2 cups fresh bread crumbs
1 tablespoon snipped parsley
½ teaspoon salt
⅛ teaspoon pepper
½ teaspoon celery salt
½ teaspoon dried sage
2 tablespoons butter
1 tablespoon fat or oil
½ cup California
    Red Table Wine
½ cup hot water
½ teaspoon peppercorns
1 teaspoon garlic wine vinegar
    GRAVY
½ cup California
    Red Table Wine
½ cup water
1 beef bouillon cube
¼ cup flour
6 tablespoons cold water

Have butcher score one side of steak in diamond pattern. Sauté onions in butter. Add crumbs, parsley and seasonings. Add warm water to make stuffing of desired consistency. Arrange on unscored side of steak, patting it until it nearly reaches the edges. Dot with butter. Roll up loosely, jelly-roll fashion; secure with skewers or string, leaving room for expansion of stuffing. In hot fat in Dutch oven, brown steak well on both sides—about 15 minutes. Add wine and water, peppercorns and sprinkle with vinegar. Simmer, tightly covered or bake in oven 350° for 1½ hours or until tender. Place meat on platter, remove string and slice. **Gravy:** Strain the liquid in which meat was cooked. To it add wine, water and bouillon cube. Mix flour with cold water and stir into wine and broth mixture. Heat, stirring until gravy is hot and thickened.

Editor's note: With this dish, serve the California Red Table Wine used in preparing it. **CALIFORNIA BURGUNDY** *or* **CABERNET** *is a good choice.*

Steaks Dianne

(10 TO 12 SERVINGS)

Mrs. Kay Martin, California Growers Winery, Cutler
I use an electric griddle and cook at the table at 375°, usually in two or three batches, using proportionate amounts of butter and sauce for each cooking. Green salad and a green bean or zucchini casserole make this meal complete. Pilaf is also a good accompaniment.

Steak buns
1 beef tenderloin
    sliced in ¼ inch slices
½ cup butter
1 cup California Burgundy
1 teaspoon salt
¼ teaspoon freshly ground
    pepper
1 clove garlic, minced
1 tablespoon chopped parsley

Have buns hot and the rest of the dinner ready to serve before cooking the steaks. Cook the steaks quickly in butter, then pour over them the rest of the ingredients and heat through. Serve two steaks on each bun. Spoon some of the heated sauce over the meat.

My choice of wine to accompany this dish:
CALIFORNIA SPARKLING BURGUNDY

International Angus Steak

(6 SERVINGS)

Mrs. William Perelli-Minetti, A. Perelli-Minetti & Sons, Delano
Editor's note: This way of cooking cube steaks is well named. It starts off in an oriental manner, but the Bulgur wheat (instead of the rice one would expect) gives it a middle European flavor.

- 6 cube steaks
- ¼ cup soy sauce
- Flour
- Salt, pepper
- ¼ cup cooking oil
- ½ cup chopped onion
- ½ cup chopped green pepper
- ⅔ cup bulgur wheat
- 4 teaspoons cornstarch
- 1 cup California Burgundy
- ½ cup water
- 2 tablespoon chopped parsley

Cut the cube steaks into strips 2″ long by 1″ wide. Sprinkle soy sauce on each side. Roll the strips in flour, then season with salt and pepper. Brown steak in a large electric frypan in hot cooking oil. When partly brown add onion and green pepper; sauté until barely tender. Cover browned ingredients with bulgur. Blend cornstarch, wine and water; add to ingredients in pan. Sprinkle parsley on top. Simmer about 30 minutes at low temperature until wheat is done. A little more wine or water may be added to keep it from getting too dry.

 Editor's note: Try a **CALIFORNIA BURGUNDY** *or* **GAMAY** *with this dish.*

Korean Steaks

(12 TO 15 SERVINGS)

Mrs. Kay Martin, California Growers Wineries, Cutler
These steaks are the specialty of Korean friends of ours. We have substituted wine for half of the soy sauce they used. With the steaks we serve plain boiled rice (using the marinade as a sauce) or a pilaf, green salad and hot buttered French bread. We have fresh fruit for dessert as this is usually prepared in the summer barbecue season. Otherwise, sherbet is good.

- 1 (5 to 6-lb.) standing rib roast
- 1 package sesame seeds
- 1 cup soy sauce
- 1 cup California Burgundy
- ½ cup oil
- 2 cloves garlic, minced
- 1 bunch green onions, minced, including part of the tops
- ½ green pepper, minced
- 1 teaspoon monosodium glutamate
- 1 teaspoon freshly ground pepper
- 1 tablespoon sugar

Have butcher bone roast and remove part of the fat, then cut in 3/16-inch slices. (My butcher uses the slicing machine and gets about 5 steaks per pound.) Toast the sesame seeds in a dry frying pan, stirring constantly until they are a light brown. Put them between two sheets of waxed paper and crush thoroughly with a rolling pin. Mix with all other ingredients to make marinade. Put a layer of steaks in a shallow dish and cover with marinade, being sure to get some of the solids on each steak. Add another layer of steaks with marinade until all steaks and marinade are used. Marinate at least six hours, turning the steaks over occasionally so the liquid can be kept distributed. Cook steaks over a hot barbecue fire. Cook on first side until brown shows through (only a few minutes), then flip and cook on other side briefly. These cook so fast that it is a good idea to have your guests already seated and served with their other food before you start the cooking process. Most guests will eat two of these steaks.

 My choice of wine to accompany this dish: **CALIFORNIA BURGUNDY** *or on especially festive occasions* **SPARKLING BURGUNDY**

Beef Burgundy

(6 SERVINGS)

Mrs. Arthur Caputi, Jr., E. & J. Gallo Winery, Modesto
Re-heating even improves the flavor of this already rich dish. So this is a perfect make-ahead company recipe. Favorite accompaniments are Caesar salad, French bread, and lemon sherbet with raspberry sauce.

- ¼ cup butter
- 2½ pounds boneless stew meat, cut into 1-inch cubes
- ½ lb. small white onions, peeled
- ½ lb. small fresh mushrooms
- 4 tablespoon flour
- 2½ teaspoons beef stock base
- 2 tablespoons tomato paste
- 1½ cups California Burgundy
- ¾ cup California Dry Sherry
- ¾ cup California Ruby Port
- 2 tablespoons California Brandy
- 1 (10½-oz.) can condensed beef bouillon, undiluted
- ⅛ teaspoon pepper
- 1 bay leaf

Melt half the butter in 4-quart Dutch oven and brown beef cubes well all over. Lift out beef as it browns. Add remaining butter to Dutch oven and add onions; cook over low heat, covered, until slightly browned. Add mushrooms and cook for about 3 minutes. Remove from heat and add flour, beef stock base and tomato paste. Stir until well blended. Stir in wines, Brandy and beef bouillon. Bring wine mixture just to boiling, stirring, remove from heat and add beef, pepper and bay leaf. Bake in 350° oven, covered, for approximately 1½ hours.

My choice of wine to accompany this dish:
CALIFORNIA BURGUNDY *or* **CABERNET SAUVIGNON**

Napa Valley Meat Roll

(4 SERVINGS)

Mrs. William Bonetti, Charles Krug Winery, St. Helena
This dish can be made a day in advance and reheated very slowly before serving.

- 1 (2-lb.) piece round steak (about ½ inch thick)
- Salt, pepper
- 2 onions, sliced
- ¼ pound mushrooms
- 1 green pepper, sliced
- 3 tablespoons butter
- 1½ cups fine, dry bread crumbs
- 1 (2-oz.) jar stuffed olives, drained and sliced
- Flour
- 2 tablespoons butter
- 6 tablespoons olive oil
- Few leaves of sage, rosemary, oregano and a sprig of parsley
- 2 cups California Burgundy

Pound steak until thin; rub in salt and pepper. Sauté onions, mushrooms, and green pepper with 3 tablespoons butter and spread it on steak; cover with bread crumbs; blanket with a layer of sliced olives. Roll meat and tie roll firmly. Flour outside. Brown in butter and olive oil. Add herbs. Add wine, bring to boil, then cover and simmer about 3 hours.

My choice of wine to accompany this dish:
CALIFORNIA ZINFANDEL *or* **GAMAY**

Steak Bordelaise, Vermouth

(6 TO 8 SERVINGS)

Miss Helen V. Reynolds, United Vintners, San Francisco
This recipe has been a long-time favorite with the Eyrud family in Paris and is usually served at family gatherings.

6 to 8 medium size
    tenderloin tips
    (or tender top round)
    Salt and pepper
⅓ cup sifted flour
¼ cup olive oil
1 (4 to 6-oz.) can mushrooms, sliced, or ½ pound fresh button mushrooms, sliced
2 cloves garlic, finely chopped
¼ cup finely chopped parsley
½ cup California Dry Vermouth
¼ cup olive oil

Roll tenderloin tips in seasoned flour, and brown in olive oil. Add mushrooms, chopped garlic, parsley and liquid from mushrooms (if canned mushrooms are used). Add Vermouth, cover and simmer over low heat for 10 to 15 minutes, or until liquid has cooked down.

Note: If there is not enough liquid after Vermouth and water from mushrooms have been added, a small amount of Burgundy may also be added. The idea is to have enough liquid for the garlic and parsley to cook in.

 My choice of wine to accompany this dish:
CALIFORNIA VIN ROSÉ *or* **PINOT NOIR**

Entrecote with Watercress

(6 SERVINGS)

Mrs. Janet Schultz, Fromm and Sichel, San Francisco
Editor's note: Good steaks deserve a good wine sauce. This one is easy and excellent.

Olive oil
2 sirloin steaks,
    large enough for 6 persons
    Salt and pepper
2 tablespoons chopped shallots
1 tablespoon butter
¾ cup California Sauterne
3 tablespoons chopped parsley
    Watercress

Barely cover the bottoms of 2 large frying pans with olive oil and heat. Trim most of the fat from the steaks. Season with salt and pepper. Cook in hot oil, 5 minutes on each side. Remove steaks to hot platter. Meanwhile, in small saucepan brown shallots in butter. Add wine and parsley. Cook, stirring occasionally, until wine is reduced by half. Serve steaks topped with shallots and wine sauce and surrounded with watercress.

Editor's note: A worthy wine accompaniment is either a
CALIFORNIA BURGUNDY *or* **CABERNET SAUVIGNON.**

Wine Short Ribs

(5 TO 6 SERVINGS)

Mrs. Kenneth Huff, Wine Institute, San Francisco
Editor's note: The tartness of the red table wine along with the acid of the wine vinegar improve the flavor and cut the richness of these braised short ribs.

2 pounds lean short ribs
    Salt and pepper
    Flour
3 tablespoons bacon fat
    or cooking oil
½ cup California
    Red Table Wine
3 tablespoons catsup
2 tablespoons California
    red wine vinegar
1 tablespoon minced onion

Season short ribs with salt and pepper and dust with flour. In a heavy roasting pan, heat fat or oil and brown meat thoroughly. Discard any excess fat. Meanwhile, combine remaining ingredients. Pour over meat. Cover and bake in 375° oven for 1¼ to 1½ hours until meat is tender. Baste with the wine sauce during the baking period.

 My choice of wine to accompany this dish: **CALIFORNIA BURGUNDY**

Flaming Beef Grenadine

(6 SERVINGS)

Mrs. Jack Matthews, Wine Institute, San Francisco

- 6 slices fillet of beef tenderloin
- ⅓ cup butter
- 6 shallots, chopped
- ¾ pound fresh mushrooms, sliced
- ⅔ cup California Port
- ⅔ cup California Brandy
- Dash each: salt, pepper, monosodium glutamate
- Dash Worcestershire sauce

Sauté fillets in butter until browned well on both sides; add and brown shallots and mushrooms; add Port. Add Brandy (at table if you want maximum eye appeal) ignite and let flame burn out. Add seasonings.

🍷 *My choice of wine to accompany this dish:*
CALIFORNIA CABERNET SAUVIGNON

Boeuf à la Bourguignonne

(6 GENEROUS SERVINGS)

Harry G. Serlis, Wine Institute, San Francisco
Editor's note: This takes two days, but it's worth the time. It has superb flavor and appearance.

- 5 lbs. round or chuck steak cut into large cubes (approx. 2½ x 2½ x 2″)
- Flour
- 5 tablespoons olive oil
- ¼ cup butter
- Salt, pepper
- ½ cup warm California Brandy
- ½ lb. bacon, cut up
- 2 cloves garlic, minced
- 2 carrots, minced
- 2 leeks, chopped
- 6 scallions or green onions, chopped
- 2 medium onions, chopped
- 1 lb. mushrooms
- 1 lamb shank, split (or calves foot)
- ½ teaspoon dried thyme
- 2 bay leaves
- 1 stalk celery and leaves
- 4 sprigs parsley
- 1 fifth bottle California Burgundy
- Water
- 2 tablespoons flour
- 1 tablespoon kitchen bouquet
- 1 tablespoon butter
- 6 small onions, peeled
- Sugar
- 1 tablespoon butter
- 1 tablespoon olive oil
- Lemon juice
- Chopped parsley

Roll cubes of beef in flour. Heat 5 tablespoons oil and half of the butter in a large skillet over a high heat and brown the meat well on all sides. Sprinkle the meat with salt and pepper, pour Brandy over it, ignite and let flame die out. Transfer contents of skillet to a large oven-proof casserole or Dutch oven (preferably clay). Sauté the diced bacon in the skillet until crisp and brown. Add garlic, carrots, leeks, scallions, onions and chopped mushroom stems. Save mushroom caps. Cook, stirring occasionally until all the vegetables are lightly browned. Transfer vegetables to the casserole with the meat. Add to the casserole the lamb shank, and the thyme and bay leaf, celery stalk and some of the parsley tied into a bouquet garni. (You can leave the lamb shank loose if you wish. However, later you will have to remove the bones and gristle from the stew. Do this if you would like the meat from the lamb shank in the stew.) Add all but one cup of the wine and add enough water to cover contents. Cover and bake in 350° oven for 2 hours. (Let stand overnight in refrigerator.) Next morning remove fat from the top of the stew. Stir in flour mixed into a paste with water or some melted butter, stir in kitchen bouquet and continue to bake at 350° for another 2 or 3 hours. Just before serving, melt 1 tablespoon butter in a saucepan; add the small onions, sprinkle with a little sugar, cook stirring until onions are browned, add a little of the remaining wine. Cover and simmer for 20 minutes. In a skillet heat the remaining 1 tablespoon butter and the 1 tablespoon olive oil and in it place the mushrooms, cap side down. Sprinkle with lemon juice and sauté mushrooms for 2 minutes longer. Add a little wine to the skillet and keep mushrooms warm. When ready to serve, remove excess fat, again, from the top of the liquid. Discard calf's foot (or lamb shank) and the bouquet garni. Stir in the remaining wine, thicken gravy if desired, adjust seasonings and arrange onions and mushrooms around the meat and garnish with parsley.

🍷 *My choice of wine to accompany this dish: A robust red table wine such as*
CALIFORNIA CLARET *or* **CABERNET SAUVIGNON**

Sweetbreads Vermouth

(6 SERVINGS)

Mrs. B. C. Solari, United Vintners, San Francisco
We call this a Sunday brunch dish. Sometimes we serve it with scrambled eggs and sometimes we surround the sweetbreads with crisp bacon, link sausages or broiled slices of ham.
Fresh fruit or juice starts the brunch. Toasted, buttered French bread completes the menu.

2 pounds sweetbreads
⅓ cup butter
½ pound sliced mushrooms
  Salt, pepper
½ cup California Dry Vermouth
½ teaspoon fresh, broken
    sage leaves
  Chopped parsley
  Grated lemon peel

Prepare sweetbreads in the usual manner, soaking in cold water briefly, then blanching in boiling water for 10 to 20 minutes. Cool. Remove all fat and membranes, and cut into one or 1½-inch cubes. Melt butter. When bubbling slowly, add sweetbreads. Cook, turning frequently, until golden brown. Add mushrooms (I prefer these also blanched for about 5 minutes) and cook about 10 minutes. Stir in seasonings, Vermouth and sprinkle with sage. Simmer 10 or 15 minutes more. Remove to heated platter and sprinkle with parsley and lemon peel.

My choice of wine to accompany this dish:
CALIFORNIA CHENIN BLANC *or* **JOHANNISBERG RIESLING**

La Lunga

(6 TO 8 SERVINGS)

Miss Jacqueline Guimina, The Christian Brothers, Reedley
Editor's note: A dry white wine gives beef tongue such an excellent flavor, it's good hot or cold.
Serve gravy separately if some of the tongue is to be reserved for a second meal.

1 large beef tongue
    (3 to 4 pounds)
2 medium onions
3 tablespoons butter
¼ cup chopped parsley
1 teaspoon Italian seasoning
½ teaspoon salt
⅛ teaspoon pepper
½ pound fresh mushrooms,
    sliced
4 tablespoons flour
1 (13¾-oz.) can chicken broth
1 teaspoon beef extract
¾ cup California Dry Sauterne

Cover tongue with cold water. Add one chopped onion and salt. Bring to boil and simmer for approximately 2½ hours, or until tender. Sauté one minced onion in butter; add chopped parsley, seasonings, and mushrooms. Cook for 5 minutes while slowly adding flour and 2 cups of broth from tongue. Add chicken broth, beef extract and wine; simmer for 30 minutes. Skin tongue while hot and slice on a platter. Pour the hot gravy over tongue slices and garnish with parsley.

My choice of wine to accompany this dish:
A hearty **CALIFORNIA RED WINE**
Editor's note: **CALIFORNIA BURGUNDY, PINOT ST. GEORGE** *or* **CABERNET SAUVIGNON** *are especially suitable.*

Ernie's Tenderloin Brochette with Bordelaise Sauce

(4 SERVINGS)

Mrs. George Al Berry, E. & J. Gallo Winery, Modesto
I am indebted to my good friend, Paul Quiarud, the chef at Ernie's restaurant in San Francisco, for this recipe. To complete the menu I serve Vischyssoise, then a crisp lettuce salad with Gourmet Dressing (Page 68). With the beef, I serve a risotto of wild rice and for dessert, Strawberries Romanoff.

- 2 pounds tenderloin of beef
- 2 green peppers
- 4 slices bacon
- 16 whole mushrooms
- Salt and pepper
- Olive oil

BORDELAISE SAUCE
- 1 stalk celery
- ½ small carrot
- ½ small onion, chopped
- 2 cloves garlic, minced
- ¼ cup butter
- 1 teaspoon pickling spice
- Pinch of rosemary
- ½ cup tomato puree
- ½ cup strong beef stock (or canned beef bouillon)
- ½ cup California Red Table Wine
- Juice of 1 lemon
- Pinch of nutmeg
- 2 egg yolks, well beaten
- Salt and pepper
- ¼ cup melted butter
- Chopped parsley

Cut beef into 16 pieces, each about one inch thick. Parboil green peppers in boiling water; drain, cool and cut into 16 squares. Cut each bacon slice into 4 pieces. Using four 10-inch skewers, first spear a piece of meat, then a square of green pepper, then bacon, then a mushroom. Repeat until each skewer contains 4 pieces of meat. Sprinkle with salt and pepper and roll in olive oil, then put on rack of preheated broiler. Broil two minutes for medium-rare or 1½ minutes for rare. Serve with Bordelaise Sauce and wild rice. **Bordelaise Sauce:** Cut celery and carrot in one-half inch lengths. Add onions and garlic and sauté in butter. Add pickling spice and rosemary and cook until vegetables are well browned. Then add tomato puree, beef stock, wine, lemon juice, and nutmeg. Boil and reduce to half its volume. Strain and discard vegetables and spices. Add strained sauce to well-beaten yolks, beating constantly until thoroughly mixed and slightly thickened. Adjust seasoning. Keep hot, but do not allow to boil. Just before serving, beat in melted butter and parsley.

 My choice of wine to accompany this dish:
A **CALIFORNIA RIESLING** *or* **CHABLIS** *is good with first two courses, and* **CALIFORNIA PINOT NOIR** *with the main course.*

Wild Boar Larkmead

(10 SERVINGS)

Mr. B. C. Solari, United Vintners, San Francisco
This is a rare taste treat. We get the wild boar from Mr. Stuyvesant Fish of Palo Corona Ranch in Carmel, California.

- 2 Haunches of a 35 to 40 pound wild boar
- Garlic
- Rosemary
- Salt and pepper
- Olive oil
- 1 (7½-oz.) can unpitted black olives
- 1½ cups California Dry White Wine

Cut boar like leg of lamb. Cut several slits in meat and insert small pieces of garlic, several needles of rosemary, salt and pepper in the little pockets (3 or 4 to the haunch). Place haunches on large flat baking pan. Pour olive oil over all leaving about ⅛ inch depth in pan. Put in very hot oven (500°) until brown for 15 or 20 minutes. Lower oven to 400° and cook 45 minutes or longer, until done. During last 20 minutes, add 1 can of black olives, with pits, and add wine.

My choice of wine to accompany this dish:
CALIFORNIA CABERNET SAUVIGNON *or* **CHARBONO**

Kidneys Hunter Style

(6 SERVINGS)

Mrs. Philip G. Smyser, Wine Advisory Board, San Francisco
This is excellent for a party breakfast or brunch with omelets. It makes a good dinner dish also.

- 6 veal or 12 lamb kidneys
- ½ cup butter
- 1 teaspoon chopped parsley
- 1 teaspoon onion (or chives)
- 1½ tablespoons flour
- ½ cup each California Madeira, dry white wine, chicken broth
- ½ pound mushrooms, thinly sliced
- ¼ cup butter

Plunge kidneys into boiling water, drain them immediately, and remove the thin skins and tough centers. Cut kidneys into thin slices. Sauté slices in ½ cup butter, until lightly browned. Add parsley and onion and cook mixture over high heat for 2 minutes. Sprinkle with flour and blend well. Add wines and broth and bring to a boil, reduce heat and simmer, stirring constantly, for 5 minutes. Sauté mushrooms in ¼ cup butter until soft. Add them to kidneys and cook whole mixture for another 3 minutes. Serve garnished with parsley on toasted English muffins.

 My choice of wine to accompany this dish: **CALIFORNIA CHAMPAGNE**

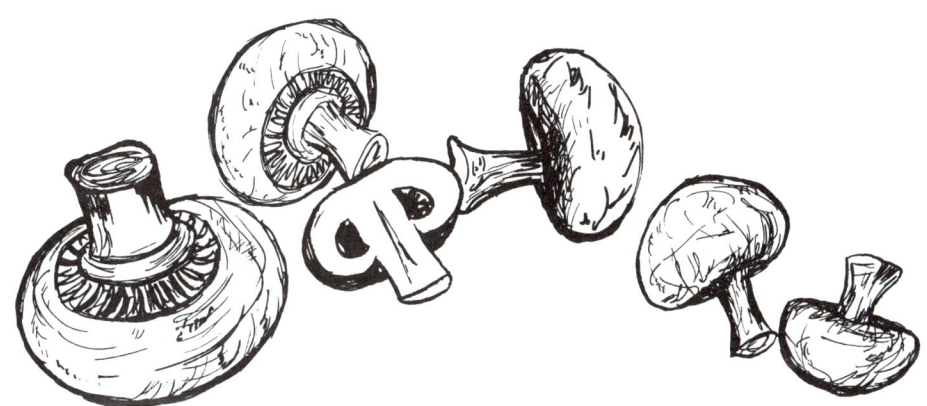

Beef Heart Pinot Blanc

(4 TO 6 SERVINGS)

Mrs. N. C. Mirassou, Mirassou Vineyards, San Jose
Editor's note: Dry white wine and more-than-a-little garlic give beef heart plenty of flavor. After long simmering, it is finished off with Brandy.

- 3 to 4 pounds beef heart
- 1 bottle California Pinot Blanc
  Salt, pepper, monosodium glutamate
- ¾ cup parsley, chopped very fine
- ½ cup chives
- 5 or 6 small cloves garlic, chopped very fine
- 15 large button mushrooms, sliced into 3 parts
- ⅓ cup California Brandy

Wash heart and cut into ½-inch strips. Use electric fry pan, set at 300°. Put 2 cups wine in fry pan, then add heart, salt, pepper and monosodium glutamate. Cook for 25 minutes before turning. After turning, add parsley, chives, garlic and mushrooms. Add more wine as needed. Cover and simmer until tender (about 2 hours). Just before done add California Brandy.

 My choice of wine to accompany this dish: **CALIFORNIA PINOT BLANC**

Puchero Chollo

(6 TO 8 SERVINGS)

Mr. and Mrs. Ferrer Filipello, Italian Swiss Colony, Asti
Editor's note: Meat and vegetables are cooked together for a hearty one-dish meal. The stock makes an excellent first course for this or another meal. Asked what they like to serve to complete the menu, the contributors said, "serve with some sour dough French bread."

- 4 quarts water
- 1 teaspoon salt
- ⅛ teaspoon monosodium glutamate
- ⅛ teaspoon black pepper
- 2 pounds beef short ribs
- ½ pound lean salt pork, sliced
- 1 chicken, disjointed
- 3 chorizo (Spanish sausage)
- 6 peeled carrots
- 2 cups canned garbanzo (chick peas) No. 303 can, drained
- 6 medium onions
- 6 small cloves garlic, minced
- 1 zucchini squash, sliced
- 6 tomatoes
- 1 head cabbage, cut in eighths
- 1 green pepper, chopped
- 6 peeled potatoes
- 6 green onions
- 2 tablespoons chopped parsley
- 1 cup California Dry Sherry

Bring to a slow boil 4 quarts water. Add salt, monosodium glutamate, pepper, beef, pork, chicken and simmer for 1½ hours. Add chorizo and carrots. Simmer 30 minutes. Add all other vegetables and cook until potatoes are tender. Add Sherry. Arrange meat on platter, surround with vegetables. Serve stock as soup.

 Our choice of wine to accompany this dish:
CALIFORNIA DRY SHERRY *with the soup,*
CALIFORNIA CLARET *with the meat.*

Veal Scallops, Roman Style

(6 SERVINGS)

Mrs. George Pentek, The Christian Brothers, Fresno
Editor's note: The sage and white wine are traditional seasonings for veal in this recipe of Italian ancestry.

- 6 thin serving-size pieces veal round (about 1½ pounds)
  Salt, pepper, powdered sage
- 6 wafer-thin slices prosciutto, ham or Canadian bacon
- 3 tablespoons butter
- ¼ cup California White Table Wine
- 6 thin slices natural Swiss or mozzarella cheese

Pound pieces of veal steak with mallet to make as thin as possible. Sprinkle lightly with salt, pepper and powdered sage, or use a leaf of fresh sage. Cover each piece with prosciutto or ham. Pin into place with picks, or roll and tie with string. Cook gently in butter over moderate heat until golden brown on all sides, a total of 6 to 8 minutes (overcooking toughens and dries out veal). Place on heatproof platter; keep hot. Add wine to pan; scrape up bottom. Heat until bubbly and pour over veal. For extra embellishment, before adding pan sauce, top each serving with a slice of cheese. Run under broiler to glaze.

 My choice of wine to accompany this dish: **CALIFORNIA VIN ROSÉ**

Loin of Pork, Larkmead

(6 SERVINGS)

B. C. Solari, United Vintners, Inc., San Francisco
This pork roast is cooked in a covered barbecue oven, but can also be done on a rotating grill, if it is basted frequently. Our menu in summer for a distinguished luncheon when guests are males with hearty appetites: cold Vichyssoise or hot chicken broth with a slice of lemon; the roast, presliced and served on a platter garnished with parsley; sauce in a separate bowl; fresh applesauce; asparagus with hollandaise sauce; green salad with oil and wine vinegar dressing. For dessert, fresh fruit, assorted cheese, French bread.

1 12-rib pork loin
1 cup soy sauce
2 tablespoons Worcestershire sauce
1 cup honey (or maple syrup)
1 cup California Red Table Wine
¼ cup dry mustard
1 cup wine vinegar
Salt and pepper

Have butcher remove bone from pork loin, then tie bone to the meat to add flavor during cooking. Prepare marinade by combining all remaining ingredients in blender and mixing thoroughly. Marinate pork in a large flat baking dish for 4 or 5 hours. Turn occasionally. In covered barbecue oven, build a slow fire of coals. Place aluminum foil in an old pan on grate. Set roast on foil. Baste generously and often with marinade. Cook, covered, 1½ hours. During last 15 minutes, heat remaining marinade until it thickens slightly. Serve as sauce for meat.

 My choice of wine to accompany this dish:
CALIFORNIA PINOT NOIR *or* **PINOT CHARDONNAY**

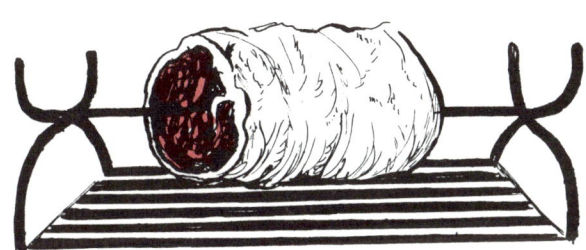

Cream Sherry Porkchops

(4 SERVINGS)

Mrs. Richard Nagoaka, The Christian Brothers, Napa
Editor's note: Both the sweetness and the caramel flavor of Cream Sherry enhance porkchops simmered and served in a creamy sauce. To take best advantage of the sauce, serve this dish with rice or noodles. Round out the meal with brussels sprouts, orange and grapefruit sections tossed with salad greens, and Apple-Brandy Cake (Page 88) for dessert.

Flour
Salt and pepper
1 teaspoon sage, crumbled or powdered
4 porkchops (about 1½ pounds)
¼ cup onions, diced
1 (10½-oz.) can cream of mushroom soup
½ cup milk or water
¾ cup California Cream Sherry
½ cup sliced mushrooms
1 cup dairy sour cream

Flour and season porkchops. Brown porkchops and add onions. Combine mushroom soup, milk, and Sherry. Pour sauce over porkchops. Add sliced mushrooms. Cover and simmer 45 to 50 minutes or until tender, stirring occasionally. Add the sour cream 2 minutes before serving. When the gravy is at preferred consistency, serve with steamed white rice. If the gravy becomes too thick, add more milk.

 My choice of wine to accompany this dish:
CALIFORNIA GAMAY, CHABLIS *or* **PINOT CHARDONNAY**

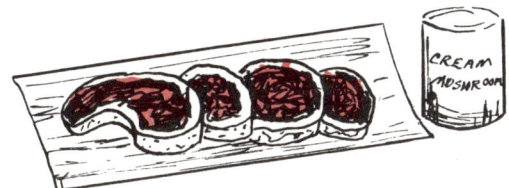

Mib's Lamb Shanks

(6 SERVINGS)

Mrs. John G. Laucci, Franzia Brothers Winery, Ripon
These lamb shanks seem to call for curried rice. We usually add a tossed green salad with olive oil and wine vinegar dressing, and serve cheesecake or lemon pie for dessert.

- 6 lamb shanks
- 1½ teaspoons salt
- 1 teaspoon pepper
- 1 teaspoon powdered oregano
- 1½ teaspoons sweet basil
- 1 tablespoon monosodium glutamate
- 1 large clove garlic
- 1½ tablespoons fresh or dry rosemary
- ¼ cup olive oil
- 3 tablespoons wine vinegar
- ½ cup water
- ½ cup California Sauterne or Chablis
- ½ cup olive oil
- 1 cup flour
- 1 large red onion, sliced thin
- 6 to 8 red potatoes, quartered
- 6 to 8 pieces dry mushrooms soaked in water then chopped or ½ pound fresh mushrooms, sliced
- ½ cup water
- ¾ cup California Sauterne or Chablis
- 1 (10-oz.) package frozen carrots
- 1 (10-oz.) package frozen peas

Place lamb shanks in deep platter or large bowl in single layer, if possible. Pour over a marinade made by combining salt, pepper, oregano, basil, monosodium glutamate, garlic, rosemary, ¼ cup olive oil, wine vinegar, ½ cup water and ½ cup wine. Allow to stand at least 1 hour, turning several times. In a large, heavy skillet, heat ½ cup olive oil. Flour shanks and cook in oil over medium heat until they are brown on all sides, about 20 minutes. Pour off all fat drippings. Add mushrooms, onions, potatoes, ½ cup water and ¾ cup wine. Allow to simmer over low heat for about 2½ hours. Add more wine and water if necessary. About 20 minutes before shanks are ready, add frozen carrots and peas. Stir gently. To serve: Place cooked curried rice on plate with shank in center. Spoon vegetables and juice around shank. Top with 1 sprinkling of fresh parsley.

 My choice of wine to accompany this dish: **CALIFORNIA CHABLIS**

Baked Ham Steak

(6 TO 8 SERVINGS)

Mrs. Jon B. Shastid, E. & J. Gallo Winery, Modesto
Editor's note: Ham steak is moist and flavorful when cooked in this way with a mixture of wine and milk. Made with these proportions, the sauce has a definite mustard flavor—complementary to the meat.

- 1 center slice of ham (about 2 inches thick)
- 1 cup milk
- 1 cup California Rhine Wine or other white table wine
- Prepared mustard

Place slice of ham in deep baking dish (8 x 12 x 2 inches is a good size). Pour over ham first milk then wine. Liquid should barely cover ham and come about half inch from top of dish. Bake in moderate oven (350°) for about one hour, turning ham steak over after 30 minutes baking. To make sauce, measure drippings in pan and add one-third as much prepared mustard.

Editor's note: Either **CALIFORNIA RIESLING** *or* **ROSÉ** *goes very well with this dish.*

Spanish Lamb

(6 TO 8 SERVINGS)

Mrs. Paul J. Lunardi, Wine Institute, San Francisco
Editor's note: Adding the wine at the end of the simmering period will preserve the wine flavor in the finished dish. Whenever wine is added earlier in the cooking period, it blends with the other seasonings and is not usually identifiable.

- 5 strips bacon, cut fine
- 4 cups boneless lamb shoulder, cut in 1-inch cubes (3 pounds)
- ⅓ cup flour
- Salt, pepper
- 1½ cups sliced peeled onions
- 3 cups diced celery
- ¾ teaspoon powdered sugar
- 1½ tablespoons lemon juice
- 3 cups tomato juice, canned or strained canned tomatoes
- 1½ teaspoons Worcestershire sauce
- 1½ teaspoons salt
- ⅛ teaspoon pepper
- ½ cup California Red Table Wine
- 3 cups green peas, uncooked

In a deep skillet or Dutch oven, cook bacon until light brown, about 5 minutes. Sprinkle lamb with flour, salt and pepper. Brown in bacon fat along with onions. Add remaining ingredients, except wine and peas, bring to a boil, then simmer 1 hour or until tender. Add wine and peas about 10 minutes before it is completely done.

 My choice of wine to accompany this dish:
CALIFORNIA CABERNET SAUVIGNON

Roasted Lamb Shanks with Potatoes

(4 TO 6 SERVINGS)

Mrs. Michael Filice, San Martin Vineyards, San Martin
This recipe originated in Calabria, Italy, and was handed down many generations in our family. Lamb is a favorite meat, especially at Easter. There always was a shaker of red hot pepper on the table, and the old timers would sprinkle their roast generously with it.

- 4 lamb shanks (about 3 pounds)
- 1 large clove garlic
- 2 teaspoons salt
- Oregano
- Monosodium glutamate
- Pepper
- 1 cup California Sauterne
- 3 tablespoons lemon juice
- Pinch chopped fresh rosemary
- 4 to 6 medium potatoes

Have butcher cut bone in 3 places. Wash shanks and place in large shallow pan. Place bits of garlic between cut bone and press together. Sprinkle with salt, oregano, monosodium glutamate and pepper. Bake in 450° oven. Mix wine, lemon juice and rosemary. As meat browns baste with wine mixture. Brown slowly and well on all sides, about ¾ hour. Then add a little of the wine mixture to bottom of pan. Cover with foil, and bake 350° for about 45 minutes. During this time prepare 4 to 6 medium potatoes, season and add alongside shanks. If pan is dry, add a little more wine or water, cover and bake until potatoes are tender, about 45 minutes.

 My choice of wine to accompany this dish: **CALIFORNIA BURGUNDY**

Sherried Lamb in Patty Shells

(6 SERVINGS)

Mrs. George Al Berry, E. & J. Gallo Winery, Modesto
I usually serve this recipe as a luncheon dish, preceded by cold consomme and accompanied by a grapefruit-cucumber molded salad and hot rolls. If dessert is served, it should be on the light side. I usually choose fresh fruit in season, such as strawberries or melons, or if none is available, ice cream or sherbet.

1 (10-oz.) package frozen patty shells
¼ cup sliced green onions
¼ lb. mushrooms, sliced
¼ cup butter or margarine
¼ cup flour
1 teaspoon salt
¼ teaspoon rosemary leaves
⅛ teaspoon pepper
½ cup milk
1 cup light cream
2 cups diced, cooked lamb
2 tablespoons diced canned pimiento
¼ cup California Dry Sherry

Prepare frozen patty shells according to directions on package. Sauté onions and mushrooms in butter until tender. Stir in flour and seasonings. Gradually add milk and cream; cook, stirring constantly until sauce thickens and boils. Add lamb, pimiento, and Sherry; mix and heat thoroughly. Spoon into hot patty shells on serving plate.

My choice of wine to accompany this dish:
CALIFORNIA GREY RIESLING or CHABLIS

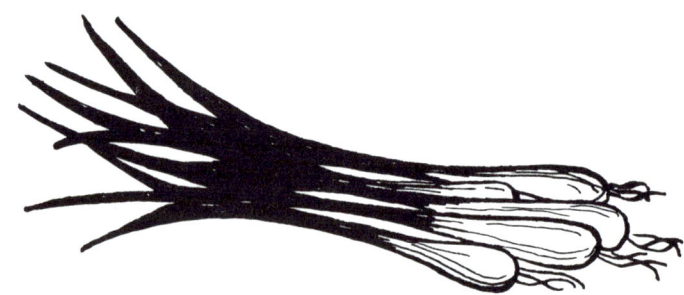

Rabbit à la Borghese

(5 TO 6 SERVINGS)

Mrs. Armand E. Bussone, Almaden Vineyards, Los Gatos
This is a northern Italian recipe brought to America by my mother-in-law. When she originally gave it to me, the recipe contained terms such as "a handful of this and a pinch of that." After years of experimentation, I feel these measurements are equivalent to the original quaint ones. This recipe can be prepared a day in advance because it tastes even better after being refrigerated 24 hours. It goes well with baked potatoes (mashed, whipped and replaced in skins) and a tossed salad plus any other favorite vegetable.

1 (2½-lb.) rabbit, cut up
3 tablespoons oil
½ medium red onion, finely chopped
¼ cup parsley, finely chopped
2 tablespoons butter
¼ cup California Chablis
Juice of ½ lemon
1 teaspoon flour
1 (10½-oz.) can consomme
Salt and pepper

Brown the rabbit in oil. In another skillet, slowly sauté onion and parsley in butter. Add rabbit. In the original browning pan, combine wine, lemon juice, and the flour mixed with water to form a paste so that it will blend smoothly with the other liquids. Simmer for three minutes. Add this to rabbit mixture. Finally, add the consommé and enough water to cover rabbit. Season with salt and pepper. Cover and cook slowly for 1 hour and 20 minutes. Note: If you're looking for a new tasty chicken dish, simply substitute a chicken for the rabbit in the above recipe and change the name to Chicken a la Borghese.

My choice of wine to accompany this dish: **CALIFORNIA RIESLING**

Veal Vermouth

(4 SERVINGS)

Mrs. Herbert L. Grosswendt, Brookside Vineyard Company, Agoura
I love this company recipe because it can all be prepared ahead of time. A little extra time on the stove won't hurt the flavor either. Finding this recipe in a magazine many years ago changed my cooking reputation overnight from "Bridal" to "Gourmet."

1½ pounds veal cutlet
1 clove garlic
　Flour
¼ cup margarine
½ pound fresh mushrooms, thinly sliced
½ teaspoon salt
　Pepper
⅓ cup California Dry Vermouth
1 teaspoon lemon juice
¼ cup snipped parsley

Wheedle the butcher into cutting your veal into very thin slices, then pound them even thinner. Rub veal all over with cut garlic clove and dip slices in flour. Heat margarine and add veal, several slices at a time, until they're golden brown on each side. Heap mushrooms on meat; sprinkle with salt, dash pepper and Vermouth. Cover and simmer 20 minutes or until fork tender. Just before serving, sprinkle lemon juice and parsley over all.

 My choice of wine to accompany this dish: **CALIFORNIA VIN ROSÉ**

Veal Steaks, Sauterne

(6 SERVINGS)

Miss Diana Weibel, Weibel Champagne Vineyards, Mission San Jose
Editor's note: These breaded veal steaks are well-seasoned and exceptionally tender, thanks to the wine and tomato sauce in which they are simmered.

1 onion, finely chopped
1 green pepper, finely chopped
3 tablespoons butter
2 tomatoes, sliced
10 mushrooms, sliced
2 (8-oz.) cans tomato sauce
1 teaspoon sweet basil
1 teaspoon oregano
1 teaspoon salt
½ teaspoon pepper
6 veal steaks
1 egg, well beaten
　Fine, dry bread crumbs
　Cooking oil
½ cup grated Parmesan cheese
1 cup California Sauterne
　Juice of 1 lemon
6 slices mozzarella cheese

Sauté onion and green pepper in butter until golden brown. Then add tomatoes, mushrooms, tomato sauce and seasonings. Simmer while preparing meat. Dip veal steaks in egg, then in bread crumbs. Fry in oil until golden brown. Place in a casserole and pour tomato mixture over meat. Sprinkle Parmesan cheese over top. Pour on wine and lemon juice. Cover and bake in slow oven, 325° for 45 minutes or until tender. Just before serving, place a slice of mozzarella cheese on top of each steak and broil until cheese melts.

 Editor's note: Either a **CALIFORNIA PINOT CHARDONNAY** *or* **ROSÉ** *would be a perfect complement to this dish.*

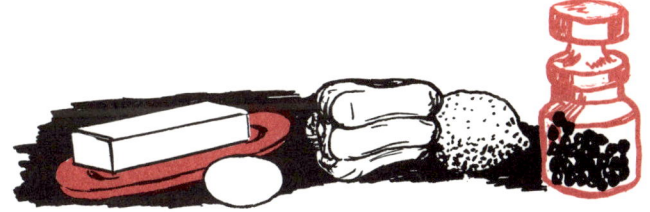

Veal Sauté

(18 SERVINGS)

Mrs. Frank Franzia, Sr., Franzia Brothers Winery, Ripon
This is our favorite recipe. We have used it many times for dinner parties—buffet style. Editor's note: It's too good to be reserved only for company. Cut it in half or thirds for an excellent family meal. Serve it with rice or noodles, peas or other green vegetable, and a salad of mixed greens with a sharp wine vinegar and olive oil dressing.

- 8 pounds veal stew meat, cut in 1½-inch cubes
- 4 teaspoons salt
- ½ teaspoon pepper
- ¼ cup salad oil
- 2 (4-oz.) cans sliced mushrooms, drained or ½ pound fresh mushrooms, sliced
- 2 cloves garlic, minced or mashed
- 1½ cups coarsely chopped onion
- 1 cup diagonally sliced celery
- 2 medium green peppers, cut in strips
- 2 (1-lb. 13-oz.) cans solid pack tomatoes
- 1 cup California Dry Red Table Wine
- 4 tablespoons cornstarch or 8 tablespoons flour
- Water

Season meat with salt and pepper and brown in oil. Remove from pan. Sauté mushrooms and garlic in drippings for 5 minutes; add onion and celery and sauté until onion is clear. Stir in green pepper, tomatoes, wine and browned meat. Cover and simmer until meat is tender, about 1½ hours. Mix cornstarch or flour with enough water to make a paste and stir in. Bring to a boil and cook, stirring, about 5 minutes, until thickened.

My choice of wine to accompany this dish:
CALIFORNIA BURGUNDY or **VIN ROSÉ**

Veal with Peas

(4 SERVINGS)

Mrs. Robert Diana, Villa Armando, Pleasanton
This recipe must have originated among the frugal French peasantry, to whom veal and peas are, after bread and onion soup, one of the most readily available and inexpensive food combinations. Like most peasant dishes, it is both satisfying and filling.

- 3 pounds veal cutlets, one inch thick
- 3 tablespoons butter
- Salt, pepper
- 2 tablespoons flour
- 1 (10½-oz.) can beef broth
- ½ cup California Dry Sherry
- Pinch of thyme
- 2 tablespoons chopped parsley
- 1 (No. 303) can early peas

Cut veal into 1-inch cubes. Melt butter in saucepan, add veal, salt and pepper, and brown meat well. Reduce heat, stir in flour. Remove from heat and gradually stir in broth. Cook until sauce is medium-thick. Add wine, thyme, parsley and peas. Continue cooking for about 15 minutes to blend flavors.

My choice of wine to accompany this dish: **CALIFORNIA ROSÉ**

Braised Veal Roast

(6 TO 8 SERVINGS)

Mrs. Frank Lico, San Martin Vineyards, San Martin
Editor's note: This is a meal-on-a-platter, with the succulent veal surrounded by vegetables and served with the sauce in which the meat was braised. Wine blends the many flavors deliciously and seems to moderate the large amount of garlic.

- 4 to 6-pound boned veal shoulder or leg, rolled
- Salt and pepper
- ¼ cup oil or butter
- 2 cups chopped onion
- 1 stalk celery, diced
- 1 cup diced carrots
- 6 peppercorns
- 1 bay leaf
- ¼ cup chopped parsley
- 3 cloves garlic, minced
- ½ cup California White Table Wine
- 1 (8-oz.) can tomato sauce
- ½ cup chicken broth
- 2 tablespoons oil or butter
- 2 large onions, cut in eighths
- 3 green peppers, cut in strips
- 2 sliced zucchini
- 1 small egg plant (sliced and cut in cubes)
- 1 (No. 303) can tomatoes
- 2 teaspoons salt

Season veal roast with salt and pepper. In deep, heavy skillet or Dutch oven, brown roast in oil or butter. Remove meat. In same pan, sauté chopped onion, celery and carrots for 5 minutes. Add peppercorns, bay leaf, parsley, 1 clove garlic, wine, tomato sauce and chicken broth. Cook over medium heat, uncovered, until liquid is reduced by half. Return roast to pan. Cover and bake in 350° oven 2 to 3 hours (about 30 minutes per pound). Add more broth or wine if necessary. About 20 minutes before roast is to be done, heat oil in skillet and sauté onions and green pepper until onion changes color. Add zucchini, egg plant and tomatoes. Season with salt. Cover and simmer 10 to 15 minutes. Add remaining garlic. Cook two minutes more. To serve, remove veal to a heated platter, surround with cooked vegetables. Sieve sauce in which meat was cooked and pour over meat or pass separately in a bowl.

 My choice of wine to accompany this dish:
A CALIFORNIA DRY WHITE TABLE WINE *or* **ROSÉ**

Roast Suckling Pig

(8 TO 10 SERVINGS)

Mrs. Alvin Ehrhardt, Allied Grape Growers, Fresno
I serve this with sauerkraut steamed in Champagne seasoned with garlic and coarse, black pepper and with ice cold applesauce with a dash of cinnamon in it.

- 12 to 14 pound pig
- 5 tablespoons butter
- 2 medium onions, chopped
- 2 cloves garlic minced very fine
- Pig's liver, finely chopped
- 5 to 6 cups dry bread crumbs
- ¼ cup chopped parsley
- 1 tablespoon basil or rosemary
- ½ cup pistachio or pine nuts
- ½ cup California Sherry or Brandy
- 2 tablespoons butter

Melt the 5 tablespoons butter in a skillet and add onion and garlic. When they are soft, but not colored, add pig's liver and sauteé 1 to 2 minutes. Add cooked mixture to bread crumbs along with remaining ingredients; mix together well. Drain pig, pat dry, salt and pepper cavity lightly, stuff pig with mixture and sew it up securely. Rub skin well with oil. Sprinkle with salt, freshly ground pepper and a little oregano or sweet basil. Arrange pig on spit so that it is perfectly balanced. Roast 2 to 2½ hours, basting often with pan drippings. (Be sure to have a drip pan at least as long as the pig.) Roast it until it is crisp and beautifully browned. Serve with a sauce made with the pan drippings, ¼ lb. finely chopped parsley and 1 teaspoon dry mustard with seasoning to taste. Make a necklace of dark red Tokay grapes, two Tokay eyes and an apple in the mouth. To carve: cut along spinal column, cutting the pig in half. Remove each ham, slice the hams and cut through the ribs.

 Editor's note: Such a festive dish almost requires that
CALIFORNIA CHAMPAGNE *be served with it.*

Poultry

Stuffed Wild Ducks

(2 SERVINGS)

Mrs. Joseph Concannon, Jr., Concannon Vineyard, Livermore

This is the only way to cook duck. Since the birds are a meal in themselves I keep the menu simple with a tossed salad (with a light dressing) and a green vegetable. Dessert is usually sherbet or fruit.

DUCKS
- 2 wild ducks
- Orange juice
- Brandy

STUFFING
- 1 cup uncooked wild rice
- 4 cups boiling water
- 1 teaspoon salt
- 1 cup boiling chicken broth
- 4 tablespoons sweet butter
- 1½ tablespoons minced chives
- 1½ tablespoons minced parsley
- 1½ tablespoons minced small green onions
- 1½ tablespoons minced celery tops
- 1½ tablespoons minced sweet basil
- 1 teaspoon gin
- Salt and freshly ground pepper
- Pinch of nutmeg
- Duck giblets

BASTE AND SAUCE
- 1 cup orange juice
- 2 cups California Red Table Wine
- 2 teaspoons lemon juice
- 1 teaspoon grated orange rind
- 3 tablespoons curacao

Ducks: Rub drawn and cleaned ducks with an equal portion of orange juice and Brandy, inside and out. Set aside while preparing stuffing. **Stuffing:** Wash wild rice. In upper part of double boiler, over direct heat, add rice slowly to boiling, salted water. Cook 5 minutes. Add chicken broth, cover and continue cooking, over boiling water in lower part of double boiler, for 20 to 45 minutes until rice is tender. While rice is steaming, cream butter with chives, parsley, green onions, celery tops and basil. Season with gin, salt and ground pepper to taste, and a tiny pinch of nutmeg. Put the creamed butter mixture into large saucepan, melt and add wild rice and chopped giblets. Cook briefly, tossing rice until thoroughly mixed. Then stuff ducks with mixture. Put ducks into open roasting pan (I use a Dutch oven without top). **Baste and Sauce:** Pour into the pan with ducks, orange juice, 1 cup red wine, lemon juice and grated orange rind. Roast in 400° oven for 20 to 40 minutes until birds are tender, basting frequently. (It depends on age and size of birds.) Remove ducks to hot platter. Add remaining cup of red wine and curacao to juices in roaster, scraping pan well. Bring to boil on top of stove, stir briefly, then pour sauce over ducks and serve.

My choice of wine to accompany this dish:
CALIFORNIA CABERNET SAUVIGNON *or* **PETITE SIRAH**

Chicken Tortilla

(8 SERVINGS)

Mrs. Reginald Gianelli, East-Side Winery, Lodi
Editor's note: This casserole dish is assembled in layers—chicken, tortillas, cheese and green chiles—with a dry white table wine as the seasoning that blends the unusual flavors together. It's ideal for the main dish of a buffet supper

- 4 whole chicken breasts (or 8 halves)
- 1 (10½-oz.) can cream of celery soup
- 1 (10½-oz.) can cream of mushroom soup
- 1¼ cups California Chablis or other White Table Wine
- 1 large onion, diced
- 12 tortillas
- 1 (7-oz.) can green chiles (seeds removed)
- 1 pound Cheddar cheese, shredded

Wrap chicken breasts in foil and bake 1 hour in a moderately hot oven (400°). Cool, bone and break into large pieces. Mix soups with wine and onion. Cut tortillas and chiles in strips. Layer ingredients in a casserole, starting with small amount of liquid and ending with cheese, in this order: liquid, tortillas, chicken, chile, cheese. Bake uncovered in a moderate oven (350°) for 1 hour.

Editor's note: Serve a **CALIFORNIA CHABLIS, ROSÉ,** *or a light red wine such as* **GRIGNOLINO** *with this dish.*

Epicurean Chicken Livers

(4 SERVINGS)

Mrs. James Gott, United Vintners, San Francisco
We tried unsuccessfully for many years to obtain a chicken liver recipe from a fine restaurant at Lake Tahoe. Finally we gave up and developed this recipe. We, and our guests, think it is wonderful. With the livers we serve a rice casserole, Chinese pea pods, and limestone lettuce salad.

- 1½ pounds frying chicken livers
- Flour
- 5 tablespoons butter
- Garlic powder, salt and pepper
- ½ pound fresh mushrooms, sautéed in butter
- ⅓ cup California Dry Sherry
- ⅓ cup chopped green onion
- ⅓ cup chopped fresh parsley

Soak livers in cold water for 30 minutes. Drain and dry on paper towels. Very lightly dust livers with flour. Melt butter in frying pan which can be covered tightly. Brown livers quickly over fairly high heat so livers remain pink inside. Reduce heat to low. Add seasonings, sautéed mushrooms and Sherry. Stir until slightly thickened (more Sherry may be added as required). Sprinkle onions and parsley over top. Cover and steam for two minutes. Serve immediately.

 My choice of wine to accompany this dish: **CALIFORNIA CHABLIS**

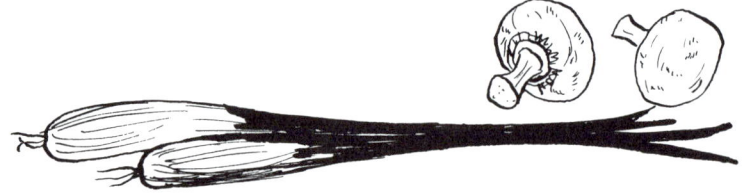

Chicken Hearts in Sour Cream

(3 TO 4 SERVINGS)

Mrs. Philip Smyser, Wine Advisory Board, San Francisco
I serve this over noodles with a salad and homemade muffins.

- 1 pound chicken hearts, split lengthwise
- ½ pound fresh mushrooms, halved
- ½ green pepper, chopped
- 1 pimiento, chopped
- ½ onion, chopped
- 3 tablespoons butter
- Garlic salt, salt, pepper, basil, spiced pepper, oregano, poultry seasoning to taste
- ¼ cup California White Table Wine
- 2 cups medium white sauce (homemade, canned or use a sauce mix)
- ½ cup dairy sour cream

Sauté chicken hearts, onion, green pepper, mushrooms, and pimiento in butter until almost done. Add wine and seasonings. Cook until tender. Mix white sauce and sour cream with the above. Serve.

 My choice of wine to accompany this dish:
CALIFORNIA WHITE TABLE WINE

Franzia Baked Chicken

(4 TO 6 SERVINGS)

Mrs. Frank Franzia, Jr., Franzia Brothers Winery, Ripon
I threw this recipe together one night when I was in a rush to get dinner started. It turned out so well, and was so simple to make, I now serve it often—even when I have plenty of time.

- 1 (3-lb.) broiling chicken
- Salt, pepper, garlic powder
- 1 (4-oz.) can mushroom pieces
- 1 medium onion, cut in wedges
- ¼ cup melted butter
- 5 medium potatoes, sliced in ¼-inch slices
- ½ cup California Sauterne
- ½ cup water

Rub whole chicken with seasonings all over and in cavity. Tuck mushrooms between thighs and breast, put remainder in cavity along with onion. Brush entire chicken with melted butter then pour rest into chicken cavity. Bake in moderate oven (350°) for 30 minutes, then place sliced potatoes around chicken in pan. Mix wine and water together and pour over all. Bake for 30 minutes more, basting once.

 My choice of wine to accompany this dish: **CALIFORNIA CHABLIS**

Chicken with Burgundy and Black Cherry Sauce

(4 SERVINGS)

Mrs. Philip Smyser, Wine Advisory Board, San Francisco
This is an impressive party dish, although it is quite easy to prepare. With it we serve rice pilaf, a steamed green vegetable like broccoli with lemon and mayonnaise sauce, and something elegant for dessert.

- 1 (2½ to 3½-lb.) frying chicken, cut up
- 1 (20-oz.) can dark, sweet, pitted cherries (reserve juice)
- 1 cup California Burgundy
- 3 tablespoons lemon juice
- 2 or 3 cloves garlic, crushed
- ¼ teaspoon ground ginger
- ½ teaspoon oregano
- 2 teaspoons salt
- Dash pepper
- 1 chicken bouillon cube
- ¼ cup shortening or oil
- ⅓ cup cornstarch
- Parsley

Wash and dry chicken. Drain cherries and save liquid. Into large kettle combine cherry juice, wine, lemon juice, garlic, ginger, oregano, salt, pepper and bouillon cube. Add chicken and simmer until tender (about one hour). Remove chicken, drain, brown in oil. Mix cornstarch with cold water to make a paste. Add to sauce, cook and stir until thickened. Add chicken and cherries to sauce, simmer till cherries are hot through. To serve, heap chicken on platter, top with cherries and sauce. Garnish with lots of parsley. Serve extra sauce on the side.

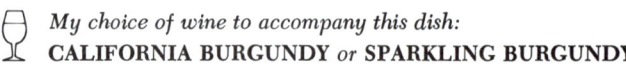
My choice of wine to accompany this dish:
CALIFORNIA BURGUNDY or **SPARKLING BURGUNDY**

Honolulu Chicken

(6 TO 8 SERVINGS)

Mr. and Mrs. Rudy Windmiller, Almaden Vineyards, San Francisco
This is our own combination, especially appreciated because it does not have any added fat.
Editor's note: A touch of spice, and the use of red table wine for flavoring is unusual and good.

- 2 large fryers, cut up
- 2 cups California Burgundy or Claret
- ½ cup soy sauce
- 1 teaspoon ground ginger
- ½ teaspoon nutmeg
- 1 tablespoon sugar
- 1 teaspoon grated orange rind, fresh or dried
- 1 (8½-oz.) can pineapple slices
- Crushed garlic or garlic salt to taste

Place chicken, skin side down, in oven pan (about 16 x 11 x 2½ inches). Prepare marinade of wine and all other ingredients including syrup from pineapple slices. (Keep slices for garnishing.) Pour marinade over chickens. Leave several hours or overnight in refrigerator. Bake 1½ to 2 hours or just until tender in moderate oven (350°), turning pieces after one hour. About 15 minutes before serving, put quartered pineapple slices into the baking dish; use later for garnishing; add sprig of parsley on plate. This is also excellent for serving cold because the marinade jells.

My choice of wine to accompany this dish:
CALIFORNIA JOHANNISBERG RIESLING or **GEWURZTRAMINER**

Delicious Chicken Casserole

(5 SERVINGS)

Mrs. Aldo Nerelli, Pesenti Winery, Templeton
Editor's note: This chicken casserole is easy to prepare and to serve because it's made of chicken breasts—one for each serving. The seasonings are subtle so they don't overpower the dry white wine that makes this dish outstanding.

- 5 large chicken breasts, boned
- 1 teaspoon monosodium glutamate
- 1 teaspoon salt
- Pepper
- Flour
- ⅓ cup butter
- 1 cup fresh mushrooms
- ¼ cup chopped green onions, including tops
- 1 clove garlic, thinly sliced
- ½ cup California White Table Wine
- 1 (7-oz.) can artichoke hearts

Sprinkle chicken with monosodium glutamte, salt and pepper and coat well with flour. Brown in ¼ cup of the butter. Remove chicken, add remaining butter; brown mushrooms, onions and garlic. Return chicken to pan and add wine and simmer gently 45 minutes or until tender. Add drained artichoke hearts and heat thoroughly.

My choice of wine to accompany this dish:
CALIFORNIA DRY SAUTERNE or **CHABLIS**

Chicken Stroganoff

(6 SERVINGS)

Kelli Ellis, Almaden Vineyards, San Francisco
Editor's note: Wine, sour cream and mushrooms give this chicken specialty excellent flavor. As an alternate method of cooking, add wine and mushrooms together, simmer 25 minutes, then add sour cream and simmer 10 minutes more. There's less chance for the cream to curdle in this shorter cooking time.

- 8 chicken breasts, boned
- 2 eggs, beaten
- Salt and pepper
- 4 tablespoons oil
- ⅓ cup California White Table Wine
- 1 pint dairy sour cream
- 1 cup fresh sliced mushrooms
- Water

Have butcher bone chicken breasts. Roll the chicken in beaten eggs, and seasonings. Brown in oil (or use half oil and half butter) slowly on all sides, approximately 15 minutes per side at 250°. Turn heat down to "simmer" and let the meat set for 10 minutes. Pour wine over, and allow to stand for a few minutes. Then stir in sour cream and mushrooms. Add water as desired so the sauce is consistency of gravy. Allow meat and sauce to simmer for 45 minutes, and serve over noodles.

Editor's note: Try a **CALIFORNIA GEWURZTRAMINER** *or* **PINOT CHARDONNAY** *with this dish. Either one goes very well with it.*

Chicken à la Waleski

(4 SERVINGS)

Mrs. Geneva Shuflin, Wine Institute, San Francisco
This is a successful copy of a heavenly dish served at L'Omelette in Los Altos, California. With it I serve rice steamed in chicken broth, tossed green salad with a mild dressing, French bread to soak up some of the delicious gravy and flaming Mandarin oranges over vanilla ice cream for dessert.

CHICKEN
- 2 broiler-fryer chickens, cut up
- 2 carrots
- 2 onions
- 2 (13¾-oz.) cans chicken broth
- 4 tablespoons chopped parsley
- 2 pinches thyme
- Bay leaf
- 2 whole cloves
- 4 peppercorns
- 4 tablespoons butter

SAUCE
- 6 tablespoons butter
- 4 tablespoons flour
- 1 cup California White Table Wine
- 2 egg yolks
- 4 tablespoons heavy cream
- 1 pound fresh mushrooms
- 4 tablespoons butter
- Juice of 2 lemons

Chicken: Simmer chicken pieces gently until tender with carrots, onions, chicken broth, parsley, thyme, bay leaf, cloves and peppercorns. When chicken is done, drain and save broth. Dry chicken on a cloth and brown in the 4 tablespoons butter. **Sauce:** Blend 6 tablespoons butter with flour and stir over heat for a few minutes. Gradually add 2 cups reserved chicken broth and wine, stirring into a smooth sauce; bring to a boil. Remove the fat and strain through a sieve. Let sauce simmer and reduce. Add egg yolks mixed with cream. Sauté mushrooms in butter until a light brown. Place browned chicken in serving dish, place mushrooms all around, cover with a little gravy. Pour the lemon juice over all. Serve remaining gravy separately.

 My choice of wine to accompany this dish:
CALIFORNIA EMERALD RIESLING *or* **CHENIN BLANC**

Blazing Chicken

(4 SERVINGS)

Mrs. Alfred Fromm, Fromm & Sichel, San Francisco
Editor's note: Like many fine old recipes, this one uses a wine glass measurement. It adds a certain flair to the cooking and flaming. In standardized measurement, a wine glass measurement equals about one-third cup.

- ¾ cup sweet butter
- 1 roasting chicken (about 3 lbs.)
- 1 wineglass California Brandy
- 1 wineglass California Port
- 1 tablespoon flour
- 1½ cups heavy cream, warmed
- Salt and pepper

Butter a baking dish and put remainder of butter inside chicken. Bake in 350° oven, turning the bird first on one side and then on the other. Baste frequently. At the end of 35 minutes, pour Brandy over chicken. Light it and when the blaze is burning brightly extinguish it with the glass of Port. Finish baking the chicken, approximately 30 minutes longer. Remove chicken and keep warm. Place baking dish over medium heat on top of stove, stir in flour, cook for a minute or so, then add the cream. Stir just a moment and pour over the chicken, when served.

 Editor's note: **CALIFORNIA PINOT CHARDONNAY**
is a distinguished partner for this dish.

Chicken Breasts Mandarin

(6 SERVINGS)

Mrs. Frank Bartholomew, Buena Vista Winery, Sonoma
Mrs. Frederick Voigt, who is a frequent visitor at Buena Vista Vineyards has been kind enough to share one of her favorite recipes with us.

- 3 chicken breasts, halved
- Flour
- ½ teaspoon monosodium glutamate
- Pepper
- 3 tablespoons butter
- ¾ cup chicken broth
- ½ cup California White Table Wine
- 3 tablespoons cornstarch
- 2 teaspoons soy sauce
- ½ teaspoon grated orange rind
- ¾ teaspoon paprika
- 1 (11-oz.) can Mandarin orange segments and juice

Skin chicken; dust with flour seasoned with monosodium glutamate and pepper. Brown in melted butter; place in baking dish. Add chicken broth to pan drippings; simmer while scraping up crusty bits from bottom and sides. Pour wine in small covered jar with cornstarch; shake smooth. Add to sauce; stir until smooth. Add remaining ingredients, except oranges, and simmer until well blended and slightly thickened. Pour sauce over chicken. Cover. Bake at 325° for 45 minutes or until tender. Add drained orange segments last 10 minutes.

My choice of wine to accompany this dish:
CALIFORNIA PINOT CHARDONNAY

Squabs in White Wine

(6 TO 8 SERVINGS)

Mrs. August Sebastiani, Samuele Sebastiani Winery, Sonoma
Editor's note: Either squabs or small chickens, cooked whole are good seasoned in this way with white wine and shallots. Mrs. Sebastiani says that an extra special touch for this dish is wild rice. Also a watercress salad in season is an excellent addition to this meal.

- 6 squabs or small chickens
- 3 tablespoons olive oil
- 3 tablespoons butter
- 2 cups California White Table Wine
- 6 squab livers
- 2 chicken livers
- 8 shallots, finely chopped
- 1 (8-oz.) can sliced button mushrooms
- Salt and pepper
- Chopped parsley

Truss squabs. In a large heavy skillet, heat olive oil and butter and brown birds lightly on both sides. Add wine and salt and pepper to taste. Cover the pan loosely and cook birds for 15 minutes. Add birds' livers, chicken livers, shallots and mushrooms with their liquid, and cook this mixture, covered, for 15 minutes longer, or until the birds are tender. Transfer the birds to a heated platter, pour the pan juices over them, and sprinkle with chopped parsley.

My choice of wine to accompany this dish:
CALIFORNIA GREEN HUNGARIAN

Petite Poulette au Vin

(4 SERVINGS)

Mrs. Richard Peterson, Beaulieu Vineyard, Rutherford
Editor's note: One teaspoon of mixed dry Italian herbs substitutes for the Fines Herbs in this recipe, though fresh herbs from the garden are, of course, delightful whenever available.

- 2 chickens, cut in halves
- ½ cup oil
- ½ cup butter
- 1 cup California Dry Sherry
- Fines Herbs
- Paprika
- Salt and pepper
- Sautéed mushrooms

Put oil in large baking dish, arrange chicken, dot with butter and pour on Sherry. Add seasonings. Bake in moderate oven (350°) 45 minutes to 1 hour. Garnish with mushrooms.

Editor's note: **CALIFORNIA JOHANNISBERG RIESLING** *is a wonderful accompaniment to this chicken dish.*

Pheasant Surprise

(4 TO 5 SERVINGS)

Mrs. Rene Baillif, Concannon Vineyard, San Francisco
Pheasant cooked in this way makes a sumptuous dish. Start the meal with sliced tomatoes and anchovies. Serve wild rice with the pheasant and Camembert and pears for dessert.

- ¼ cup oil
- ¼ cup butter
- 2 pheasants boned, skinned and cut in pieces
- Flour
- 2 shallots, minced
- ½ pound mushrooms, sliced
- 1 cup bouillon or chicken broth
- 1 cup California Dry Sherry
- 2 jiggers (¼ cup) California Brandy
- 1 small stalk celery
- 1 sprig parsley
- 1 small green onion

Heat the oil and butter in a deep skillet or Dutch oven over medium heat. Slightly coat pheasant pieces with a little flour, brown them evenly to a golden color, add shallots, mushrooms, bouillon, Sherry, Brandy, celery, parsley and onion. Cover and cook slowly 1½ to 2 hours.

 My choice of wine to accompany this dish: **CALIFORNIA PETITE SIRAH**

Mandarin Pheasant

(6 SERVINGS)

Mrs. Jack Farrior, Jr., Almaden Vineyards, Los Gatos
We like this pheasant with wild rice, Green Peppers Florentine, (page 64) a tossed green salad, and fried apples.

6 pheasant breasts, split
2 (10½-oz.) cans chicken broth
⅓ cup soy sauce
1 clove garlic
1 teaspoon fresh grated ginger
1 (6-oz.) can frozen concentrated orange juice
1 cup brown sugar
1 teaspoon salt
1 cup California Chablis
2 (11-oz.) cans Mandarin oranges, drained

Place breasts in large baking dish with all ingredients except oranges and cover. Bake in moderate oven (350°) for 1½ hours. Arrange orange segments over pheasant breasts. Continue baking uncovered for ½ hour or until there is a golden glaze.

 My choice of wine to accompany this dish: **CALIFORNIA CHABLIS**

Blossom Hill Pheasant

(2 GENEROUS SERVINGS)

Mrs. E. Jeff Barnette, Martini & Prati Winery, Santa Rosa
We serve this pheasant with asparagus or another green vegetable, and Lemon Meringue Pie.

1 pheasant
2 cups California Red Table Wine
5 tablespoons melted butter or margarine
Salt and pepper
3 stalks celery, sliced
3 sprigs parsley, chopped
½ cup each, sliced onions and carrots
2 slices bacon
1 cup light cream
2 tablespoons currant jelly

Wash and drain pheasant. Marinate several hours or overnight in wine, turning several times. Remove and dry with paper towels. Brush inside and out with melted butter. Season with salt and pepper. In 450° oven, roast pheasant, 20 minutes, until golden brown. Place celery, parsley, onions, carrots and bacon in bottom of casserole. Place pheasant on top, add about half of the wine marinade and bake covered in 350° oven for 30 minutes. Pour cream over the bird and bake covered until tender. Remove cover from pan and return to very hot oven (500°) until brown, about 10 minutes. Baste several times. Strain the pan gravy and mix with currant jelly, beating until smooth. Serve the gravy separately.

My choice of wine to accompany this dish: **CALIFORNIA CABERNET SAUVIGNON, PINOT NOIR** *or* **SPARKLING BURGUNDY**

Roast Stuffed Pheasant

(8 SERVINGS)

Mr. Robert Diana, Villa Armando, Pleasanton
Editor's note: The sausage and other seasonings give these whole roasted pheasants a definite Italian character. The birds are moist and very flavorful.

STUFFING
- ¾ pound Italian sweet sausage
- ½ cup uncooked wild rice
- 2 slices bread
- ¼ cup milk
- ¼ cup olive oil
- 7 tablespoons butter, melted
- 1 ounce salt pork, diced
- ¼ pound onions, diced
- 1 bay leaf, crumbled
- 1 small garlic clove, mashed
- ½ cup California White Table Wine
- 2 eggs, lightly beaten
- ½ cup chopped parsley
- ¼ cup grated Parmesan cheese

PHEASANTS
- 2 pheasants
- 3 thin slices salt pork
- ¼ teaspoon minced fresh rosemary
- Salt and pepper
- ¼ cup hot chicken broth

Prepare Stuffing: Remove casing from sausage and cut meat into 1-inch pieces. Soak rice in lukewarm water for 15 minutes, then drain and cook in lightly salted water for about 20 minutes or until tender, but not mushy; drain. Soak the bread in milk, squeeze out the liquid and crumble the bread. Combine 3 tablespoons of the oil and 4 tablespoons of the butter and the diced salt pork in a skillet; heat. Add the onions and sauté to medium brown. Add sausage pieces, chopped giblets, the bay leaf and garlic. Cook 20 minutes. Add the wine, cover and cook 3 minutes. Remove mixture from the heat and cool 10 minutes. Take the ingredients from the skillet; chop very fine. Do not lose juices. Place all back in the skillet, add the bread, beaten eggs, parsley, cheese and drained rice. Mix well.

Pheasants: Fill the birds with the stuffing. Truss the birds and place them breast side down in oiled roasting pan. Roast at 450° for 10 minutes. Turn the birds and cover breasts with the sliced salt pork. Sprinkle seasonings over the birds and pat remaining oil on parts not covered with salt pork. Reduce heat to slow (300°) and cook 45 minutes basting occasionally. The whole cooking time should not be longer than 1 hour. Remove from oven and keep warm. Discard fat from roasting pan. Add remaining butter and hot broth to the drippings in the pan and simmer for 10 minutes until mixture is reduced to a gravy. Strain, spoon gravy over birds and serve immediately.

 My choice of wine to accompany this dish:
CALIFORNIA BURGUNDY *or* **BARBERA**

Theresa's Sherry-Flavored Chicken

(3 SERVINGS)

Mrs. Enzo Casazza, Cambiaso Winery and Vineyards, Healdsburg
This is my mother's recipe. We serve it over steamed rice with a sprinkle of cheese. It's even delicious reheated the next day. Editor's note: The Sherry flavor is subtle. If you like it more dominant, increase the Sherry ingredient to ½ cup and cut the water to ¾ cup.

- 1 (2½-lb.) chicken, cut up
- ½ cup butter
- 1 medium onion, sliced
- ⅓ cup California Sherry or Marsala
- 1 cup water
- 1 (8-oz.) can tomato sauce
- ½ teaspoon paprika
- Salt and pepper

Fry chicken slowly in butter till browned on all sides. Remove chicken to oven baking dish, sauté onion in butter in which chicken has been browned and add wine, water, tomato sauce and paprika. Bring to a boil, add seasonings and pour over chicken. Bake 50 to 60 minutes at 375°.

My choice of wine to accompany this dish:
CALIFORNIA CHABLIS *or* **GRENACHE ROSÉ**

Flaming Cornish Hens

(6 SERVINGS)

Mrs. Earl G. Harrah, Wine Advisory Board, San Francisco

Flaming Cornish Hens is the main dish of our favorite Epicurean dinner. I enjoy cooking and serving this menu on very special occasions and Earl enjoys serving it at the table. First there is a crab and avocado cocktail seasoned lightly with Sherry, then come the birds, garnished with spiced peaches. The vegetable is green beans amandine. Strawberries in Champagne top off the meal.

6 Rock Cornish Hens (14 to 16 oz. each), fresh or frozen
1 tablespoon salt
2 (6-oz.) packages wild rice (6 cups cooked)
3 (2½-oz.) cans whole button mushrooms, drained
1 cup finely chopped onion
1 cup finely chopped celery
½ cup butter or margarine
1 cup California White Table Wine
Salt and freshly ground pepper
Melted butter
California Brandy
Spiced peaches
Wine gravy (below)

WINE GRAVY
2 tablespoons butter or margarine
½ cup flour
¾ cup California White Table Wine
¾ cup water
1 (4-oz.) can mushrooms
2 tablespoons chopped parsley
1 tablespoon chopped onion
½ tablespoon paprika
½ teaspoon salt
¼ teaspoon freshly ground pepper
1 cup dairy sour cream

Wash birds and dry thoroughly, inside and out. Rub inside cavity of each with ½ teaspoon salt. Prepare wild rice stuffing: Cook rice according to package directions. Sauté drained mushrooms, onion, and celery in melted butter. Then add to cooked rice along with the wine and seasonings. Mix lightly with a fork. Stuff body and neck cavity of each bird loosely with stuffing. (A scant cup stuffing for each is usually sufficient.) Skewer openings together. Brush outside of hens with melted butter. Place on rack in shallow pan and bake in moderate oven (350°) until tender, about 1¼ hours. Brush with additional butter as needed. **Wine Gravy:** Melt Butter or margarine in pan in which birds were cooked. Blend in flour. Mix wine and water and gradually add to flour-butter mixture, stirring constantly. Cook until thick and smooth. Add mushrooms with liquid, parsley, onion, paprika, salt and pepper. Just before serving add sour cream at room temperature. Heat thoroughly, but do not boil. Makes about 3½ cups wine gravy. To serve: Place birds in a circle on a large fire-proof serving plate (a round chop plate is best). Garnish with spiced peaches. Pour warmed Brandy over hens and peaches, ignite and bring to the table in flames.* Serve with wine gravy.

My choice of wine to accompany this dish: **CALIFORNIA SPARKLING BURGUNDY, CHAMPAGNE or CABERNET SAUVIGNON**

Editor's note: White and wild-rice mix may be substituted for the wild rice specified in this recipe, or brown rice mixed with a small amount of wild rice may also be used.

* Note: Be sure to warm the Brandy in a double boiler over hot water, never in an open pot over flame.

Fish and Shellfish

Sole with Shrimp and Crab Filling

(6 SERVINGS)

Mrs. Morris Katz, Paul Masson Vineyards, Saratoga
Editor's note: Sole fillets form rolls around a savory shrimp and crab stuffing. The wine sauce tops each serving.

FISH
- 3 large fillets of sole (1½ lbs.)
- ½ teaspoon salt
- ⅛ teaspoon white pepper
- Filling (below)
- Wine Sauce (below)
- Melted butter
- Parsley for garnish
- 12 whole shrimp for garnish

FILLING
- 1½ teaspoons butter
- 1½ tablespoons flour
- ½ cup milk
- ½ cup flaked crabmeat, canned or fresh
- ½ cup cooked chopped shrimp, canned or fresh
- ¼ cup chopped celery
- ¼ cup chopped green onions
- 1 teaspoon chopped parsley
- ½ teaspoon salt

SAUCE
- 1 tablespoon butter
- 1 teaspoon flour
- ½ cup California White Table Wine
- ½ cup light cream
- ¼ teaspoon salt
- Dash pepper
- Hot sauce to taste
- 2 egg yolks, lightly beaten
- 1 teaspoon lemon juice

Fish: Season the fillets with salt and pepper. Lay flat on baking sheet.
Filling: Melt butter and stir in flour. Gradually add milk and cook, stirring constantly, until sauce thickens. Remove from heat and stir in crabmeat, shrimp, celery, onions, parsley and salt. Divide the filling equally among the fillets, spreading it generously. Roll the fillets carefully and secure with picks. Cut each roll in half and place in shallow baking dish. Bake in moderately hot oven (400°) for 30 minutes. Baste often with melted butter. Meanwhile, prepare **Wine Sauce:** In upper part of double boiler, melt butter, stir in flour, then gradually mix in wine and cream. Season with salt and pepper. Heat over boiling water, stirring constantly, about 5 minutes, until sauce thickens slightly. Add a few spoonfuls of hot sauce to the slightly beaten egg yolks. Then stir egg mixture into sauce. Continue cooking a few minutes longer, stirring, until eggs thicken sauce. Add lemon juice and pour over sole rolls on serving plates. Garnish with parsley and whole cooked shrimp.

 My choice of wine to accompany this dish:
CALIFORNIA EMERALD RIESLING

Oysters Provençales

(AS FIRST COURSE: 4 SERVINGS. AS MAIN DISH: 2 SERVINGS)

Mrs. Leon S. Peters, Valley Foundry, Fresno

1 onion, chopped
3 tablespoons margarine or butter
4 tablespoons flour
2 cups rich milk
¾ teaspoon salt
¼ teaspoon paprika
Dash pepper
½ teaspoon monosodium glutamate
Garlic salt to taste
3 tablespoons finely chopped parsley
¼ cup California White Table Wine
2 (8-oz.) cans oysters

Sauté onions in margarine. Toss with flour and gradually add milk and keep stirring. Add seasonings, parsley and wine. The sauce can be covered and set aside until one-half hour before you are ready to serve. When ready to serve, drain oysters, reserving liquid, and place them in individual casseroles. Reheat cream sauce with broth from oysters, and pour over oysters. Bake in 300° oven about 20 minutes.

My choice of wine to accompany this dish:
CALIFORNIA GREY RIESLING *or* **EMERALD RIESLING**

Salmon Mousse

(6 SERVINGS)

Mrs. Don Rudolph, Cresta Blanca Wine Company, Livermore
Editor's note: This elegant salmon mousse is made in two parts then layered in a ring mold.

PART I
1 (1-lb.) can salmon
½ cup lemon juice
1 envelope unflavored gelatin
2 tablespoons water
½ cup California White Table Wine

PART II
2 egg yolks
1½ tablespoons soft butter or margarine
½ teaspoon flour
1 teaspoon salt
2 teaspoons sugar
1 teaspoon Worcestershire sauce
1 teaspoon dry mustard
1 teaspoon grated onion
⅛ teaspoon cayenne
½ teaspoon fresh dill, dried dill-weed or finely chopped parsley
¾ cup milk
1 envelope unflavored gelatin
¼ cup California White Table Wine

Part I: If you have a blender, put the whole can of salmon, bones and all, in blender jar. Add lemon juice. Blend until smooth. If you have no blender, remove bones and any skin, and with a fork, flake the salmon into tiny pieces. Soften gelatin in water for five minutes. Dissolve gelatin over hot water. Allow to cool, then combine with wine and salmon. Chill while preparing second part. **Part II:** In upper part of one-quart double boiler over hot water, beat egg yolks. Smooth together the butter and flour and add to egg yolks, stirring constantly. Add salt, sugar, Worcestershire sauce, mustard, onion, cayenne, dill and milk. Add gelatin that has been soaked for a few minutes in wine. Stir until gelatin is dissolved. Let mixture cool until slightly set. Rub a 1½-quart ring mold with cooking oil. Pour in one-third of cooked gelatin mixture. Let stand 5 minutes. Add ½ of salmon mixture. Repeat with gelatin and fish until all are used. Pour last of gelatin on top. Chill until firm, about 3 hours. To serve, unmold on a chilled platter. If desired, garnish with watercress or surround with cocktail crackers.

Editor's note: Either **CALIFORNIA PINOT CHARDONNAY** *or* **CHABLIS** *would be excellent wine accompaniments for this dish.*

Fillet of Sole Florentine
(4 SERVINGS)

Mrs. Leon S. Peters, Valley Foundry, Fresno

4 tablespoons flour
4 tablespoons butter
 or margarine
2 cups rich milk
¾ teaspoon salt
 Pepper
½ teaspoon curry powder
 or more to taste
1 (10-oz.) package frozen
 chopped spinach
2 pounds fillet of sole
½ cup California
 White Table Wine
¼ cup water
 Salt
 Parmesan cheese

Make standard cream sauce by blending flour with butter or margarine, then add milk and stir constantly until thick and smooth. Season with salt, pepper and curry powder to taste. Set aside. This can be made ahead of time and reheated when ready to use. Cook spinach in very little water; drain, pressing out excess water. Simmer the sole in wine and water, in a covered fryer about 5 minutes. Butter individual casseroles or one shallow casserole. Place spinach on bottom, salt lightly, lift fish carefully and place on top of spinach. Add some sauce that fish has been cooked in to the cream sauce and reheat. Sauce should be medium thick. Correct seasoning if necessary and pour over fish. Sprinkle Parmesan cheese over top and bake in 300° oven about 20 minutes until bubbly. Put under broiler to brown lightly.

 My choice of wine to accompany this dish: **CALIFORNIA GEWURZTRAMINER**

Stuffed Fish Rolls
(6 SERVINGS)

Mrs. Herbert L. Grosswendt, Brookside Vineyard Company, Agoura

½ tablespoon minced onion
2 tablespoons butter
6 thin white fish fillets
 (about 1½ pounds)
⅛ pound fresh mushrooms,
 sliced thin (about ¼ cup)
⅛ pound tiny cooked shrimp
 (about ⅔ cup)
 Salt and cracked pepper
½ pint dairy sour cream
¼ cup California Chablis
 Paprika

Cook onion in butter until transparent. Sprinkle fish fillets with mushrooms, shrimp, onion, salt and pepper. Roll up fillets and secure with picks. Put in greased baking dish and top with sour cream thinned with wine. Sprinkle with paprika, and bake in moderate oven (350°) for 20 minutes or until fish flakes easily.

My choice of wine to accompany this dish: **CALIFORNIA CHABLIS**

Winemasters' Swordfish
(6 SERVINGS)

Mrs. Robert M. Ivie, Guild Wine Company, San Francisco

6 swordfish steaks
 (about 1 inch thick)
1 tablespoon minced onion
1 teaspoon oregano
2 tablespoons chopped parsley
½ teaspoon salt
 Freshly ground pepper
 to taste
2 tablespoons lemon juice
1 cup California Sauterne

Marinate swordfish steaks for two hours or longer in a mixture of all remaining ingredients, turning occasionally. For barbecuing: When coals are ready place steaks on buttered rack. Cook about 5 minutes on each side, using the marinade to brush on heavily during cooking. For broiling: Place steaks on buttered rack 3 inches from heat. Do the same as for barbecuing. Swordfish should be golden brown and firm, but flaky, when done.

 Editor's note: Any **DRY CALIFORNIA WHITE TABLE WINE** *is a good choice to accompany this dish.*

Artichoke and Shrimp Casserole

(4 SERVINGS)

Mrs. Jack Welsch, The Christian Brothers, San Francisco
This is a slight variation of a dish reported to have been a favorite of Adlai Stevenson, former U.S. Ambassador to the United Nations. It is also one of our favorites, and I have made it for just family and for large parties. I serve it buffet style at parties in a Dansk casserole, with a matching one for Turmeric rice.

- 1 (8-oz.) package frozen artichoke hearts, cooked according to directions
- 1 pound medium-size fresh shrimp, cooked and cleaned
- ¼ pound fresh or canned mushrooms
- 1 (5-oz.) can water chestnuts
- 2 tablespoons butter
- 1 tablespoon Worcestershire sauce
- ¼ cup California Dry Sherry
- 1½ cups medium cream sauce (made with 3 tablespoons flour and light cream)
- ¼ cup grated Parmesan cheese
- Salt and pepper
- Dash of paprika

Cook and drain artichoke hearts and arrange in buttered casserole. Spread the cooked shrimp over them. Sauté sliced mushrooms for 6 minutes and add them to baking dish. Slice water chestnuts and add to baking dish. Add Worcestershire sauce, salt, pepper and Sherry to cream sauce and pour over contents of baking dish. Sprinkle the top with Parmesan cheese, dust with paprika, and bake for 20 to 25 minutes in 375° oven.

 My choice of wine to accompany this dish: **CALIFORNIA CHENIN BLANC**

Crab Coquille

(4 TO 6 SERVINGS)

Mrs. Arthur Caputi, Jr., E. & J. Gallo Winery, Modesto
We serve this crab dish with rice pilaf, homemade yeast rolls and green salad with Parmesan cheese dressing. Because this is a fairly simple meal, we prefer to serve a rich dessert, such as a chocolate soufflé with creme chantilly or chocolate sauce.

- ⅔ cup California Sauterne, Chablis, or other white table wine
- ⅓ cup water
- 1 sprig parsley
- 1 small onion, halved
- 2 (7½-oz.) cans Alaskan King Crab
- 2 tablespoons butter
- ¼ pound mushrooms, sliced
- 2 tablespoons flour
- 1 (10-oz.) can condensed cream of chicken soup
- ⅓ cup heavy cream
- 2 tablespoons lemon juice
- 4 to 6 baked pastry shells

Combine wine, water, parsley and onion and heat to boiling. Add crab and simmer 5 minutes. Drain, reserving 1 cup of the liquid. Cut the crab meat into bite-size pieces. Melt butter in saucepan, add mushrooms and brown lightly. Blend in flour. Gradually add soup, cream and lemon juice; cook, stirring constantly, until thickened. Gradually stir in the reserved wine broth. Fold in crab. Spoon into pastry shells.

 My choice of wine to accompany this dish: **CALIFORNIA RIESLING**

Wine Baked Fish

(6 SERVINGS)

Mrs. Frank Franzia, Sr., Franzia Brothers Winery, Ripon

2½ pounds fillets of halibut
    or other white fish
½ cup halved mushroom caps
1 carrot, diced
2 tablespoons chopped leek
    or onion
¼ cup olive oil
1 cup California
    White Table Wine
½ cup water or fish stock
    Salt and pepper

Place fillets in well-greased pan. Sauté mushrooms, carrot and leek in olive oil for 5 minutes. Add wine, water. Season to taste. Simmer until the vegetables are tender, but still firm. Remove vegetables, reserving liquid, and arrange on top of fish; cover. Bake in moderate oven (350°) 15 to 20 minutes. Boil the liquid briskly to reduce by half; pour over fish just before serving.

My choice of wine to accompany this dish:
CALIFORNIA CHABLIS *or* **SAUTERNE**

Scampi Delectable

(3 TO 4 SERVINGS)

Mrs. Maury Baldwin, Owens-Illinois Glass Co., Sacramento

2 pounds fresh jumbo prawns
3 cloves garlic, finely minced
¼ teaspoon salt
2 tablespoons chopped parsley
¼ cup olive oil
¼ cup melted butter
½ cup California White Wine
2 tablespoons lemon juice
⅛ teaspoon freshly ground
    pepper

Shell and devein prawns, leave tail on. Split lengthwise, 1 inch from head, forming butterfly. Combine remaining ingredients and mix well. Marinate prawns in mixture for several hours. Arrange prawns in single layer in shallow pan. Pour remaining sauce over. Broil for 6 to 8 minutes, 3 inches from heat. Remove prawns to warm platter and pour drippings from pan over all. Be sure to remove from broiler while prawns are still "chewy"; do not overcook.

 My choice of wine to accompany this dish:
CALIFORNIA GREY RIESLING *or* **GREEN HUNGARIAN**

Baked Striped Bass Fillets

(4 TO 6 SERVINGS)

Miss Marjorie Lumm, Wine Institute, San Francisco
Leon Adams, author of "Striped Bass Fishing" and "The Commonsense Book of Wine,"
generously shares his catch of Stripers with his neighbors. On one such memorable occasion,
he gave me his favorite recipe for baking the fillets.

2 pounds striped bass fillets
    Salt and pepper
1 large onion,
    sliced into thin rings
2 teaspoons sweet basil
2 cups California Sauterne or
    other White Table Wine
2 teaspoons Worcestershire
    sauce
3 tablespoons butter
2 tomatoes, sliced
½ green pepper, sliced

Sprinkle fish fillets with salt and pepper. Lay fillets in oven-proof baking dish. Cover with onion rings. Sprinkle with basil. Pour on wine and Worcestershire sauce and allow to marinate several hours or over night. If the wine does not cover the fillets, turn them occasionally. Preheat oven to 375°. Dot fish with butter, distribute tomatoes and green pepper over and around fish. Bake 35 minutes or until fish flakes when tested with fork. Baste frequently with wine mixture in baking dish. Do not overcook.

 My choice of wine to accompany this dish:
CALIFORNIA RIESLING, PINOT CHARDONNAY *or* **DRY SEMILLON**

Shellfish Thermidor

(4 SERVINGS)

Miss Margaret Shahenian, Guild Wine Company, San Francisco
With this rich dish, I serve plain boiled rice, sliced tomato salad with wine vinegar and oil dressing, and for dessert, pineapple sherbet with a sugar cookie.

- 4 tablespoons chopped onion
- 1 cup fresh mushrooms, sliced
- ¼ cup butter
- ¼ cup sifted flour
- ½ teaspoon salt
- ¼ teaspoon pepper
- ¼ teaspoon paprika
- 1 cup light cream
- 1 cup chicken broth
- 1 teaspoon Worcestershire sauce
- 1 egg yolk, beaten
- ¼ cup California Dry Sherry
- 2 lobster tails, cooked
- 1 pound prawns, cooked and cleaned
- 1 pound crab meat
- Fine dry bread crumbs

Preheat oven to 450°. Sauté onion and mushrooms in butter. Blend in flour and seasonings. Cook over low heat until bubbly. Remove from heat and stir in cream, chicken broth, Worcestershire sauce. Bring sauce to boil, stir in egg yolk, Sherry and prepared shellfish. Place mixture in shells or baking dish. Sprinkle with fine bread crumbs. Bake 5 minutes or until topping is brown.

 My choice of wine to accompany this dish: **CALIFORNIA SAUTERNE**

Crab Pie with Almonds

(6 TO 8 SERVINGS)

Mrs. E. A. Kirkman, Jr., Wente Bros., Livermore
I suggest that this be served as the fish course at dinner or as an entree for a luncheon.
The recipe started when I tried to persuade a homemaking class of girls to make a Quiche Lorraine. They didn't like the idea at all, but when I presented them with this recipe, without the wine, they were delighted. That was my incentive to further develop this recipe with the addition of wine.

PASTRY
- 1 cup sifted flour
- ½ teaspoon salt
- ½ cup shortening
- 2 tablespoons California White Table Wine

FILLING
- 1 (7½-oz.) can crab meat
- ½ cup California White Table Wine
- 1 cup shredded Swiss cheese
- 1 green onion with tops, chopped
- 3 eggs, beaten slightly
- ¾ cup light cream
- ½ teaspoon salt
- Dash mace
- ½ cup sliced almonds

Pastry: Combine flour, salt, shortening, wine as for a regular pie crust, and roll very thin, then place in an 8-inch glass pie plate. Bake in a hot oven, 425°, for 5 minutes to insure a crisp crust. **Filling:** Marinate the crab in the wine at least 2 hours. When ready to prepare, sprinkle the shredded cheese into the partially baked pie crust. Drain wine from crab and set aside. Spread crab over cheese, sprinkle on onion. Combine eggs, cream, reserved wine, salt and mace and pour into pie shell. Sprinkle almonds on top. Bake at 325° for 45 minutes. Serve warm.

 My choice of wine to accompany this dish: **CALIFORNIA GREY RIESLING**

Wine Marinated Cracked Crab

(4 SERVINGS)

Mr. Vernon L. Singleton, University of California, Dept. Viticulture and Enology, Davis

- 2 medium-size Dungeness crabs
- ½ cup California Dry White Table Wine
- ½ cup lemon juice
- ½ cup salad oil
- ¾ teaspoon dry mustard
- 1 teaspoon salt
- ⅛ teaspoon pepper
- 1 small clove garlic, finely grated
- 1 egg

If possible have crabs cleaned and cracked at the market. You may need to recrack any difficult spots to make easy eating. Combine all ingredients except egg and crab in a bowl and mix well. Add egg and mix with a fork until well blended. Add cracked crab. Marinate in a covered bowl in refrigerator for at least 1 hour, mixing several times. Serve cracked crab with a little container of marinade and small forks or picks. An added touch is a small hot terry cloth rolled with a sprig of fresh mint to wipe the fingers.

My choice of wine to accompany this dish:
CALIFORNIA WHITE RIESLING *or* **CHARDONNAY**

Old Rancho Shrimp Creole

(6 SERVINGS)

Mrs. Joseph A. Filippi, Jr., Thomas Vineyards, Cucamonga

- 3 quarts water
- 2 teaspoons cooking oil
- 3 teaspoons salt
- 40 medium shrimp (2 to 2¼ lbs.)
- ½ cup butter or olive oil
- 1 medium onion, diced
- 2 cloves garlic, minced
- 1 medium green pepper, diced
- 3 stalks celery, diced
- 1 bay leaf
- 1 (8-oz.) can tomato sauce
- ½ cup water
- ½ cup California Sauterne
- 1 teaspoon salt

In large pan, boil water. Add oil and salt. Devein and clean shrimp. Let drain and drop into boiling water for only 5 minutes or until they turn pink. Drain and place on paper towel to dry. In large skillet or deep roasting pan, sauté in butter, onion, garlic, green pepper, celery and bay leaf for 5 minutes. Add tomato sauce, water, wine and salt. Simmer for 10 minutes. Add one shrimp at a time until all are in pan. Bake in a moderate oven (350°) 45 minutes or until sauce thickens and coats shrimp. There should be enough sauce left to serve over rice.

My choice of wine to accompany this dish:
CALIFORNIA SAUTERNE *or* **CHABLIS**

Crab Omelette Supreme

(3 SERVINGS)

Mrs. Sam J. Sebastiani, Samuele Sebastiani Winery, Sonoma

- 6 eggs
- 3 tablespoons California Dry Sherry
- 1½ cups finely chopped fresh Alaskan King Crab or 1 (7½-oz.) can crabmeat
- Dash of salt
- ¼ cup cream
- ½ teaspoon minced parsley
- 1 tablespoon butter

Separate egg whites from yolks. Beat egg whites until stiff. Add wine, salt and cream to yolks and beat until smooth. Fold yolks into stiffly beaten whites. Heat skillet over low flame, until hot but not smoking. Add butter, tip skillet back and forth until butter spreads evenly. Add combined egg mixture to skillet and spread evenly with fork. When omelette is slightly cooked but not firm, spread crabmeat mixed with parsley over center. Fold omelette and slide onto heated platter. Brush top with melted butter, place in preheated oven, 250°, for 15 minutes and serve immediately.

My choice of wine to accompany this dish:
CALIFORNIA GREEN HUNGARIAN

Skewered Shrimp In White Wine

(4 SERVINGS)

Mrs. George Pentek, The Christian Brothers, Fresno
Editor's note: This is a light and flavorful dish for lunch or supper and it is very good with risotto.

20	raw jumbo shrimp
	Canadian bacon or prosciutto, in wafer thin slices
3	tablespoons salad oil
1	tablespoon California Brandy
¼	cup light cream
¼	cup California Dry White Table Wine
⅓	cup consomme
2	teaspoons minced parsley
2	teaspoons lemon juice
½	teaspoon Worcestershire sauce
	Dash cayenne pepper
	Salt to taste

Shell and devein shrimp, leaving tail intact. Rinse and pat dry on paper towels. On each of 4 skewers thread 5 shrimp alternately with small squares of bacon or ham, piercing shrimp so flat sides lie flat in pan, brown lightly in hot salad oil on each side. Sprinkle with Brandy; add rest of ingredients. Cover lightly; simmer gently about 10 minutes. Remove to warm plates. Pour sauce over shrimp.

 My choice of wine to accompany this dish: **CALIFORNIA RIESLING**

Shrimp Tiffany

(4 SERVINGS)

Mrs. Maury Baldwin, Owens-Illinois Glass Co., Sacramento
My very dear friend, Grace Tiffany, who also happens to be my husband's girl Friday, gave me this recipe. We know good food and good wine keep him happy. This is excellent for large groups. Prepare almost completely a day or two ahead of time. At the last moment, add sour cream, blend and heat. Serve in chafing dishes. Very colorful, especially if sprinkled with finely chopped parsley.

1	(10-oz.) can frozen shrimp soup
2	tablespoons chopped onion
½	cup sliced fresh or canned mushrooms
2	tablespoons butter
1	tablespoon flour
⅓	cup California Dry Sherry
1	cup dairy sour cream
	Dash pepper
1	pound medium-size fresh, cooked prawns

Thaw frozen shrimp soup. Sauté onions and mushrooms in butter. Add flour and blend. Add soup, Sherry (and liquid, if canned mushrooms used) and cook until thick. Add sour cream, pepper and prawns which have been deveined and cut into halves or quarters.

 My choice of wine to accompany this dish: **CALIFORNIA PINOT CHARDONNAY**

Scallops in Wine Cream Sauce

(6 SERVINGS)

Miss Gyl Rheingans, Sanger Winery Association, Sanger
Editor's note: Scallops in a wine-cream sauce, embellished with mushrooms and bacon bits are usually served with (or over) rice.

- 2 pounds sea scallops, fresh or frozen
- 8 slices bacon, diced
- 2 tablespoons butter or margarine
- 2 tablespoons minced onion
- 3 tablespoons finely diced green peppers
- ¼ cup flour
- ¾ cup chicken broth
- 1 cup light cream
- 1 (3-oz.) can sliced broiled mushrooms
- ½ teaspoon salt
   Pepper
- 3 tablespoons California Marsala
   Chopped parsley

Defrost scallops, if frozen; cut in half, crosswise, cover with boiling water, simmer 5 to 7 minutes or until tender; drain. Cook bacon until crisp, drain. Return 2 tablespoons bacon drippings to skillet, add butter, onion and green pepper. Cook until vegetables are soft but not brown. Blend in flour. Add broth, cream and liquid from mushrooms; stir until thickened. Add mushrooms, scallops, salt, pepper and wine. Heat to serving temperature. Sprinkle crisp bacon bits and parsley on top.

 My choice of wine to accompany this dish:
CALIFORNIA JOHANNISBERG RIESLING

Sherry and Parmesan Scampi

(2 SERVINGS)

Mrs. D. C. Turrentine, Wine Advisory Board, San Francisco
This recipe is much easier and better than others I have tried for scampi. I serve it with fresh French bread and green salad.

- ½ cup butter or margarine
- 1 clove garlic, crushed
- 2 teaspoons Worcestershire sauce
   Juice of ½ lemon
- ¼ cup California Dry Sherry
- 1 teaspoon sugar
- 2 teaspoons fresh dill, chopped
- 1 pound raw shrimp, shelled and deveined
- ¼ cup minced parsley
- 2 cups hot cooked rice
   Parmesan cheese

In shallow pan, melt butter over low heat. Add next 6 ingredients; mix well. Arrange shrimp in a single layer in the sauce. Spoon sauce over shrimp. Broil at low heat 8 minutes. Remove from broiler. Let stand for 15 minutes. Sprinkle on parsley. Broil at high heat for 3 minutes. Spoon sauce over rice. Sprinkle with Parmesan cheese. Arrange shrimp over rice.

 My choice of wine to accompany this dish:
CALIFORNIA CHABLIS *or other* **DRY WHITE TABLE WINE**

Specialty Main Dishes

Eggs à la Monsignor Gerald Cox

(4 SERVINGS)

Mrs. Edmund A. Rossi, Jr., Italian Swiss Colony, Asti
This was served to us for brunch by our good friend, Monsignor Gerald Cox of Sonoma County. He prepared this delicious dish and served it with hot buttered rolls and a chilled bottle of champagne. It is easy to make but yummy! Our whole family thought it was terrific.

1 dozen eggs ¼ cup California Dry White Table Wine 1 or 2 bell peppers, seeded and chopped ½ pound fresh mushrooms, sliced 3 or 4 green onions, chopped ¼ cup oil or butter 3 or 4 Italian sausages, cut in bite-size pieces 2 tablespoons oil or butter Salt and pepper	Beat eggs with fork, add wine, set aside. Sauté all three vegetables in ¼ cup oil or butter until tender. In a separate frying pan, sauté sausage for 10 to 15 minutes. Drain off all grease and remove sausage. Over medium heat add 2 tablespoons oil or butter to pan, pour in eggs. As they start to set, add all other ingredients. Stir constantly until eggs are cooked to desired consistency.

 My choice of wine to accompany this dish: **CALIFORNIA CHAMPAGNE**

Regina Fritata

(6 SERVINGS)

Mrs. John B. Ellena, Regina Grape Products Co., Etiwanda
This recipe may be used as a meat substitute, considering the amount of cheese and the number of eggs in it. However, I believe, it is best served with a light meat such as lamb roast or chicken. It's also good with a spaghetti dinner.

1 (10-oz.) package frozen chopped spinach
1 medium onion, finely chopped
2 tablespoons butter or margarine
8 eggs
⅓ cup California Dry Sherry
¼ teaspoon salt
¼ teaspoon pepper
Dash of powdered rosemary
Pinch of sweet basil leaves
1 cup Parmesan cheese

Cook spinach as directed on package. Drain well, pressing out as much liquid as possible. Sauté onion in butter or margarine until golden brown. Beat eggs in mixing bowl and add all ingredients except ¼ cup cheese and mix well. Pour mixture into an 8 x 12-inch greased baking dish. Sprinkle ¼ cup Parmesan cheese over top. Bake at 325° for 25 minutes, then place under broiler for 5 minutes to get top golden brown.

 My choice of wine to accompany this dish: **CALIFORNIA ROSÉ**

Fisherman's Soup

(8 TO 10 SERVINGS)

Mrs. Robert Diana, Villa Armando, Pleasanton
If you like variety in your seafood, this is your dish. For any of the fish mentioned you can substitute any others you may prefer. But do not use crab meat, it tends to disintegrate and loses its flavor unless left in the shell.

½ pound red snapper
½ pound bass
½ pound halibut
½ pound cod
12 cherrystone clams in shell
1 pound jumbo shrimp
1 cup flour
3 beaten eggs
½ cup bread crumbs
½ cup olive oil
½ cup butter
3 firm tomatoes, sliced thin
3 cloves garlic, mashed
12 sprigs parsley
½ teaspoon crushed red pepper
½ teaspoon black pepper
1 teaspoon salt
2 bay leaves crumbled
2 cups California Dry White Table Wine
2 cups boiling water
2 loaves Italian bread

Cut the 4 kinds of fish into 2-inch pieces. Do not open the clams. Wash them under cold running water and scrub with a vegetable brush. Discard any open ones. Shell shrimp, wash and devein them while still raw. Split down middle lengthwise. Sprinkle fish with flour then dip into beaten eggs. Roll in bread crumbs. Place 6 tablespoons of oil in a skillet and heat. Sauté fish pieces on each side for 5 minutes. Remove skillet from heat. Place butter and remaining oil in bottom of large soup pot. Heat, add shrimp, clams in shell and sliced tomatoes. Cover and cook 10 minutes. Chop mashed garlic and parsley together and add to soup with red and black pepper, salt and bay leaf. Add sautéed fish and pour in oil and juices from skillet. Add wine. Cover and cook 5 minutes. Add boiling water and cook another 10 minutes uncovered. Turn off heat but keep pot covered. Slice bread and toast in oven. Place 2 slices of toast in each large soup plate. On this arrange pieces of fish, then clams and shrimp, then the juice.

 My choice of wine to accompany this dish: **CALIFORNIA DRY MUSCAT**

Risotto Italiene

(5 SERVINGS)

Mrs. Aldo Nerelli, Pesenti Winery, Templeton
An exciting change from potatoes, this risotto is a good accompaniment with any type of meat.
Editor's note: This cheese and rice specialty is also hearty enough to serve as a main dish at a luncheon or family supper.

¼ cup butter
½ cup finely cut onions
1 clove garlic, thinly sliced
1 (2-oz.) can mushrooms
1 cup long grain rice, uncooked
2 tablespoons chopped parsley
Salt and pepper
3 to 4 cups beef broth from boiled meat
¾ cup California Dry White Wine
⅛ teaspoon saffron
½ cup Parmesan cheese, grated
½ cup Cheddar cheese, grated

Melt butter, add onions, garlic, drained mushrooms, and sauté until light brown. Add rice, parsley and salt and continue cooking until brown. Add hot broth, wine and saffron, a little at a time, until rice becomes tender. Continue cooking over medium heat. When rice is cooked stir in cheese and heat gently just until cheeses melt.

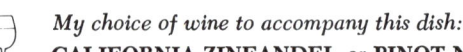 *My choice of wine to accompany this dish:* **CALIFORNIA ZINFANDEL** *or* **PINOT NOIR**

Rice with Mushrooms

(6 SERVINGS)

Mrs. Robert Weaver, University of California, Dept. Viticulture and Enology, Davis

- 1 cup raw regular rice, uncooked
- 1 cup chopped tomatoes
- 1 pound mushrooms, sliced
- ½ cup chopped onion
- ½ cup butter
- 3 cups chicken broth
- ½ cup California Red Table Wine
- 2 teaspoons salt
- ⅛ teaspoon pepper
- 1 cup cooked green peas
- ¼ cup grated Parmesan cheese

In a large skillet, cook rice, tomatoes, mushrooms and onion in butter for about 10 minutes, stirring occasionally. Add broth, wine and seasonings; mix well. Cover. Simmer for about 45 minutes, or until rice is tender and liquid is absorbed. Stir in peas. Heat until peas are warmed through. Sprinkle with Parmesan cheese. Serve.

My choice of wine to accompany this dish:
CALIFORNIA CABERNET, PINOT NOIR, *or* **ZINFANDEL**

Omelet with Artichokes

(1 SERVING)

Mrs. William Bonetti, Charles Krug Winery, St. Helena

OMELET
- 2 eggs
- 2 tablespoons cream
- Salt
- 3 canned artichoke hearts, sliced very thin
- 1 tablespoon butter

CHEESE SAUCE
- ½ cup shredded cheese (fontina or similar)
- 1 teaspoon cornstarch
- 3 tablespoons California Chablis

Omelet: Beat eggs, cream and salt together with a fork until well blended. Mix with artichokes. In a skillet heat the butter until golden; pour in the egg mixture and tilt the skillet until the bottom is covered. Cook to desired consistency. **Sauce:** Coat the cheese with cornstarch; heat wine in heavy saucepan until it bubbles; turn heat to simmer; add the cheese, stirring constantly until melted. To serve, slide omelet onto a preheated plate; pour the sauce over it and fold in half; serve immediately.

 My choice of wine to accompany this dish:
CALIFORNIA JOHANNISBERG RIESLING

Valley Royal Eggs

(12 SERVINGS)

Mr. Joseph J. Franzia, Franzia Brothers Winery, Ripon

- 12 egg yolks
- Boiling water
- 1¾ cups sugar
- 2½ cups water
- 1 (3-inch) cinnamon stick, broken into small pieces
- ⅓ cup California Sherry

Preheat oven to 350°. Butter bottom and sides of a 9″ x 5″ loaf pan. In small bowl of electric mixer, at medium speed, beat egg yolks until very thick and lemon-colored, about 7 minutes. Pour into prepared pan. Place loaf pan in shallow baking pan. Pour boiling water to 1-inch depth around loaf pan. Bake 20 minutes or until cake tester inserted in center comes out clean. Remove to wire rack, and let cool in pan. In medium saucepan, combine sugar, water and cinnamon stick. Bring to a boil, stirring until sugar is dissolved. Boil 5 minutes. Cut cooled egg mixture into 12 even-sized serving pieces. Put a piece of cinnamon stick from syrup in each. Turn cubes into syrup; simmer gently, uncovered, 10 minutes. Remove from heat, stir in Sherry. Cool, then refrigerate, covered, at least 24 hours.

 My choice of wine to accompany this dish: **CALIFORNIA CHAMPAGNE**

Moussaka Tsapralis

(10 TO 12 SERVINGS)

Mrs. Don Rudolph, Cresta Blanca Wine Company, Livermore
This recipe was given to me by Cleo Tsapralis, an excellent cook.

- 1 eggplant
- ½ cup shortening
- 2 tablespoons butter
- 4 medium onions, thinly sliced
- 3 cloves garlic, chopped
- 1½ pounds ground beef
- 1 teaspoon salt
- ½ teaspoon thyme
- ½ teaspoon oregano
- ½ cup canned tomatoes
- ½ cup California White Table Wine
- 2 egg whites, slightly beaten
- ½ cup bread crumbs
  SAUCE
- 2 tablespoons butter
- 2 tablespoons flour
- 1½ cups milk
- ½ teaspoon salt
- 2 egg yolks, slightly beaten
- ⅛ teaspoon nutmeg

Cut unpeeled eggplant in lengthwise slices, fry in shortening until brown then transfer to platter lined with absorbent paper. Melt butter and add sliced onions and chopped garlic, fry until limp, add ground beef, salt, thyme, oregano, tomatoes and wine, cook slowly for 30 minutes. Cool, mix in egg whites and half bread crumbs. While mixture cooks, make sauce.
Sauce: Melt butter. Stir in flour, add milk and salt, stir until thick. Add egg yolks to sauce, stir until blended well, add nutmeg. Butter large casserole, cover bottom with remaining bread crumbs, arrange a layer of eggplant, then a layer of meat mixture, repeat layers then cover with sauce. Bake uncovered at 350° for 1 hour.

 My choice of wine to accompany this dish:
ANY CALIFORNIA RED TABLE WINE

Shell Macaroni in Curried Clam Sauce

(4 TO 6 SERVINGS)

Mr. and Mrs. Ferrer Filipello, Italian Swiss Colony, Asti

- 5 tablespoons butter
- 1 (8-oz.) can sliced mushrooms, drained
- 1 (7-oz.) can minced clams, drained, save liquid
- ¼ teaspoon monosodium glutamate
- ½ teaspoon salt
- ½ cup California Vermouth
- 1 teaspoon curry powder
  Pinch cayenne pepper
- 1 tablespoon oyster sauce (may be purchased at a Chinese grocery)
- ½ cup grated dry Monterey cheese
- ½ cup grated Cheddar cheese
- 1 tablespoon parsley, chopped
- 1 tablespoon chives, chopped
- 1 (12-oz.) package large shell macaroni
  Water
  Salt

Melt butter in skillet over low heat. Add drained mushrooms and sauté for 3 minutes with occasional stirring. Add drained minced clams, monosodium glutamate, salt and stir. Add clam liquid and Vermouth and allow to simmer. Add curry, cayenne and oyster sauce. Stir in cheese, parsley and chives. If sauce becomes too sticky, stir in more Vermouth. Cook macaroni in salted boiling water for 15 to 20 minutes until cooked but **not** mushy soft. Drain well and mix with sauce.

 My choice of wine to accompany this dish:
CALIFORNIA PINOT BLANC or CHAMPAGNE

This section provides the accents to a meal — the soups, the salads, and the vegetables. If the main dish is the star of an Epicurean presentation, then these accompaniments are the supporting players. They have strength but not obtrusiveness. They don't compete with the main dish, they complement it.

ACCOMPANIMENTS TO MAIN DISHES

Vegetables

Bear Mountain Zucchini

(4 TO 6 BIG SERVINGS)

Mrs. Hector Castro, Bear Mountain Winery, Di Giorgio
One year I grew zucchini and having more than we or the whole neighborhood could use, I asked all my friends for their recipes for using zucchini. This recipe evolved from three recipes and this is the first time I've even written it down. It is now one of our family favorites.

1½ pounds zucchini, sliced
3 tablespoons cooking oil
2 tablespoons olive oil
1 (8-oz.) can tomato sauce
1 clove garlic, chopped
Dash sweet basil
½ cup California
    Red Table Wine
¼ pound Jack cheese, sliced
3 tablespoons grated
    Parmesan cheese

Fry zucchini in oil and drain. In same pan (drain off excess oil), combine olive oil, tomato sauce, garlic, basil and wine and cook until thickened. In greased, 2-quart baking dish, put zucchini, sauce and cheese slices in layers. Pour remaining sauce over top and sprinkle with Parmesan cheese. Bake at 350° 30 to 40 minutes or until it bubbles.

My choice of wine to accompany this dish:
either **CALIFORNIA RED** *or* **WHITE TABLE WINE**, *depending on the main dish.*

Scalloped Onions

(6 TO 8 SERVINGS)

Mrs. Joseph Concannon, Jr., Concannon Vineyard, Livermore
This recipe is a cinch to prepare. It can be done well ahead of time and the results are superb. It is an excellent accompaniment for baked ham.

3 tablespoons butter or
    margarine
3 tablespoons flour
1 cup canned consomme
¼ cup California Dry Sherry
¼ cup grated Parmesan cheese
2 tablespoons chopped parsley
Salt, pepper
2 (1-lb.) cans small whole
    onions, drained
¼ cup fine dry bread crumbs
    mixed
2 teaspoons melted butter

Melt butter and stir in flour; add consomme and Sherry; cook, stirring constantly, until mixture boils and thickens. Add cheese, parsley, salt and pepper. Combine this sauce with the onions. Turn into a greased casserole. Mix bread crumbs with melted butter and sprinkle on top. Bake in moderate oven (350°–375°) for about 25 minutes.

My choice of wine to accompany this dish:
CALIFORNIA JOHANNISBERG RIESLING *or* **MOSELLE**

Fresh Broccoli with Cream Cheese Sauce

(6 TO 8 SERVINGS)

Mrs. Peter Mirassou, Mirassou Vineyards, San Jose
This recipe was given to me by a good friend whose family is a large producer of broccoli in the Salinas Valley. This is one of her favorite ways of serving it.

- 2 pounds broccoli
- 2 teaspoons salt
- 4 tablespoons butter (½ cube)
- 4 tablespoons flour
- 1 cup cream
- 1 bouillon cube
- ¾ cup hot water
- 2 tablespoons California Dry Sherry
- 2 tablespoons lemon juice
- Pepper
- ½ teaspoon monosodium glutamate
- ¼ cup grated Parmesan cheese
- ½ cup grated Cheddar cheese
- ¼ cup slivered almonds

Separate broccoli and wash. Then cook with small amount of water until barely tender. Drain. Arrange in shallow baking dish. While broccoli is cooking, melt butter and blend in flour. Pour in cream and bouillon cube, dissolved first in the hot water. Stirring, cook until smooth and thickened. Add Sherry, lemon juice, pepper and monosodium glutamate. Pour sauce over broccoli. Sprinkle grated cheeses and almonds over top. Bake 20 minutes or until hot.

 My choice of wine to accompany this dish: Any wine that would complement whatever meat is served with the broccoli; perhaps **CALIFORNIA ZINFANDEL** *if a red meat or* **CHENIN BLANC** *if poultry.*

Egg Plant Parmigiana

(8 SERVINGS)

Mrs. Leon A. Kirschenmann, East-Side Winery, Lodi
I have discovered that people who think they don't care for egg plant really go for this.
Editor's note: This dish is rich enough to serve as a main dish, accompanied by a tossed green salad.

EGG PLANT
- 1 large egg plant, sliced in ¼-inch slices
- 1 egg
- Flour
- Oil

TOMATO SAUCE
- 1 large onion, chopped
- 2 tablespoons oil
- 1 (1 lb. 12-oz.) can whole plum tomatoes
- ¾ cup California Marsala
- ½ (1½-oz.) package spaghetti sauce mix
- 1 teaspoon instant minced garlic
- Salt and pepper
- 2 cups fresh bread crumbs
- 1½ cups grated Monterey Jack cheese
- 2 tablespoons dry or fresh chopped parsley

Egg Plant: Dip slices of egg plant in slightly beaten egg. Roll in flour and brown in oil on both sides. Set aside while preparing tomato sauce. **Tomato Sauce:** Sauté 1 large onion in oil in pan in which you browned egg plant. When onion is soft add tomatoes, wine, spaghetti sauce mix, minced garlic, and salt and pepper. Simmer mixture until thick. Toss together bread crumbs, 1 cup grated cheese and parsley. Arrange layer of egg plant slices in 9 x 13" flat baking pan. Sprinkle ½ crumb mixture over slices, pour ½ tomato sauce over crumb layer. Repeat process and sprinkle top with remaining ½ cup grated cheese. Bake at 350° until heated through.

 My choice of wine to accompany this dish: **CALIFORNIA RUBY CABERNET** *or* **EMERALD RIESLING** *or* **CHENIN BLANC**

Sherried String Beans

(8 SERVINGS)

Mrs. Jack H. Farrior, Jr., Almaden Vineyards, Los Gatos
Editor's note: This vegetable casserole dish with the delicate Sherry flavor is an excellent accompaniment for baked ham, hot or cold.

2 (10 to 12-oz.) packages frozen, French-style string beans
½ cup California Dry Sherry
1 (1-lb.) can whole onions
1 (10½-oz.) can mushroom soup
½ teaspoon nutmeg
¼ teaspoon salt
⅓ cup slivered almonds

Cook string beans according to directions on package. Drain and add Sherry, onions, mushroom soup, nutmeg, salt and almonds. Place in baking dish and bake at 350° for ½ hour.

*Editor's note: If this dish is served with ham, **CALIFORNIA ROSÉ** is the ideal accompanying wine.*

Le Celeri à la Eschscholtzia

(6 SERVINGS)

Dr. Salvatore P. Lucia, University of California, School of Medicine, San Francisco
Editor's note: Braised celery with wine and caraway flavorings is an unusual vegetable accompaniment for slices of cold roast beef or tongue. The short simmering period is important, because the celery is already cooked, and longer heating will make it less attractive.

12 canned celery hearts with juice
¼ cup butter
Juice of 1 lemon
½ cup California Sherry
1 teaspoon whole caraway seed

Drain celery, reserving liquid. Braise celery in butter in a covered frying pan. Then add half of the juice in which the celery was canned. When thoroughly heated, add lemon juice, Sherry and sprinkle caraway seed evenly over celery. Replace cover on pan and simmer slowly for 3 to 5 minutes. Serve immediately on warmed plates.

 My choice of wine to serve with this dish: **CALIFORNIA CHARDONNAY**

Broccoli Crown

(8 TO 10 SERVINGS)

Mrs. Paul L. Halpern, United Vintners, Madera
This is a very tasty dish. I serve it with a prime rib roast menu or butterfly leg of lamb.

1 bunch broccoli (1¼ to 1½ pounds)
1 small onion, chopped
4 tablespoons butter
4 tablespoons flour
1 teaspoon seasoned salt
½ cup grated Parmesan cheese
3 eggs
1 cup milk
½ cup mayonnaise
¼ cup chopped parsley
3 tablespoons California Dry Sherry

Trim outer leaves and tough ends and peel stems. Chop flowers and stems in ½-inch slices. Cook in small amount of boiling salted water 10 minutes. Drain. Sauté onion in butter until soft. Stir in flour and salt. Cook stirring constantly until bubbly. Stir in milk and continue stirring until it thickens and boils one minute. Beat eggs slightly and stir in ½ cup of the heated sauce. Then stir egg mixture back quickly into remaining sauce. Cook, stirring constantly until mixture thickens again. Remove from heat. Stir in mayonnaise, Sherry and parsley. Fold in broccoli. Spoon into a well-greased 3-quart ring mold and sprinkle on Parmesan cheese. Bake for 30 minutes or until set at 350°. Let ring stand several minutes. Loosen with knife and invert onto serving plate.

Editor's note: **CALIFORNIA BURGUNDY** *is good with prime rib roast and* **ROSÉ** *is good with leg of lamb.*

Artichoke Hearts in Wine

(4 TO 6 SERVINGS)

Mrs. Sam J. Sebastiani, Samule Sebastiani Winery, Sonoma
This recipe originated among families who lived in the artichoke center of the world, the Castroville area of California. It is a food that many have never tasted, but so far all new-comers that I have served this to have really enjoyed it.

12 small artichokes
½ cup olive oil
½ cup California
    Dry White Table Wine
2 cloves garlic,
    minced or mashed
½ teaspoon salt
Dash of pepper and garlic salt

Cut slice off top of each artichoke, then cook artichokes in boiling salted water for 25 minutes, or until almost tender; drain. Pull off all tough outer leaves, and cut off stem so that only the hearts of the artichokes remain. Cut hearts in half lengthwise and scrape out choke. Combine olive oil and wine in a heavy saucepan with a tight fitting cover. Add pepper, garlic salt and artichoke hearts. Cover and simmer, turning occasionally, for 20 to 30 minutes or until artichokes are thoroughly done. Add a little more wine and oil if the sauce gets dry.

 My choice of wine to accompany this dish:
CALIFORNIA RED *or* **WHITE TABLE WINE**,
depending on the complete meal.

Madeira Onion Rings

(4 SERVINGS)

Mrs. N. C. Mirassou, Mirassou Vineyards, San Jose
Editor's note: These glazed onion rings make an interesting change from the creamed onions served with most turkey or roast beef. They'll also add distinction to meat loaf or hamburgers.

4 tablespoons butter
4 large onions,
    sliced ¼-inch thick
    and separated into rings
⅔ cup California Madeira
1 tablespoon chopped parsley
Salt and pepper

Melt butter in heavy skillet. Toss onions in the hot butter, but do not sauté long enough to make onions soft. Add ½ cup of wine; cover pan. Raise heat and let onions cook over a medium flame until they are tender. Remove cover and let the wine reduce to a glaze in the pan. Stir in the remaining Madeira and chopped parsley.

Editor's note: Serve a **CALIFORNIA RED** *or* **WHITE TABLE WINE**
depending on the main dish of the meal.

Green Peppers Florentine

(8 SERVINGS)

Mrs. Jack H. Farrior, Jr., Almaden Vineyards, Los Gatos
This is our favorite vegetable to serve with Mandarin Pheasant. Editor's note: (see page 41).

6 green peppers
2 tablespoons olive oil
1 tablespoon wine vinegar
½ teaspoon sugar
3 tablespoons capers
2 tablespoons chopped olives
¼ teaspoon oregano
½ cup California Sauterne

Slice green peppers lengthwise, sauté until limp in olive oil. Add wine vinegar, sugar, capers, chopped olives, oregano and Sauterne. Simmer 20 minutes.

 My choice of wine to accompany this dish: **CALIFORNIA SAUTERNE**

Canneloni with Spinach Souffle Filling

(8 TO 10 SERVINGS)

Mrs. Louis P. Martini, Louis M. Martini Winery, St. Helena
This dish may be prepared 3 or 4 hours ahead of time and refrigerated.
I serve it as a first course, for luncheon or for a buffet.

VELOUTE SAUCE
- 2 cups canned chicken broth
- 3 tablespoons each, sliced onion, carrot, celery
- ½ cup California Sauterne or Vermouth
- 3 sprigs parsley
- 1 bay leaf
  Pinch of thyme
- 2 tablespoons butter
- 3 tablespoons flour

SPINACH FILLING
- 2 (10-oz.) packages spinach frozen in butter sauce, partially thawed
- 2 tablespoons arrowroot powder
- 2 cups ricotta cheese
- 2 eggs
- 2 tablespoons grated Parmesan cheese
- ¼ teaspoon nutmeg
- ½ teaspoon celery salt
- ¼ teaspoon garlic salt
- 20 crepes (see page 85)
  Swiss or Gruyere cheese, grated

Veloute sauce: Simmer broth, onion, carrot, celery, wine, parsley, bay leaf, thyme together about 30 minutes; taste and strain. Bring stock back to boiling point. In heavy-bottomed pan, melt butter and work in flour stirring constantly until flour is cooked but not browned. Add stock, stirring vigorously with a wire whip until the sauce is thickened. **Filling:** Cook spinach. When cooked and still hot, drain and put in blender and blend in arrowroot. Place spinach in large mixing bowl. In blender place ricotta cheese, eggs, Parmesan cheese, nutmeg, celery salt and garlic salt. Blend and mix with spinach mixture. Spread not more than half of the Veloute sauce in the bottom of a flat square baking dish. Holding crepe in palm of one hand, spoon filling down center, fold over ends and place with lapped-over portion face down in baking dish. Spread over with remaining sauce. Sprinkle generously with shredded Swiss or Gruyere cheese. When ready to serve, heat in a hot (400°) oven for 20 minutes. Cheese should be melted, sauce bubbling. It may be browned for a minute under the broiler.

My choice of wine to accompany this dish:
CALIFORNIA DRY SEMILLON

Green Beans Française

(6 SERVINGS)

Mrs. Alessandro Baccari, Baccari Wine Festival, San Francisco

- 1 pound green beans, cut French style
- ⅓ cube butter
- 2 tablespoons olive oil
- 1 large clove garlic, cut in 3 sections
- 4 slices lemon
- 1 drop Worcestershire sauce
- ⅓ cup toasted slivered almonds
- ½ teaspoon salt
- ⅛ teaspoon pepper
- 1 tablespoon chopped minced parsley
- ½ cup California Dry Sherry
- ½ cup California Dry Sauterne

Boil green beans until tender (do not over-cook). Set aside. Melt butter and oil together; add garlic, lemon, almonds, Worcestershire sauce, salt and pepper and sauté slowly on very low fire; stir with fork, making sure not to break up garlic; press on lemon slices to remove juice. Add parsley, Sherry and Sauterne and cook slowly for about 25 minutes. Remove garlic and lemon, add green beans and simmer 10 to 12 minutes longer. If sauce gets too thick, add more wine.

Editor's note: If this dish is served with roast beef, **CALIFORNIA PINOT NOIR** *or* **CABERNET SAUVIGNON** *is a good choice as the accompanying wine.*

Soups and Salads

Charbonnet Soup Supreme

(6 SERVINGS)

Mrs. Edmund G. Carbone, Carbone Napa Valley Winery, Napa
I made this recipe up. It's wonderful for the busy woman as it serves as a main course.
This is a rich soup, almost a meal itself. One could serve Italian bread with garlic and a dash
of Parmesan cheese mixed with butter to spread on the bread before heating it.
A light dessert such as a cheesecake would do the trick.

1 pound chicken wings	Cook chicken wings in water, wine and tomato juice with salt and peppercorns added. Cook until tender, 20 to 30 minutes. Cool. Remove meat from bones, discarding skin, and chop or cut meat in small pieces. There will be about ¾ cup. Strain peppercorns from broth and reserve broth. In a saucepan, heat butter, add onion and celery and sauté until tender, but not brown. Stir in flour, reserved chicken broth and cream. Bring to a boil, stirring constantly. Add diced chicken. Reheat before serving. This is great to make and freeze.
1 cup water	
1 cup California Burgundy	
1 cup tomato juice	
1 teaspoon salt	
10 peppercorns	
¼ cup butter	
1½ cups finely chopped onion	
1½ cups finely chopped celery	
2 tablespoons flour	
1½ cups light cream	

 My choice of wine to accompany this dish: **CALIFORNIA DRY SHERRY**

Mushroom Cream Soup

(6 SERVINGS)

Mrs. Charles van Kriedt, California Wineletter, San Francisco

1 pound fresh mushrooms	Slice mushrooms into pan with a tight lid. Pour on wines and bring to a boil. Cover tightly and steam until mushrooms are soft, about 10 minutes. Drain mushrooms, reserving liquid, and puree them through a food mill or swirl a few seconds in a blender. Hold. Slice carrot, celery, garlic and onion. In another saucepan, melt butter and brown vegetables, adding a few sprigs of parsley. Now stir in flour and slowly add heated milk, stirring constantly to keep sauce smooth as it thickens. Add nutmeg, salt, pepper and monosodium glutamate to taste. Hold just under a boil for 10 minutes, then cool and strain out vegetables. Combine mushrooms, strained milk sauce and wine bouillon. Add cream and reheat, preferably in a double boiler, as the soup must not boil. Adjust seasoning and serve very hot, garnished with chopped parsley.
1 cup California White Table Wine	
¼ cup California Dry Sherry	
1 carrot	
1 stalk celery with leaves	
1 clove garlic	
1 onion	
3 tablespoons butter	
Parsley	
3 tablespoons flour	
3 cups milk, heated	
Pinch nutmeg	
Salt, pepper, monosodium glutamate to taste	
1 cup cream	

Editor's note: Serve **CALIFORNIA DRY SHERRY** *with this mushroom soup and you'll taste again how well these two flavors complement each other.*

Pink Strawberry Soup
(8 SERVINGS)

Mrs. Richard W. Wilson, Vie-Del Company, Fresno

- 1 cup fresh ripe strawberries, washed, hulled and sliced
- 4 cups California Port
- 1 cup water
- ¼ cup sugar
- Pinch of salt
- 3 tablespoons arrowroot
- ¼ cup water
- Hot cream

In a saucepan, mix strawberries, wine and water. Bring to boil. Stir in sugar and salt. Mix arrowroot with water, add a few spoonfuls of hot soup, then stir into hot soup. Cook stirring frequently until soup thickens. Chill. Serve cold, topped with hot cream. Frozen raspberries can also be used, omitting the sugar.

Editor's note: **CALIFORNIA ROSÉ** *or* **LIGHT SWEET MUSCAT** *would be good wine accompaniments for this fruit soup.*

Vichyssoise
(6 SERVINGS)

Mrs. George Al Berry, E. & J. Gallo Winery, Modesto
This makes an excellent first course followed by a green salad with Gourmet Dressing [see below] and Ernie's Tenderloin Brochette [see Page 22]. I usually serve this course in the living room before sitting down in the dining room. It simplifies the table-clearing process.

- 4 cups coarsely diced raw potatoes
- ½ cup finely chopped green onions
- 2½ cups chicken consomme
- ¼ cup crumbled blue cheese
- ½ teaspoon celery salt
- ½ cup California Riesling
- 2 cups light cream

Combine potatoes, green onions and chicken consomme in a saucepan; bring to a boil. Cover and cook until potatoes are tender, 10 to 15 minutes. Then put mixture in a blender, add the blue cheese and blend about 30 seconds. Add celery salt, wine and cream. Blend and chill thoroughly. Serve in soup cups with a sprinkling of minced chives.

 My choice of wine to accompany this dish: **CALIFORNIA RIESLING**

Gourmet Salad Dressing
(2 CUPS)

Mrs. George Al Berry, E. & J. Gallo Winery, Modesto
This dressing over plain lettuce, can serve as the salad course for virtually any dinner menu. It also makes an excellent luncheon dish served on wedges of crisp lettuce with slices of tomato, whole shrimp, and cooked asparagus spears. Accompany with crisp rolls and glasses of the same California wine used in the dressing.

- 2 (3-oz.) package cream cheese
- 1 teaspoon grated onion
- ¼ teaspoon garlic salt
- ½ teaspoon salt
- ⅛ teaspoon paprika
- ¼ cup California Dry White Wine
- ½ cup dairy sour cream
- 2 tablespoons chili sauce
- 1 (7½-oz.) can undrained minced clams
- ¼ cup finely chopped green onions

Beat cheese until soft. Blend in grated onion, garlic salt, salt, paprika, and wine. Add remaining ingredients. Beat until well blended. Refrigerate until ready to use.

My choice of wine to accompany this dish: **CALIFORNIA DRY WHITE TABLE WINE**

Tangy Tuna Mold

(4 TO 6 SERVINGS)

Mrs. Richard Peterson, Beaulieu Vineyard, Rutherford
Editor's note: This Sherry-flavored tuna mold is smooth and rich. Serve it as a main dish salad for luncheon or supper, accompanied by a dry white wine, chilled to a refreshingly cool temperature.

- 1 envelope unflavored gelatin
- ¼ cup California Sherry
- 1 cup dairy sour cream
- 2 tablespoons catsup
- ¾ teaspoon salt
- ½ cup finely chopped green pepper
- ½ cup finely chopped celery
- 1 (7-oz.) can drained tuna
- 2 tablespoons lemon juice
- ¼ cup chopped green onion

Soften gelatin in Sherry, dissolve over hot water. Combine with remaining ingredients, pour into mold and chill. Garnish with ripe olives and fresh parsley.

 Editor's note: CALIFORNIA RIESLING would enhance the flavor of this salad.

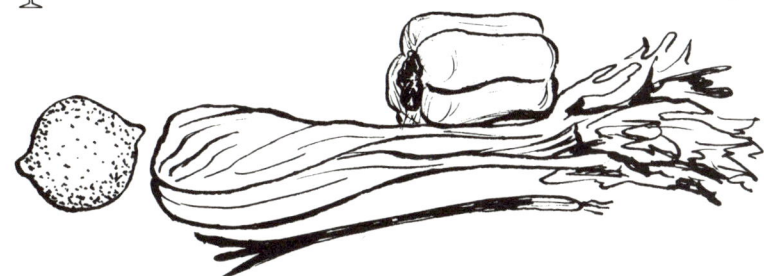

Lentil Soup

(7 TO 8 CUPS)

Mrs. Clifton Chappell, Thomas Vineyards, Cucamonga

- 1¼ cups lentils
- 1 teaspoon salt
- Water (to cover)
- ½ cup California Burgundy
- ½ green pepper, diced
- ½ onion, diced
- 1 (16-oz.) can tomatoes or 2 small (6-oz.) cans vegetable juice

Rinse lentils and cook covered in salted boiling water (at simmering) for about an hour. Add remainder of ingredients and simmer another hour or until lentils are tender.

 Editor's note: When presented as a dinner course, serve this soup with a glass of CALIFORNIA DRY SHERRY.

Tomato Aspic

(8 TO 10 SERVINGS)

Mrs. William B. Hewitt, U.C. San Joaquin Valley Research and Extension Center, Lodi
Editor's note: This is a light salad, delicately flavored with white wine.

- 2 envelopes unflavored gelatin
- ½ cup cold water
- 1 (8-oz.) can tomato sauce
- ½ cup water
- 1 (16-oz.) can stewed tomatoes
- 2 tablespoons chopped parsley
- 2 cups California Gewurztraminer

Soften gelatin in ½ cup cold water; set aside. Pour tomato sauce in saucepan, rinse can out with ½ cup water and add to tomato sauce. Mix in stewed tomatoes and parsley and bring mixture to boil. Strain into measuring cup. Reheat 1½ cups strained mixture to boiling point then stir in softened gelatin and wine. Pour into 2-quart mold or glass utility pan and refrigerate until firm. Serve on butter lettuce with a mayonnaise salad dressing thinned with Gewurztraminer wine.

Editor's note: The same wine used in preparation, CALIFORNIA GEWURZTRAMINER, would be a good choice for the accompanying beverage.

Fruit Wine Compote
(6 TO 8 SERVINGS)

Christine Pedroncelli, J. Pedroncelli Winery, Geyserville
This salad makes a spectacular centerpiece when served in a scooped out watermelon half with the edges cut in a sawtooth border. I serve it with a chicken or crab casserole. It can also be served as a dessert.

- 1 cup diced fresh cantaloupe
- 1 cup diced fresh watermelon
- 1 cup diced fresh pineapple
- 1 cup mandarin orange sections
- 2 cups fresh strawberries
- 1 cup Thompson Seedless grapes
- 1 cup California Sauterne

Mix ingredients together — refrigerate and serve cold. The variations on fruit are endless, using any fresh or canned fruit.

My choice of wine to accompany this dish: **CALIFORNIA CHABLIS**

Seasoned Wine for Salad Dressing
(1 FIFTH)

Mrs. Walter S. Richert, Richert & Sons, Morgan Hill
This recipe came to me from Lew Largent of Pacific Grove, California, in 1960.

- 1 Fifth bottle California Zinfandel
- Handful of parsley
- 5 cloves of garlic
- Lemon juice

Remove ¼ of the bottle of wine. (This portion may be consumed while completing this recipe.) Chop parsley, peel and halve garlic cloves; add to wine bottle. Fill remainder of bottle with lemon juice. Seal and store in refrigerator for two weeks before use.

Cream of Mushroom Soup with Sherry
(5 SERVINGS)

Mrs. August Sebastiani, Samuele Sebastiani Winery, Sonoma

- ¾ pound fresh mushrooms
- 3 tablespoons butter
- 3 tablespoons flour
- 4 cups scalded milk
- 1 egg yolk
- ½ cup California Dry Sherry
- Salt and pepper to taste

Slice mushroom caps and chop the stems. Sauté in butter until they are lightly browned, sprinkle with flour, and cook over low heat for 4 minutes. Add milk and simmer the soup, stirring for 10 minutes. Mix egg yolk, lightly beaten, and Sherry and add to the soup. Add salt and pepper to taste and cook soup for 2 minutes longer. Garnish with finely chopped parsley.

 My choice of wine to accompany this dish: **CALIFORNIA RED TABLE WINE**

Fruit Salad Dressing
(MAKES 1½ CUPS)

Mrs. Harold Berg, University of California, Department of Viticulture and Enology, Davis

- 1 cup mayonnaise
- ½ cup dairy sour cream
- 2 tablespoons chopped chutney
- 1 tablespoon capers, drained
- 1 tablespoon chopped chives
- 1 tablespoon sliced pimiento
- ¼ teaspoon curry powder
- 2 tablespoons California Sherry

Blend all ingredients well and serve with fresh fruit salad, avocado and grapefruit salad or iceberg lettuce.

Editor's note: **CALIFORNIA HAUT SAUTERNE** *is a good complement to this salad.*

Appetizer wines have been enjoyed for centuries. And modern day Epicures are finding that they make an excellent start to today's good foods. Their function, now as always, is to alert the appetite for the meal to come. For this, you can count on California dry Sherry, a sweet or dry Vermouth, one of the natural flavored wines or even on a dry Champagne. Mixed wine drinks are still a novelty to many, even though such "house specialties" as Sherry Sour, Vermouth Half-and-Half, wine lemonade, and various wine coolers have been making aperitif history in California for many years. Some additional choice wine drinks are among the recipes in this section. Another way to stimulate the appetite is to offer wine-flavored hors d'oeuvres, canapes, and dips. When accompanied by a before-dinner wine, these appetizers serve as a prelude to the delicious wine and food combinations that follow.

HORS D'OEUVRES and BEVERAGES

Hors d'oeuvres

Lobster Rumaki

(4 TO 6 SERVINGS)

Mrs. Arthur Caputi, Jr., E. & J. Gallo Winery, Modesto
Editor's note: Rumaki is the favorite cocktail-hour tidbit in the West. Count on serving several per person when planning a party.

- 1 (9-oz.) package frozen rock lobster tails, thawed
- 2 tablespoons salad oil
- ¼ cup soy sauce
- ¼ cup California Dry Sherry
- 1 teaspoon lemon peel, grated
- Small piece ginger root, or ¼ teaspoon powdered ginger
- 6 or 7 slices bacon, halved
- 1 small can water chestnuts

Remove lobster meat from shells and cut into 1-inch pieces. Combine salad oil, soy sauce, Sherry, lemon peel and ginger. Add lobster, mix, and refrigerate for at least 1 hour. To assemble, wrap a piece of bacon around a piece of water chestnut and lobster and secure with a pick or bamboo skewer. Broil 4 inches from heat, turning occasionally for 10 minutes or until bacon is crisp. Serve warm. Bacon may also be partially cooked while lobster meat is marinating. For added flavor, drain marinade and simmer until reduced slightly, then brush over cooked lobster.

 My choice of wine to accompany this dish:
CALIFORNIA COCKTAIL SHERRY

Blossom Hill Cannibal Canape

Mrs. E. Jeff Barnette, Martini-Prati Winery, Santa Rosa
This is a delicious canape and a conversational dish.

- 2 pounds choice top grade lean ground beef
- ½ cup finely chopped onion
- 1 tablespoon Worcestershire sauce
- 3 dashes tabasco
- 1 teaspoon salt
- ½ teaspoon freshly ground black pepper
- 1 teaspoon dry mustard
- 1 clove garlic, crushed
- 2 egg yolks
- ⅓ cup California Port or Sherry
- 1 tablespoon finely cut parsley or chives

Mix well chilled beef with all other ingredients. Shape mixture in a fancy mold or bowl. Refrigerate until ready to use. Unmold, surround with thin slices of rye or pumpernickel bread cut into small squares or crisp crackers. Let guests spread their own.

 Editor's note: Have plenty of **CALIFORNIA DRY SHERRY** *on hand to go with this appetizer.*

Lobster Tail Glacé à la Marguerey

(2 SERVINGS)

Mrs. Leon Peters, Valley Foundry, Fresno
We enjoyed this dish served in very small quantities in individual baking dishes as a first course at the El Tovar Hotel in Grand Canyon.
It is best served as a first course in a small quantity as it is quite rich.

- 1 whole lobster tail
- 2 tablespoons butter
- 4 mushrooms, sliced
- Pinch paprika
- 2 tablespoons flour
- 3 tablespoons California Dry Sherry
- 2 cups light cream
- Salt to taste

Boil one whole lobster tail about 10 minutes. Take out of shell and dice, then put butter in skillet and sauté lobster with mushrooms and paprika. Add flour. Add Sherry and light cream and simmer until thick. Salt to taste and pour lobster into individual shells or casseroles, pour warm sauce over and glaze under broiler until brown.

 My choice of wine to accompany this dish: **CALIFORNIA PINOT BLANC**

Oyster Appetizers

(4 TO 5 SERVINGS)

Mrs. Greg Goorigian, Vie-Del Company, Fresno

- 1 tablespoon lemon juice
- 2 tablespoons buttery oil
- 1 tablespoon instant minced onion
- ⅛ teaspoon pepper
- ½ teaspoon salt
- ¼ teaspoon dry mustard
- ¼ cup California Dry Sherry
- 1 pint fresh oysters
- ½ pound sliced bacon

Combine lemon juice, oil, onion, pepper, salt, dry mustard and wine. Pour mixture over fresh oysters and refrigerate for 2 to 3 hours, spooning mixture over oysters several times while marinating. Just before cooking, make sure oysters have been generously coated again with mixture extra-large oysters may be cut in half). Then wrap each oyster with ½ slice bacon, secure with toothpick. Put on grate and barbecue over hot coals, or if barbecue is not available use hot broiler. Brown on one side, turn, brown on other side. Serve at once.

 Editor's note: Serve the same **CALIFORNIA DRY SHERRY** *used in the preparation of these appetizers with them.*

Brandied Chicken Liver Paté

Mrs. Philip Smyser, Wine Advisory Board, San Francisco
One recipe of this paté lasts us several months since it is so rich.
I store it in small crocks and serve it as a spread on crackers or toast.

- 2 pounds chicken livers, chopped
- ½ cup butter
- 2 medium onions, quartered
- 1 teaspoon paprika
- 1 teaspoon curry powder
- ¼ teaspoon salt
- ¼ teaspoon pepper
- 1 cup softened butter
- ¼ cup California Brandy

Combine in a sauce pan the first 5 ingredients. Cover and cook over low heat for 10 minutes. Puree in a blender or force through sieve. Stir in the softened butter and Brandy. Put the paté in a crock or covered dish and chill until firm.

 My choice of wine to accompany this dish:
CALIFORNIA DRY SHERRY *or* **DRY VERMOUTH**

Oyster Stuffed Mushroom Caps

(10 TO 12 SERVINGS)

Mrs. Louis P. Martini, Louis M. Martini Winery, St. Helena
I use this as a first course or as an appetizer with a light dry white table wine.

30 large mushrooms
Butter
Lemon juice
1 pint fresh oysters
½ cup California White Table Wine
¼ teaspoon horseradish
¼ cup lemon juice
Salt and pepper
1 clove garlic
¼ cup butter

Carefully remove stems and set aside. Clean mushroom caps, being careful not to break. In a covered frying pan melt butter and squeeze in lemon juice. Place mushrooms under side down in the pan, squeeze a small amount of lemon juice over caps and cover and cook slowly until cooked, but not mushy soft. Place bottom side up on a buttered baking dish. Cut fresh oysters in small pieces and fill mushroom caps. In a cup, mix wine, horseradish, lemon juice, salt and pepper and spoon a little over each cap. Clean mushroom stems and grind together through meat grinder (or chop very fine) with one clove of garlic. Blend in softened butter. Put a small amount on each cap. Refrigerate until ready to serve (may be made a few hours ahead of time); 15 minutes before serving, place under broiler and cook until the butter melts and browns.

My choice of wine to accompany this dish:
CALIFORNIA JOHANNISBERG RIESLING

Crab Delight Dip

(TWO CUPS)

Mrs. Shelton Brown, Paul Masson Vineyards, Saratoga
Editor's note: The delicate Sherry flavor in this dip suggests it as suitable to be served with Sherry as an appetizer before dinner. The recipe is also good made with shrimp or lobster.

1 cup mayonnaise
½ cup dairy sour cream
1 tablespoon finely chopped parsley
1 (6½-oz.) can crabmeat, drained
1 tablespoon California Medium Sherry
1 teaspoon lemon juice
Salt and pepper

Combine all ingredients. Chill at least 2 hours before serving. Serve with crackers or crisp, raw vegetables for dipping.

 Editor's note: **CALIFORNIA DRY SHERRY** or **DRY VERMOUTH** *over ice is perfect with this.*

Cheese Fondue

(10 SERVINGS)

Mrs. Irvine C. Mettler, Woodbridge Vineyard, Lodi
Cheese fondue, served in the classic way with cubes of French bread to dip into the melted cheese mixture, is almost a full meal in itself. Sometimes we add salad and a simple dessert.

Garlic
2 cups California White Table Wine
1 pound Swiss cheese
1 pound Jack cheese
4 tablespoons flour
1 tablespoon California Brandy

Rub fondue pot with cut clove of garlic; pour in wine and heat. Dredge cheese in flour and in small amounts, slowly add to wine, stirring constantly. Mixture is ready when thick and smooth. Add Brandy.

 My choice of wine to accompany this dish: **CALIFORNIA CHABLIS**

Stuffed Mushroom Missouri

(5 TO 6 SERVINGS)

Dr. Salvatore P. Lucia, University of California, School of Medicine, San Francisco

20 to 30 mushrooms
    Boiling water, salted
1 cup finely ground
    sauteed or roast pork
1 tablespoon diced celery
1 tablespoon pine nuts
1 tablespoon minced chives
2 tablespoons sliced ripe olives
    Salt and pepper
1 egg, beaten
1⅓ tablespoons light cream
2 tablespoons butter
1 tablespoon California Brandy
    Sweet butter
    Sliced lemon peel

Cook mushrooms gently in water until tender, about 5 minutes. Separate stems from caps. Chop stems into fine pieces. Measure 1 cup of mushroom stems. Add pork, celery, pine nuts, chives, and ripe olives. Season to taste with salt and pepper. Moisten with egg and cream mixture, and simmer until celery is tender. Add Brandy. Fill mushroom caps. Top each with a bit of sweet butter, and grill under broiler until lightly browned. Serve with a sliver of lemon peel.

 My choice of wine to accompany this dish:
CALIFORNIA BRUT CHAMPAGNE *or* **MUSCAT DE FRONTIGNAN**

San Jose Giblets

(8 TO 10 SERVINGS)

E. A. Mirassou, Mirassou Vineyards, San Jose
This is a delightful hors d'oeuvre.
During cooking time baste the chef internally with the California Sherry or Champagne.

¼ cup butter
1 clove pressed garlic
    Salt and pepper
⅛ teaspoon monosodium
    glutamate
¼ teaspoon thyme
¼ teaspoon sage
2 pounds fresh or frozen
    chicken giblets (gizzards,
    chicken hearts and livers)
¼ cup chopped parsley
½ cup California Sherry
1 cup California Champagne
    or any California Dry
    White Wine will substitute

Melt butter in 10-inch frying pan with garlic, sprinkle ½ the dry spices over giblets. Place them in pan, seasoned side down; then add balance of dry spices to giblets. Sprinkle on parsley. Brown giblets on all sides. Reduce heat and simmer for 20 minutes or until tender. Increase heat. Pour in Sherry rapidly 1 minute later pour in Champagne. Allow to simmer in open fry pan until sauce is reduced by two-thirds. It is now ready to serve. Cut giblets in bite size pieces and serve with cocktail picks.

 My Choice of wine to accompany this dish: **CALIFORNIA CHAMPAGNE**

Mushrooms Catalan

(4 TO 5 SERVINGS)

Mrs. Joseph Heitz, Heitz Wine Cellars, St. Helena
Editor's note: An easy and elegant hors d'oeuvre.
Choose small cloves of garlic so the flavor won't be too potent.

1½ pounds firm fresh mushrooms
½ cup olive oil
1 onion, sliced
4 small garlic cloves, sliced
Bouquet garni (several sprigs of fresh herbs, such as parsley, thyme, basil)
Salt and pepper
½ cup California White Table Wine
Finely chopped parsley

Remove stems from mushrooms and reserve for another use. Wash the caps and dry them well. In a skillet heat olive oil, add onion and cook very slowly until onion is soft, but not browned. Add garlic, bouquet garni, salt and pepper, and wine. Heat to simmering. Add mushroom caps. Boil them for 5 minutes. Then remove from heat and allow mushrooms to cool completely in the liquid. Drain the mushrooms and serve them sprinkled with finely chopped parsley as an hors d'oeuvre.

 Editor's note: **CALIFORNIA DRY SHERRY, VERMOUTH** *or* **BRUT CHAMPAGNE** *goes well with this hors d'oeuvre.*

Mushrooms Bourguignon

(6 SERVINGS)

Mrs. Cecil P. Kahmann, Wine Institute, San Francisco
You can serve this as a hot appetizer with cocktail picks,
or thicken the wine sauce slightly and serve over steak or chops.

¼ cup butter
1 clove garlic
2 shallots, minced (or green onions)
1 pound medium-size whole mushrooms
1 cup California Burgundy
1 tablespoon minced parsley
Dash of mace
Salt and freshly ground black pepper

Melt butter in skillet and add crushed garlic and minced shallots. Toss a couple of minutes until tender and golden brown. Add mushrooms, wine, parsley and seasonings. Simmer about 5 to 10 minutes. Serve from a chafing dish or other heated buffet server as a hot hors d'oeuvre. Have cocktail picks available, or serve on small plates with forks.

 Editor's note: **CALIFORNIA DRY VERMOUTH** *complements this appetizer perfectly.*

Wine Olives

Mrs. Frank Bartholomew, Buena Vista Vineyards, Sonoma
Whenever we were served an aperitif in Portugal or Spain, these wine olives accompanied it.
Editor's note: A jar of these olives can be kept in the refrigerator for use any time.
They make a good relish as well as an appetizer.

Olives
Sherry or Madeira

Put olives, either green or ripe, in a small serving bowl and cover with Sherry or Medeira. Refrigerate at least two hours until thoroughly chilled. Serve from bowl in the middle of a canape tray.

Editor's note: Serve **CALIFORNIA DRY SHERRY** *with these olives for an appetizing combination, or try one of California's Special Natural Wines.*

Beverages

Evergreen Delight

(6 SERVINGS)

        Mrs. E. A. Mirassou, Mirassou Vineyards, San Jose
A warm nightcap for a cool evening, this drink also makes a delightful summer nightcap when the honey, whipped cream and nutmeg are omitted. Serve it over ice cubes.

- 6 jiggers California Brandy
- 6 tablespoons honey
- 6 cups hot milk (don't boil)
- Whipped cream
- Nutmeg

Preheat 6 mugs and add 1 jigger of Brandy to each. Stir honey into milk until dissolved. Pour hot milk mixture into Brandy. If calories don't count, add a squiggle of whipped cream and top with a sprinkle of nutmeg.

A Lion's Kiss

(1 4-OUNCE SERVING)

        Fred E. Weibel, Jr., Weibel Champagne Vineyards, Mission San Jose
Editor's note: A bright and cheerful summer taste treat, the proportions can be increased to serve as a punch if desired.

- 3 ounces California Champagne
- 1 ounce California Tangerine-flavored Wine

To a chilled Champagne glass, add Tangerine-flavored Wine and Champagne. Stir lightly and serve. If desired, garnish with a slice of orange or tangerine.

Winemaker's Champagne Punch

(25 TO 30 SERVINGS)

        Mrs. Catherine Menth, California Wine Association, San Francisco
Various frozen fruit juices can be added to this recipe as desired. Sometimes I add frozen orange juice concentrate and frozen pink lemonade concentrate.

- 1 fifth California White Table Wine
- 1 cup California Brandy
- 1 fifth California Champagne
- 1 large bottle (quart) lemon-lime carbonated beverage

Pre-chill ingredients. Mix wine and Brandy in punch bowl. Pour Champagne and lemon-lime beverage in punch bowl simultaneously. Serve immediately.

Frosted Fruit Juice

(4 SERVINGS)

Mrs. N. C. Mirassou, Mirassou Vinyards, San Jose
Editor's note: This fruity combination makes a light, refreshing and frothy drink, nice for mid-afternoon or evening. The natural grape sugar in the Sherry makes it pleasantly sweet.

1 cup orange juice
1 cup California Sweet Sherry
½ cup pineapple juice
½ cup crushed ice
2 egg whites
  Fresh mint sprigs

Combine juices and wine in a shaker with crushed ice. Beat egg white slightly and add to shaker. Shake until frothy. Strain into glasses garnished with mint and serve.

Nectar of the Sea

(1 SERVING)

David R. Wilcox, Wine Advisory Board, San Francisco
This was the result of a successful experiment. I have always enjoyed the three beverages separately and I wondered one day how they would taste together.

¼ cup tomato juice
¼ cup clam juice
½ cup California Rhine Wine

Chill all ingredients well, mix together thoroughly in a glass and garnish edge with a thick wedge of lemon.

Bombay Punch

(ABOUT 30 SERVINGS)

Mrs. Shelton Brown, Paul Masson Vineyards, Saratoga
Editor's note: This punch has a very pleasant flavor and considerable authority. When you want to present a truly festive drink for a memorable occasion, such as a wedding reception, try this one.

1 pint California Brandy
1 pint California Sherry
3 ounces maraschino liqueur
3 ounces Orange Curacao
  Fresh fruits for garnish
1 quart carbonated water
2 quarts California Champagne

Mix Brandy, Sherry and liqueurs in punch bowl with large block of ice. Garnish with slices of fresh fruit. Add carbonated water and Champagne just before serving.

Rosé Fruit Punch

(16 4-OUNCE SERVINGS)

Mrs. John Franzia, Sr., Franzia Brothers Winery, Ripon
Editor's note: This light, pitcher punch refreshes marvelously on a warm afternoon.

4 cups California Vin Rosé
4 cups fresh or frozen grapefruit juice
4 tablespoons grenadine syrup

Combine all ingredients and chill thoroughly. Makes 2 quarts of punch.

A glass of dessert wine is the sweet way to end an Epicurean meal. Sometimes it is paired with fresh fruit and nuts, sometimes with cheese. There's great variety in each of these foods, so the combination can be new every time. Among the wines, there are Port, Sweet Sherry, several Muscats, Angelica and Tokay. These are heavy bodied, rich in flavor and color. Another group, perhaps less well known, are the light sweet wines such as Haut Sauterne or its varietal counterparts Sweet Semillon and Sweet Sauvignon Blanc. Light sweet muscats are fruity and delicious, and sweet Champagne, either pink or the more familiar pale golden, ends a meal in style. We Americans like "made" desserts, and here, too, wine can play an important role as the recipes in this section prove.

DESSERTS

Desserts

Classic Zuppa Inglese

(16 TO 20 SERVINGS)

Mrs. Robert Diana, Villa Armando, Pleasanton

Zuppa Inglese (English Soup) probably has more variations and stories about its origin than any other Italian food including macaroni. When Eighteenth-Century English tourists went to Italy they grew nostalgic for their trifle (Tipsy Cake). So Italian cooks tried to please them by soaking sponge cake with rum or Sherry. There was a great deal of the liquid, so much so that it had to be eaten with a spoon. They referred to the cake, among themselves, as a soup—"English Soup." Some stories say that the Zuppa was first served to Lord Nelson and Lady Hamilton. I reserve this dessert for special occasions such as for a birthday, graduation party or even for a bridal party. To serve it, I cut a large circle in the center and cut the outer ring into serving pieces first.

9	eggs
1½	cups sugar
1½	teaspoons vanilla
1½	cups self-rising flour, sifted
4	tablespoons cornstarch
1	cup sugar
	Pinch of salt
4	cups milk
6	egg yolks, slightly beaten
1	ounce baking chocolate, melted
½	cup California Cream Sherry
1	pint whipping cream
	Sugar
	Vanilla
¼	cup California Cream Sherry
	Candied cherries

In large bowl of electric mixer, combine eggs, 1½ cups sugar and 1½ teaspoons vanilla and beat at high speed for not less than 20 minutes, until lemon colored. With spatula fold in sifted flour ¼ cup at a time. Place equal amounts of batter in four 8-inch cake pans that have been lightly greased and floured. Bake in moderate oven (350°) for 20 minutes, or until sides of cake shrink from pans. Cool 10 minutes on racks, then remove from pans. Meanwhile, make fillings. In top of double boiler, mix cornstarch, 1 cup sugar and salt. Add milk and egg yolks; set over boiling water; cook, stirring constantly, until thickened. Divide the filling in half. To one half, add melted chocolate and blend thoroughly. Cool fillings thoroughly, then add ¼ cup Sherry to each. Whip the cream until peaks form when you raise the beaters. Flavor to taste with sugar and vanilla. Set aside. To assemble the cake, sprinkle an additional ¼ cup Sherry evenly over the 4 layers. Spread first layer with half the chocolate filling; second layer with the white filling; third, with remaining chocolate, and fourth, with the remaining white filling. Directly on top of the white filling place some of the whipped cream, then cover the sides also. Decorate the top and sides by forcing the remainder of the whipped cream through pastry bag and No. 27 star decorating tip. Garnish with candied cherries. Refrigerate for several hours or even overnight before serving.

Editor's note: **CALIFORNIA MEDIUM SWEET CHAMPAGNE** *is the perfect beverage to go with this dessert.*

Macaroon Trifle

(4 OR 5 SERVINGS)

Mrs. August Sebastiani, Samuele Sebastiani Winery, Sonoma
This recipe comes from a good friend, Mrs. Mark Pasquini of San Francisco, who is one of the greatest Epicurean cooks I know. We enjoy sharing our recipes.
I have served this dessert with a great variety of menus.

- ¼ pound almond macaroons
- ¼ pound ladyfingers
- ½ cup raspberry jam
- Custard sauce (below)
- ¼ cup California Medium Sherry
- ¼ cup California Brandy
- Maraschino cherries
- Whipped cream

CUSTARD SAUCE
- 2 tablespoons cornstarch
- 2 cups milk
- 3 tablespoons sugar
- 3 egg yolks
- 3 tablespoons water

Use a small bowl (about 6-cup size). Break macaroons and ladyfingers in two and mix together. Line bowl with part of jam. Add part of cakes to lining of bowl. Spread with remaining jam. Add wine and Brandy to custard sauce and whip all 3 together. Add custard sauce to the remainder of the cakes, and fill the bowl. Cover and refrigerate overnight. Just before serving, decorate with maraschino cherries and whipped cream. **Custard Sauce:** Blend cornstarch with ½ cup cold milk. Heat 1½ cups milk in double boiler, stir in cornstarch mixture. Beat together the sugar, egg yolks and water. Add hot milk, stirring constantly. Cook 5 to 10 minutes to a thin custard consistency. Cool and use as directed above.

 My choice of wine to accompany this dish: **CALIFORNIA CHAMPAGNE**

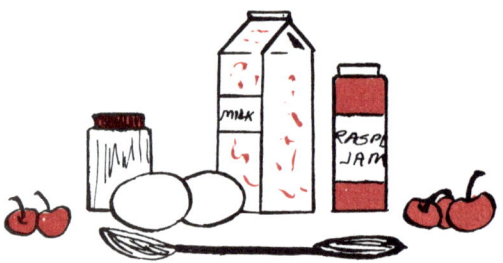

Cenci

(8 DOZEN)

Mrs. Joe Carrari, Paul Masson Vineyards, Soledad
Cenci may be served with most any type of dessert in place of cake or cookies.
They are excellent served with wine for guests.

- 4 cups unsifted cake flour
- ¼ cup butter or margarine
- ⅓ cup granulated sugar
- 4 eggs
- ½ cup California Cream Sherry
- Salad oil or shortening for deep-frying
- Powdered sugar

Place flour in a large bowl. With pastry blender, cut in butter until mixture resembles coarse crumbs. Then stir in granulated sugar. In small bowl, lightly beat eggs with Sherry. Add to flour mixture, stirring until all flour is moistened. On lightly floured surface, knead dough until smooth (about 5 minutes). Cover, and let rest 10 minutes. In deep-fat fryer or heavy saucepan, slowly heat salad oil (4 inches deep) to 400° on deep-frying thermometer. Meanwhile, cut off one-sixth of dough at a time, and roll to paper thinness. With pastry cutter or knife, cut into strips 8 inches long and ¾ inch wide; tie some into knots by making a small cut in center of strips, then lacing one end through and pulling gently into knot. If desired, cut some into 2-inch diamonds. Gently drop dough shapes, a few at a time, into hot oil, and cook 1 minute, or until very lightly browned. With slotted utensil, lift out of oil, and drain on paper towels. Let cool. Sprinkle with powdered sugar. May be stored, loosely covered, in dry place.

 My choice of wine to accompany cenci: Any California dessert wine such as **CALIFORNIA SWEET SHERRY, PORT,** *or* **MUSCATEL**

Sherry Savarin

(10 TO 12 SERVINGS)

Mrs. Louis P. Martini, Louis M. Martini Winery, St. Helena

SAVARIN
- 4 eggs
- ¾ cup sugar
- 1 teaspoon salt
- 2 packages dry yeast dissolved in ¾ cup warm milk
- 2 cups flour
- 1 cube butter melted
- 1 cup flour

SAUCE
- 1 (11-oz.) can Mandarin orange segments
- 1 cup California Sherry
- Water
- 1 cup sugar

GLAZE
- 1½ cup apricot jam
- Flaked coconut (optional)

FILLING
- 1½ pints whipping cream
- Sugar
- Sherry

Savarin: Beat eggs until light, add sugar and salt and beat. Add dissolved yeast and milk mixture. Beat in 2 cups flour until batter is glossy. Add melted butter and 1 cup flour and beat until batter is stiff, but not stiff enough to work by hand. Let mixture raise until double in bulk. Beat down and put in mold (I use a large Bundt pan) and let raise again until double. Bake in hot oven (425°) for 30 to 40 minutes. If getting too brown, lower heat to 375°. Yeast doughs are cooked when they sound hollow to a rap with the knuckles. **Sauce:** Drain the juice from Mandarin orange slices into measuring pitcher (reserve orange sections for later) add Sherry and enough water to make 2½ cups liquid. Bring to a rapid boil and add sugar. Boil 1 or 2 minutes after sugar dissolves. Cool to lukewarm. Prick Savarin with a fork and spoon sauce over cake letting it soak in. First prick bottom of cake and spoon about ⅓ of sauce over it. Then carefully turn and place on serving plate and spoon rest of sauce over top. Let stand 12 hours at room temperature. If sauce drains out of cake, carefully spoon back over cake. **Glaze:** After cake has set for 12 hours, melt apricot jam and put through sieve and spread over cake. Flaked coconut may be sprinkled over top. **Filling:** Just before serving, whip cream until stiff, flavor with sugar and Sherry to taste. Fold in reserved Mandarin orange sections (well drained) and fill center of cake with this mixture. Serve any extra whipped cream mixture separately in bowl.

 My choice of wine to accompany this dish:
CALIFORNIA SPARKLING MUSCAT

California Crepes Suzette

(4 SERVINGS)

Marc and Ze've Halperin, The Christian Brothers, Reedley
Long considered the dessert of sophisticated upper classes, Crepes Suzette are fast becoming part of the menu of the average household. For convenience, crepes may be made in advance and frozen, if necessary.

CREPES
- 1 cup sifted flour
- 2 eggs
- 1¼ cups milk
- Butter

SAUCE
- 4 tablespoons butter
- ¼ cup sugar
- 1 teaspoon strained lemon juice
- ¾ cup strained orange juice
- ½ cup California Light Sweet Muscat
- 4 tablespoons California Brandy

Crepes: Prepare batter with the flour, eggs and milk. Beat until perfectly smooth. Pour into a hot, buttered frying pan to cover bottom; pour back excess. (Pan should be hot enough so that batter sizzles). Allow to cook till crepe is brown, then flip over to brown on the other side. Crepes should be as thin as possible. As they are finished, fold into quarters and place in chafing dish or large frying pan. (Butter frying pan as needed.) **Sauce:** Melt butter in medium-hot sauce pan. Sprinkle in sugar. Using a wire blender, mix continuously until sugar is slightly browned. Remove from heat, immediately add the lemon and orange juices. Put back on heat and continue blending till sugar is completely dissolved. Add the wine and Brandy, blending thoroughly. Pour over crepes. To serve: Place chafing dish with crepes over high heat and spoon sauce over crepes until sauce bubbles. Put 4 tablespoons Brandy into a ladle, warm Brandy by setting ladle in hot water, then ignite Brandy and pour over the crepes.

 Our choice of wine to accompany this dish: **CALIFORNIA CREAM SHERRY**

Brandy Mince Meat

(12 SERVINGS)

Mrs. Alvin Ehrhardt, United Vintners, San Francisco
Use this mince meat as the filling for a lattice-top pie.
It is especially good served warm with a fluffy Sherry hard sauce.
Editor's note: A quart container of mince meat will make two 9-inch pies if the mince meat is mixed with an equal amount of chopped fresh apple. To freeze the filling for one pie without adding any other fruit, put only 3 cups of mince meat into the quart container.

MINCE MEAT
- 2 pounds boneless beef stew meat cubed
- 1 pound beef suet, membrane removed
- 1 pound candied fruit peel
- 3 pounds apples, pared, cored and chopped
- 2 pounds light brown sugar
- 4 cups cider
- 1 tablespoon salt
- 1 tablespoon nutmeg
- 1 tablespoon allspice
- 1 tablespoon cloves
- 2 tablespoons cinnamon
- 1½ cups light molasses
- 3 (11-oz.) packages currants
- 1 pound each seedless raisins and golden raisins
- 2 cups California Brandy

SHERRY HARD SAUCE
- ½ cup butter or margarine
- 2½ cups sifted powdered sugar
- ⅛ teaspoon cinnamon
- ¼ cup California Sherry

Mince Meat: Cover meat with water and bring to a boil, cook until tender and almost dry, about 1½ hours. Cool and put through food chopper using medium blade. (You should have 5½ cups of ground cooked meat.) Put suet and candied fruit peel through the chopper. Mix with meat and apples. Dissolve sugar in cider in large pan, bring to a boil. Add meat mixture carefully and return to a boil. Reduce heat and simmer 5 minutes. Remove from heat. Add salt, spices, molasses, currants and raisins, mix thoroughly. Blend in Brandy, cool to room temperature. **Sherry Hard Sauce:** Beat butter or margarine until creamy. Beat in sifted powdered sugar and cinnamon alternately with Sherry. Beat until mixture forms stiff, creamy peaks. Makes 2 cups sauce. Or add Sherry to taste to commercially prepared Hard Sauce sold in jars.

 My choice of wine to accompany this dish:
CALIFORNIA PORT or **SWEET SHERRY**

Strawberry Cardinal Topping

(6 TO 8 SERVINGS)

Mrs. Charles J. Welch, Guild Wine Company, San Francisco
This topping may be served over ice cream, or over plain cake—unfrosted angel food, pound, or such.

- 1½ quarts fresh strawberries (or whole frozen may be substituted)
- ¼ to ⅓ cup sugar (omit if frozen berries are used)
- 1 (10-oz.) package frozen raspberries
- 2 tablespoons California Brandy
- 1 teaspoon lemon juice

Wash and hull fresh strawberries. Cut into bite-size pieces. Place in a bowl and sprinkle with sugar. Cover and chill. Thaw raspberries. Blend in electric blender until thoroughly pureed and slightly frothy. Strain. Stir in the Brandy and lemon juice. Drain excess liquid from strawberries. Blend raspberry mixture and berries.

My choice of wine to accompany this dish: **CALIFORNIA ROSÉ** or **WHITE TABLE WINE**, *depending on the meat course.*

Plum Wine Jelly

(6 TO 8 SERVINGS)

Mrs. Edmund Accomazzo, Cucamonga Winery, Cucamonga
Editor's note: This dessert makes a soft jelly, not firm. The consistency is part of its charm.
To make a jelly that will hold its shape, reduce the water to 1½ cups.

- 2 cups sliced purple or red plums
- 1 cup honeydew melon balls
- 2 cups water
- 5 whole cloves
- 1 stick cinnamon, broken
- ½ lemon sliced
- 1 (3-oz.) package strawberry gelatin
- 2 teaspoons lemon juice
- ¾ cup California Tokay

Combine sliced plums and melon balls in a shallow dessert bowl. In a saucepan, combine 1 cup water, cloves, cinnamon and lemon and bring to a boil. Add gelatin and stir until dissolved. Add remaining 1 cup water, lemon juice and wine. Pour over plums and melon balls in bowl. Chill until set. Spoon into dessert glasses and, if desired, top with whipped cream.

 Editor's note: The wine used in the preparation of this dish, **CALIFORNIA TOKAY,** *is a delicious accompaniment.* **CALIFORNIA PORT** *is also excellent.*

Grand Sherry Chocolate Mousse

(6 SERVINGS)

Mrs. Frank Franzia, Jr., Franzia Brothers Winery, Ripon
This grand dessert recipe was taken a few years ago from a magazine. It was said to be Raymond Burr's favorite holiday dessert. However, I replaced the liquor it called for with a California Sherry so a minor change in the name was then necessary.

- 1 (12-oz.) jar chocolate or fudge sauce
- 1 envelope unflavored gelatin
- ¼ cup cold water
- 1 teaspoon instant coffee powder
- ¼ cup California Sweet Sherry
- ½ pint whipping cream

The day before or early on the day of serving, in saucepan, heat chocolate or fudge sauce, but do not boil. Soften gelatin in cold water; heat over hot water, until dissolved. Stir in hot sauce. Refrigerate in bowl until cool, about 15 minutes. Dissolve instant coffee powder in Sherry and add to above mixture. Then gently fold it into heavy cream, whipped stiff. Spoon into 6 sherbet glasses; refrigerate until served; garnish with unsweetened whipped cream, if desired. This dessert may also be molded.

 My choice of wine to accompany this dish: **CALIFORNIA CHAMPAGNE**

Sauterne Delight

(8 TO 10 SERVINGS)

Mrs. Frank Lico, San Martin Vineyards Company, San Martin
This is a rather rich cake so it should be served with a simple meal such as baked chicken, green vegetable and oil-vinegar salad. I tried this on my husband's family and it was accepted rather well, so it must be good.

- 1 large angel food cake
- ⅔ cup California Sauterne
- 1 pint dairy sour cream
- 1 cup powdered sugar
- 1 (8-oz.) package cream cheese (at room temperature)

Cut cake crosswise in 2 layers. With a long-pronged fork or ice pick, punch about 20 holes in bottom layer. Sprinkle half the wine over that layer. Combine sour cream and sugar. Spread half the mixture on bottom layer of cake. Cover with top layer and sprinkle on remaining wine. Blend remaining cream mixture with cream cheese to make frosting. Spread on top and sides. Chill.

 My choice of wine to accompany this dish:
CALIFORNIA SAUTERNE *or* **SWEET SAUTERNE**

Apple-Brandy Cake

(9 TO 10 SERVINGS)

Mrs. Paul L. Halpern, United Vintners, Madera

- 1 large egg
- 1¾ cups chopped raw unpeeled apples
- 1 cup sugar
- ¼ cup California Brandy
- 1¼ cups chopped walnuts
- ¼ cup oil
- 1 cup sifted cake flour
- ½ teaspoon nutmeg
- 1 teaspoon soda
- ½ teaspoon salt

Beat the egg and stir in the apples to coat them. Add sugar. Add Brandy and nuts. Stir in the oil. Sift remaining dry ingredients together, then sift into the batter and stir until well mixed. Line an 8″ square pan with wax paper and pour in the cake, spreading evenly. Bake in moderate oven (350°) for 40 minutes—or until a pick inserted in cake comes out clean.

My choice of wine to accompany this dish:
CALIFORNIA CHAMPAGNE *or* **PINK CHABLIS**

Editor's note: For delicious variations, substitute California Sherry or Muscatel for the Brandy in this recipe.

Biscote

(3 DOZEN)

Mrs. Leon Kirschenmann, East-Side Winery, Lodi

- 3 eggs, well beaten
- 1 cup sugar
- ¼ cup California Brandy
- 2 cups sifted flour
- 2 teaspoons baking powder
- ½ teaspoon salt
- ¼ cup whole anise seed, washed in cold water
- 1 cup coarsely chopped almonds
- 1 teaspoon vanilla
- ½ cup butter, melted

Beat eggs until light and lemon colored. Add sugar slowly and continue beating. Add Brandy alternately with sifted dry ingredients to which anise seed and almonds have been added. Add vanilla and melted butter. Beat well. Pour ½ inch of batter into small disposable foil bread pans which have been oiled and floured. Bake in moderate oven (350°) until lightly browned on top and batter pulls away from sides of pans—about 20 to 25 minutes. Turn out on board to cool. When cool, slice loaves in ¼-inch slices, arrange slices on unoiled cookie sheets and toast in 300° oven until crisp and lightly browned. Store in tight container. I usually freeze part of the little loaves and toast them as I wish to serve them.

My choice of wine to accompany this dish:
CALIFORNIA CREAM SHERRY *or* **MARSALA**

Chadeau en Tasse Wein

(5 TO 6 SERVINGS)

Mrs. Donald Gregg, Guild Wine Company, Ukiah

- ½ cup California White Wine or California Sherry or Angelica
- 1½ tablespoons sugar
- 2 whole eggs or 3 egg yolks
- 1 small piece lemon rind

Mix all ingredients in upper part of double boiler. Set upper part on top of lower part of boiler with hot water, heat gently. Whip vigorously with egg beater until mixture comes just to the boiling point, when all should be foam. (If it boils, it will curdle and the foam will disappear again.) Pick out lemon rind and serve the wine foam immediately in teacups with a cookie or some cake. Or whip it after it is foamy until cold again. In that case use 3 yolks and add 1 white of egg, beaten stiff, before serving. If used as a pudding sauce, increase wine to 1 cup with the same ingredients. It also goes well with rice, prunes and bread pudding.

Editor's note: A **CALIFORNIA SWEET SAUTERNE** *or* **LIGHT SWEET MUSCAT** *is a pleasant accompaniment for a pudding topped with this "wine foam."*

Chocolate Muscatel Peaches

(6 TO 8 SERVINGS)

Mrs. John Franzia, Sr., Franzia Brothers Winery, Ripon
This recipe is one my mother-in-law gave me years ago. It is truly something very scrumptious to serve during the fresh peach season, especially for a Sunday dinner. Our menu then usually includes chicken with ravioli or spaghetti.

10 freestone peaches, slightly ripened, fresh, firm, medium yellow, unpeeled	Cut peaches in half. With a melon baller or a teaspoon measure, enlarge the cavity in each half slightly to hold the filling. Reserve the pulp scooped out. Arrange peaches in bowl. Pour wine over peaches and allow to marinate for about ½ hour. Meanwhile, make the filling: Crush macaroons, add sugar, beaten egg, ground chocolate, vanilla and reserved peach pulp. Crack peach pits, remove kernel, chop and add to filling. Remove peaches from wine; place in lightly buttered baking dish. Place a mound of filling mixture in the cavity of each peach half. (Mixture should be thick; if too soft add more macaroon crumbs.) Bake in moderate oven (350°) until browned, about 40 minutes. Serve hot or cold.

- 10 freestone peaches, slightly ripened, fresh, firm, medium yellow, unpeeled
- 2 cups California Muscatel
- 18 Italian almond macaroons, crumbled (1⅓ cup crumbs)
- ⅓ cup sugar
- 1 egg, beaten
- ⅓ cup ground chocolate
- 1 teaspoon vanilla
- 5 chopped peach pit kernels

Editor's note: **CALIFORNIA LIGHT, SWEET MUSCAT** *is delightful with this dessert.*

Bulgarian Brandied Fruit

(6 SERVINGS)

Mrs. Donald Gregg, Guild Wine Company, Ukiah
I serve this fresh fruit mixture either as a dessert or as an appetizer.

- 1 large pear
- 1 large apple
- 1 large orange
- 2 medium peaches
- 2 cups cubed melon
- 1 cup grapes or fresh cherries
- ½ cup powdered sugar
- ¾ cup California White Table Wine
- ¼ cup lemon juice
- ¼ to ⅓ cup California Brandy

About three hours before serving, cut pear, apple, orange sections and peaches into cubes or slices, arrange in a pretty glass bowl together with melon and grapes. Add sugar, wine and lemon juice, blending well. Refrigerate until serving time. Just before serving, toss fruit with Brandy.

Editor's note: To complement this dish, serve a **CALIFORNIA SWEET SAUTERNE** *or* **MEDIUM SWEET CHAMPAGNE.**

Curried Fruit Compote

(8 SERVINGS)

Mrs. Jack Farrior, Jr., Almaden Vineyards, Los Gatos
Editor's note: This attractive dessert can be served warm or cold. The blend of flavors is excellent.

- 1 (No. 2) can pineapple
- 1 (No. 2) can pears
- 1 (No. 2) can peaches
- ½ cup brown sugar (packed)
- ¼ cup butter, melted
- 2 teaspoons curry powder
- ¼ cup California Sauterne

Place fruits and juices in shallow baking dish and cover with remaining ingredients. Bake for ½ hour at 350°.

 My choice of wine to accompany this dish: **CALIFORNIA CHAMPAGNE**

Dessert Cream Cheese

(4 TO 5 SERVINGS)

Mrs. Philo P. Biane, Brookside Vineyard Company, Guasti

1 (8-oz.) package cream cheese
1 cup powdered sugar
½ cup California Dry Sherry or ¼ cup California Brandy
1 egg

In a blender mix cheese, sugar and Sherry or Brandy. Add one whole egg and finish blending at high speed. Pour mixture into small dessert dishes or into lightly oiled small mold. Chill well. This dessert chills to a fairly firm consistency. It can be gently unmolded and surrounded with fruit.

 Editor's note: A **CALIFORNIA LIGHT MUSCAT** or **MEDIUM-SWEET CHAMPAGNE** *complements this dish perfectly.*

Sparkling Champagne Strawberries

(6 SERVINGS)

Mrs. Stephanie DeWitt, Almaden Vineyards, Paicines

2 quarts large strawberries
Sugar
1 tablespoon Kirschwasser
1 tablespoon Cointreau
2 cups California Sec Champagne
1 tablespoon California Brandy

Stem strawberries. Do not wash as this softens the berries. Rinse away any dirt with California white table wine, drying each strawberry immediately with paper towel. Sprinkle liberally with sugar; chill. Add liqueurs shortly before serving. Just as serving begins, add the Champagne and Brandy.

 My choice of wine to accompany this dish: **CALIFORNIA SEC CHAMPAGNE**

Port Pudding

(6 TO 8 SERVINGS)

Mrs. Otto Gramlow, Beaulieu Vineyard, Rutherford
This recipe has been handed down from my great grandmother who was a pioneer in California.

2 packages unflavored gelatin
2 cups California Port
2 cups sugar
2 cups water
Cream or whipped cream

Soften gelatin in ½ cup wine. Combine all ingredients in saucepan and heat until gelatin dissolves. Pour into sherbet or dessert glasses and chill in the refrigerator until set. Serve with thin cream or unsweetened whipped cream. Sherry or Muscat de Frontignan may be substituted for the Port wine.

 Editor's note: **CALIFORNIA HAUT SAUTERNE** *makes a marvelous accompaniment to this dessert.*

Sherried Gelatin Dessert

(4 SERVINGS)

Mrs. John Franzia, Sr., Franzia Brothers Winery, Ripon

1 cup boiling water
1 (3-oz.) package orange-pineapple-flavored gelatin
½ cup cold water
½ cup California Dry Sherry

In a mixing bowl, add boiling water to gelatin. Stir to dissolve completely. Add cold water and Sherry. Pour into one layer mold or four individual molds. Chill until set. For variation, add sliced bananas or ½ cup of drained cocktail fruit.

 Editor's note: **CALIFORNIA SWEET SAUTERNE** or **LIGHT MUSCAT** *makes an excellent accompanying beverage for this dessert.*

Delicious Sherry Cream Pie

(8 TO 10 SERVINGS)

Mrs. Suzanne McKethen, Wine Advisory Board, San Francisco
This is not an original or family recipe. My mother, Mrs. G. W. Scott, copied it from a magazine about 25 years ago and she has never found anyone who is familiar with it.

- 1½ cups crisp chocolate cookies, crushed
- ½ cup butter, melted
- 1 envelope unflavored gelatin
- ¼ cup cold milk
- 3 eggs, separated
- ½ cup sugar
- 1 cup milk
- ⅛ teaspoon salt
- ¼ teaspoon nutmeg
- ½ cup California Sherry
- ½ pint whipping cream

Crush cookies on waxed paper with rolling pin until very fine. Mix with melted butter and pat mixture firmly into 10-inch glass pie plate up over edges to form pie shell. It should not be sticky, only moist. Chill 1 hour. Soften gelatin in cold milk. Put egg yolks in top of double boiler, beat slightly, then add sugar, 1 cup milk; stir well and cook 10 minutes or until mixture coats spoon. Remove from heat. Add gelatin mixture, salt and nutmeg to egg custard, stir until gelatin is dissolved. Add Sherry, very slowly, stirring constantly (if you add Sherry too fast mixture might curdle). Place custard in refrigerator to thicken. When thick, beat egg whites stiff and whip cream firm. Fold egg whites into mixture then add whipped cream to mixture. Pour into chilled, firm piecrust and sprinkle top with grated sweet chocolate or crushed cookies. Chill at least 8 hours or over night.

 Editor's note: A glass of **CALIFORNIA CREAM SHERRY** *complements this dessert beautifully.*

Wine Vinegar Cookies

(TO 10 DOZEN)

Mrs. R. Michael Mondavi, Robert Mondavi Winery, Oakville

- 1 cup butter
- 1 cup sugar
- 1 egg, beaten
- 3 tablespoons unflavored red wine vinegar
- 3 cups sifted flour
- 1 teaspoon nutmeg
- ½ teaspoon baking soda

Set oven temperature for 375°. Cream butter; gradually add sugar and cream well. Mix egg with vinegar and add to creamed mixture. Sift dry ingredients together and gradually add to creamed mixture. Fill cookie press; chill for a few minutes. Form cookies on ungreased cookie sheets. Bake 8 to 10 minutes. Cookies are done when they begin to brown at edges.

 Editor's note: **CALIFORNIA SWEET SHERRY** *or* **PORT** *complements these cookies very well.*

Tutti Fruitti

Mrs. Dinsmoor Webb, University of California, Department of Viticulture and Enology, Davis
This is a recipe given to me by my mother and it had been handed down to her by her mother.

In a heavy crock which has a close-fitting cover, combine equal parts of cut-up fresh fruit, sugar and Brandy. Store in a cool place and stir from time to time. Additional fruit, sugar and Brandy can be added at any time. This compote can be begun with the first Spring strawberries and other fruits added as the season progresses. It is delicious served over ice cream or a cream pudding. It can continue over years to become more complicated in flavor if it is operated on a solera system of each season adding fresh ingredients to replace the amounts removed for consumption.

 Editor's note: Any **CALIFORNIA DESSERT WINE** *or* **CHAMPAGNE** *is excellent with this Brandied fruit.*

A Cellar in Your Home

Imagine being able to say to a guest, "Would you like to come with me to the wine cellar and help me choose the wine for dinner." There's a conversational gambit that stimulates curiosity and heightens anticipation of the meal. Since a wine cellar is so easy to set up, why not have the fun of inviting your guests to participate in the wine selection under your guidance.

Showing off your wine cellar is only part of the fun. Maintaining a stock of wines can enrich your life in many other ways. You always have something elegant and in good taste to serve guests who drop in unexpectedly. There is no need to rush to the store for refreshments. And when you buy wine by the case ahead of time, you save money as well as time. Think of your wine cellar as an extension of your food shelf, and you always have a stock of gourmet ingredients on hand for your cooking.

When you want to give a gift that reflects personal interest and thoughtful selection, choose one or more bottles of wine from your cellar. Champagne, for instance, makes a perfect wedding gift. Some wine cellar owners have cards or labels printed up with their names under the phrase "From the private cellar of . . ." When you present a bottle of wine from your own cellar you give something of yourself.

A wine cellar continually brings you the personal satisfactions of discovery. In trying different wines you discover which ones suit you best. You discover which are the best buys, and you discover which ones age the best. The most practical way to determine how well your favorite wines age is to keep a wine cellar log. Key each bottle of wine, and then on a log sheet or in a log book keep track of when the wine was purchased, and when it was opened and consumed. You might even make notes on how it tasted when you opened it. This will provide you with a guide for future purchases.

How To Start

You can start a wine cellar for as little as $15.00.* A trial selection could include 1 bottle each of the following: a dry or cocktail Sherry; a cream (sweet) Sherry or Port; a dry Vermouth; a Burgundy or similar type (such as Pinot Noir, Gamay, Red Pinot); a Claret or similar type (such as Cabernet, Zinfandel, Grignolino); a Rosé; a Rhine Wine or similar type (such as Johannisberg Riesling, Traminer, Sylvaner); a dry Sauterne or similar type (such as dry Semillon, dry Sauvignon Blanc); a sweet or Haut Sauterne or a light Muscat type; and a medium dry or very dry Champagne. In addition, you should have a half-gallon jug of Sherry for cooking or everyday refreshment. In fact, you can save money by buying other wines in half-gallon and gallon sizes and then decanting them into smaller bottles for easy use. Many excellent wines come in these larger sizes.

* Brand selection, state taxes, transportation and other variables will raise or lower cost.

Where to Locate Your Cellar

Now that you have a fine stock of wine, where do you store it? There are only two requirements for the safe storage of wines that are pure and stable as are all California wines. The storage area must not be subject to constant, strong light and it must have a relatively stable temperature. This is why cellars are perfect for wine storage.

Strong, constant light, particularly sunlight, can harm wine. But note the qualifying word "constant." A couple of days in sunlight will not harm wine, so don't be afraid to take it on picnics or other outings. But for lengthy storage, wine should be kept in a dark area.

Wide fluctuations in temperature can also be harmful to wine. Consequently, the stability of the temperature where the wine is stored is more important than at which temperature it is stored. However a fluctuation of a few degrees will not hurt it. Any temperature in the range from 50 degrees to 60 degrees Farenheit is ideal for storing wine. But wine can be safely stored in temperatures up to 70 degrees. If the temperature rises slightly above 70 degrees for a couple of hours or so on a warm, sunny afternoon there is no cause for alarm. The temperature of wine does not change as readily as air, so the wine will not be harmed.

A wine cellar should provide for the storage of bottles on their sides and standing up. Corked bottles should be stored on their sides to keep the corks moist. This prevents the corks from drying out, shrinking and letting air into the bottle. Metal or plastic enclosed bottles can be stored either upright or on their sides. But having a place to store bottles upright will allow you to include the economical half-gallon and gallon bottles as well as screw-capped fifth bottles.

Wine racks can be purchased in various sizes and at various prices starting at about $4.00. But if you're the resourceful type, you can have fun building your own wine rack; one that fits your special requirements. If you want to improvise, there are many ways to do so. For instance, if you buy a case of wine, stand the case on its side and it makes an excellent wine rack. Cut the ends out of 56-ounce juice cans, fit them snugly between the two sides of a cupboard or cabinet and you have a safe and unique wine rack. Heavy duty mailing tubes can be used the same way. A similar approach is to use agricultural tile. It has the advantage of being a highly efficient insulator which will keep your wine at a more even temperature.

Many modern homes do not have walk-in basements. But this need not prevent your having a wine cellar, because closets, cabinets, lockers, cupboards, and drawers make excellent wine cellars. All that is required is that the storage area protect the wine from light and have a relatively cool and stable temperature.

As you can see there are many ways to obtain a wine "cellar." The important thing to remember is that you are the judge; you choose the wines that you like best. You decide how many bottles best suit your needs. And you decide what kind of "cellar" is the most practical for you.

KITCHEN NOTES

Wine Flavor

Wine is used moderately in the recipes in this book to blend with other ingredients so no one flavor dominates. However, the many who enjoy a more pronounced wine flavor can accomplish this by adding wine to a dish just before it is served.

Also, a bottle called a "wine shaker" with perforated top like a salt shaker can be placed on the table to allow guests to season their food with wine to suit their own tastes. Some hosts give their guests a choice by providing two kinds of wine in table shakers, a Sherry and a red or a white wine.

What Happens to Alcohol In Cooking?

Alcohol boils at a lower temperature (172°) than water. Consequently, when wine is used in cooking, the alcohol evaporates rapidly (in 10 minutes at the simmering temperature), leaving behind the unique flavor and rich aroma of the wine to enhance the food.

Flaming Dishes

Part of the enjoyment of Epicurean cooking is the visual effect. One of the most spectacular ways to present a dish, as well as add to its flavor, is to flame it with Brandy.

For good flaming Brandy, 100-proof is better than 80-proof Brandy. Warm briefly in a double boiler or in a ladle held in a sauce pan of simmering water. Never hold Brandy over direct heat. Pour or ladle gently over the dish and light. A few drops of lemon or orange extract on a sugar cube placed in center of dish with Brandy aids lighting—apply the match to the sugar cube and spoon Brandy gently over resulting flame.

A Good Tenderizer

Many recipes call for marinating foods in wine. With meats wine both flavors and tenderizes. Glass, porcelain, or stainless steel containers are best. Avoid marinating in aluminum containers since it might affect the taste. However, foods can be cooked with wine in aluminum with no adverse effect.

Substitution

Dry table wines are generally interchangeable when used in cooking so long as one white table wine is substituted for another or a red table wine for a different type of red. For instance, if a recipe calls for a Sauterne, and you have only Chablis in the house, there is no reason why the Chablis cannot be used. This is not true of dessert and appetizer wines such as Port and Sherry, however. Substitution of wine in these classes will cause flavor variations in the dish.

Rebottling

Because of their low alcoholic content, table wines are perishable once opened. The best way to prevent spoilage of left-over table wine is to decant it into sterilized smaller bottles leaving not more than an inch and a half of air space at the top. Many wines are sold in the tenth-gallon (12.8 oz.) and fifth gallon (25.6 oz.) sizes with either screw caps or corks. These bottles are ideal for keeping wine left over from larger bottles. If corks are used, they should be tested to see that they don't leak.

Wine Glasses

California's winegrowers recommend an all-purpose, tulip-shaped, nine-ounce, stemmed glass for any wine type. It should be perfectly clear to let the color of the wine show through.

Index of Recipes in this book by Category

BEVERAGES
  A Lion's Kiss 79
  Evergreen Delight 79
  Frosted Fruit Juice 80
  Nectar of the Sea 80
  Punches
    Bombay Punch 80
    Rosé Fruit Punch 80
    Winemaker's Champagne Punch 79
CAKES: See Desserts
CHEESE DISHES
  Cheese Fondue 75
  Risotto Italiene 56
  Regina Fritata 55
COOKIES: See Desserts
CUSTARDS: See Desserts
DESSERTS
  Biscote 88
  California Crepes Suzette 85
  Cenci 84
  Wine Vinegar Cookies 91
  Cakes
    Apple Brandy Cake 88
    Classic Zuppa Inglese 83
    Sauterne Delight 87
    Sherry Savarin 85
  Custards, Gelatins and Puddings
    Chadeau en Tasse Wein 88
    Dessert Cream Cheese 90
    Grand Sherry Chocolate Mousse 87
    Macaroon Trifle 84
    Port Pudding 90
    Sherried Gelatin Dessert 90
  Dessert Sauces, Toppings, and Fillings
    Brandy Mince Meat 86
    Strawberry Cardinal Topping 86
    Tutti Fruitti 91
  Fruit Desserts
    Bulgarian Brandied Fruit 89
    Chocolate Muscatel Peaches 89
    Curried Fruit Compote 89
    Plum Wine Jelly 87
    Sparkling Champagne Strawberries 90
  Pies
    Delicious Sherry Cream Pie 91
EGG DISHES
  Eggs à la Monsignor Gerald Cox 55
  Omelet with Artichokes 57
  Regina Fritata 55
  Valley Royal Eggs 57
FISH AND SHELLFISH
  Fish
    Baked Striped Bass Fillets 49
    Fillet of Sole Florentine 47
    Fisherman's Soup 56
    Salmon Mousse 46
    Sole with Shrimp and Crab Filling 45
    Stuffed Fish Rolls 47
    Wine Baked Fish 49
    Winemasters' Swordfish 47
  Shellfish
    Artichoke and Shrimp Casserole 48
    Crab Coquille 48
    Crab Omelette Supreme 51
    Crab Pie with Almonds 50
    Old Rancho Shrimp Creole 51
    Oysters Provençales 46
    Scallops in Wine Cream Sauce 53
    Scampi Delectable 49
    Shellfish Thermidor 50
    Sherry and Parmesan Scampi 53

    Shrimp Tiffany 52
    Skewered Shrimp in White Wine 52
    Wine Marinated Cracked Crab 51
FRUIT DESSERTS: See Desserts
GELATINS: See Desserts
HORS D'OEUVRES
  Blossom Hill Cannibal Canape 73
  Lobster Rumaki 73
  Lobster Tail Glace à la Marguerey 74
  Mushrooms Bourguignon 77
  Mushrooms Catalan 77
  Oyster Appetizers 74
  Oyster Stuffed Mushroom Caps 75
  San Jose Giblets 76
  Stuffed Mushroom Missouri 76
  Wine Olives 77
  Dips and Spreads
    Brandied Chicken Liver Paté 74
    Cheese Fondue 75
    Crab Delight Dip 75
MEATS
  Beef
    Beef Burgundy 18
    Beef Heart Pinot Blanc 23
    Beef Ragout 15
    Boeuf à la Bourguignonne 20
    Braised Stuffed Flank Steaks 16
    Entrecote with Watercress 19
    Ernie's Tenderloin Brochette
      with Bordelaise Sauce 22
    Flaming Beef Grenadine 20
    International Angus Steak 17
    Korean Steaks 17
    La Lunga 21
    Napa Valley Meat Roll 18
    Puchero Chollo 24
    Steak Bordelaise, Vermouth 19
    Steaks Dianne 16
    Sweetbreads Vermouth 21
    Wine Shortribs 19
  Ham
    Baked Ham Steak 26
  Lamb
    Kidneys Hunter Style 23
    Mib's Lamb Shanks 26
    Roasted Lamb Shanks with Potatoes 27
    Sherried Lamb in Patty Shells 28
    Spanish Lamb 27
  Pork
    Cream Sherry Porkchops 25
    Loin of Pork, Larkmead 25
    Roast Suckling Pig 31
    Wild Boar Larkmead 22
  Veal
    Braised Veal Roast 31
    Veal Sauté 30
    Veal Scallops, Roman Style 24
    Veal Steaks, Sauterne 29
    Veal Vermouth 29
    Veal with Peas 30
PASTAS
  Shell Macaroni in Curried Clam Sauce 58
PIES: See Desserts
POULTRY
  Chicken
    Blazing Chicken 38
    Charbonnet Soup Supreme 67
    Chicken à la Waleski 38
    Chicken Breasts Mandarin 39
    Chicken Hearts in Sour Cream 35
    Chicken Stroganoff 37
    Chicken Tortilla 34

    Chicken with Burgundy
      and Black Cherry Sauce 36
    Delicious Chicken Casserole 37
    Epicurean Chicken Livers 34
    Franzia Baked Chicken 35
    Honolulu Chicken 36
    Petite Poulette au Vin 40
    Theresa's Sherry-Flavored Chicken 42
  Cornish Game Hens
    Flaming Cornish Hens 43
  Duck
    Stuffed Wild Ducks 33
  Pheasant
    Blossom Hill Pheasant 41
    Mandarin Pheasant 41
    Pheasant Surprise 40
    Roast Stuffed Pheasant 42
  Squab
    Squabs in White Wine 39
PUDDINGS: See Desserts
RICE
  Rice with Mushrooms 57
  Risotto Italiene 56
SALADS AND SALAD DRESSINGS
  Salads
    Fruit Wine Compote 70
    Tangy Tuna Mold 69
    Tomato Aspic 69
  Salad Dressings
    Fruit Salad Dressing 70
    Gourmet Salad Dressing 68
    Seasoned Wine for Salad Dressing 70
SOUPS
  Chicken
    Charbonnet Soup Supreme 67
  Fruit
    Pink Strawberry Soup 68
  Seafood
    Fisherman's Soup 56
  Vegetable
    Cream of Mushroom Soup with Sherry 70
    Lentil Soup 69
    Mushroom Cream Soup 67
    Vichyssoise 68
VEGETABLES
  Artichoke and Shrimp Casserole 48
  Artichoke Hearts in Wine 64
  Bear Mountain Zucchini 61
  Broccoli Crown 63
  Canneloni with Spinach Souffle Filling 65
  Eggplant Parmigiana 62
  Fresh Broccoli
    with Cream Cheese Sauce 62
  Green Beans Française 65
  Green Peppers Florentine 64
  Le Celeri à la Eschscholtzia 63
  Madeira Onion Rings 64
  Moussaka Tsapralis 58
  Scalloped Onions 61
  Sherried String Beans 63
WILD GAME
  Boar
    Wild Boar Larkmead 22
  Duck
    Stuffed Wild Ducks 33
  Pheasant
    Roast Stuffed Pheasant 42
    Pheasant Surprise 40
    Mandarin Pheasant 41
    Blossom Hill Pheasant 41
  Rabbit
    Rabbit à la Borghese 28

Alphabetical Index of Recipes in This Book

A Lion's Kiss 79
Apple Brandy Cake 88
Artichoke and Shrimp Casserole 48
Artichoke Hearts in Wine 64

Baked Ham Steak 26
Baked Striped Bass Fillets 49
Bear Mountain Zucchini 61
Beef Burgundy 18
Beef Heart Pinot Blanc 23
Beef Ragout 15
Biscote 88
Blazing Chicken 38
Blossom Hill Cannibal Canape 73
Blossom Hill Pheasant 41
Boeuf à la Bourguignonne 20
Bombay Punch 80
Braised Stuffed Flank Steaks 16
Braised Veal Roast 31
Brandied Chicken Liver Paté 74
Brandy Mince Meat 86
Broccoli Crown 63
Bulgarian Brandied Fruit 89

California Crepes Suzette 85
Canneloni with Spinach Souffle Filling 65
Cenci 84
Chadeau en Tasse Wein 88
Charbonnet Soup Supreme 67
Cheese Fondue 75
Chicken à la Waleski 38
Chicken Breasts Mandarin 39
Chicken Hearts in Sour Cream 35
Chicken Stroganoff 37
Chicken Tortilla 34
Chicken with Burgundy and
  Black Cherry Sauce 36
Chocolate Muscatel Peaches 89
Classic Zuppa Inglese 83
Crab Coquille 48
Crab Delight Dip 75
Crab Omelette Supreme 51
Crab Pie with Almonds 50
Cream of Mushroom Soup with Sherry 70
Cream Sherry Porkchops 25
Curried Fruit Compote 89

Delicious Chicken Casserole 37
Delicious Sherry Cream Pie 91
Dessert Cream Cheese 90

Eggplant Parmigiana 62
Eggs à la Monsignor Gerald Cox 55
Entrecote with Watercress 19
Epicurean Chicken Livers 34
Ernie's Tenderloin Brochette
  with Bordelaise Sauce 22

Evergreen Delight 79
Fillet of Sole Florentine 47
Fisherman's Soup 56
Flaming Beef Grenadine 20
Flaming Cornish Hens 43
Franzia Baked Chicken 35
Fresh Broccoli with Cream Cheese Sauce 62
Frosted Fruit Juice 80
Fruit Salad Dressing 70
Fruit Wine Compote 70

Gourmet Salad Dressing 68
Grand Sherry Chocolate Mousse 87
Green Beans Française 65
Green Peppers Florentine 64

Honolulu Chicken 36

International Angus Steak 17

Kidneys Hunter Style 23
Korean Steaks 17

La Lunga 21
Le Celeri à la Eschscholtzia 63
Lentil Soup 69
Lobster Rumaki 73
Lobster Tail Glace à la Marguerey 74
Loin of Pork, Larkmead 25

Macaroon Trifle 84
Madeira Onion Rings 64
Mandarin Pheasant 41
Mib's Lamb Shanks 26
Moussaka Tsapralis 58
Mushroom Cream Soup 67
Mushrooms Bourguignon 77
Mushrooms Catalan 77

Napa Valley Meat Roll 18
Nectar of the Sea 80

Old Rancho Shrimp Creole 51
Omelet with Artichokes 57
Oyster Appetizers 74
Oyster Stuffed Mushroom Caps 75
Oysters Provençales 46

Petite Poulette au Vin 40
Pheasant Surprise 40
Pink Strawberry Soup 68
Plum Wine Jelly 87
Port Pudding 90
Puchero Chollo 24

Rabbit à la Borghese 28
Regina Fritata 55

Rice with Mushrooms 57
Risotto Italiene 56
Roasted Lamb Shanks with Potatoes 27
Roast Stuffed Pheasant 42
Roast Suckling Pig 31
Rosé Fruit Punch 80

Salmon Mousse 46
San Jose Giblets 76
Sauterne Delight 87
Seasoned Wine for Salad Dressing 70
Scalloped Onions 61
Scallops in Wine Cream Sauce 53
Scampi Delectable 49
Shell Macaroni in Curried Clam Sauce 58
Shellfish Thermidor 50
Sherried Gelatin Dessert 90
Sherried Lamb in Patty Shells 28
Sherried String Beans 63
Sherry and Parmesan Scampi 53
Sherry Savarin 85
Shrimp Tiffany 52
Skewered Shrimp in White Wine 52
Sole with Shrimp and Crab Filling 45
Spanish Lamb 27
Sparkling Champagne Strawberries 90
Squabs in White Wine 39
Steak Bordelaise, Vermouth 19
Steaks Dianne 16
Strawberry Cardinal Topping 86
Stuffed Fish Rolls 47
Stuffed Mushroom Missouri 76
Stuffed Wild Ducks 33
Sweetbreads Vermouth 21

Tangy Tuna Mold 69
Theresa's Sherry-Flavored Chicken 42
Tomato Aspic 69
Tutti Fruitti 91

Valley Royal Eggs 57
Veal Sauté 30
Veal Scallops, Roman Style 24
Veal Steaks, Sauterne 29
Veal Vermouth 29
Veal with Peas 30
Vichyssoise 68

Wild Boar, Larkmead 22
Wine Baked Fish 49
Winemakers' Champagne Punch 79
Wine Marinated Cracked Crab 51
Winemakers' Swordfish 47
Wine Olives 77
Wine Shortribs 19
Wine Vinegar Cookies 91

INDEX
to Wine Advisory Board's Six Wine Cookbooks

PUBLISHED BY THE WINE APPRECIATION GUILD

INDEX TO WINE ADVISORY BOARD'S
SIX WINE COOKBOOKS

Each recipe in all six books is listed under appropriate categories and cross-referenced where necessary. Following each recipe in the index is the code word for the title of the book in which it appears and the page. The code words and the titles of WAB's cookbooks are as follows:

CODE		TITLE OF COOKBOOK
Favorite	=	Favorite Recipes of California Winemakers
Adventures	=	Adventures in Wine Cookery
Gourmet	=	Gourmet Wine Cooking the Easy Way
Epicurean	=	Epicurean Recipes of California Winemakers
Easy	=	Easy Recipes of California Winemakers
Menus	=	Wine Cookbook of Dinner Menus

1978

These cookbooks are available in bookstores, winery tasting rooms, retail package stores and other outlets or may be obtained by mail from:

Wine Appreciation Guild
1377 Ninth Avenue
San Francisco, California 94122
(415) 566-3532

CONTENTS

APPETIZERS & HORS D'OEUVRE
    Canapes 100
    Dips and Spreads 100
    Hot and Cold Hors D'Oeuvres 100

BEVERAGES
    After Dinner Drinks 101
    Before Dinner Drinks 101
    Cold Drinks 101
    Hot Drinks 101
    Punches 102

BRANDY FLAMING 102

BREADS 102

CHEESE DISHES 102

CREPES, PANCAKES, TOAST, WAFFLES 103

CURRIES 103

DESSERTS
    Cakes 103
    Candies 103
    Cookies and Bars 103
    Dessert Pancakes 104
    Dessert Toppings and Fillings 104
    Fruit Desserts 104
    Ice Cream Desserts 105
    Pies, Tarts 105
    Puddings, Gelatin Desserts 105

EGG DISHES 106

FISH AND SHELLFISH
    Fish 106
    Shellfish 107

FONDUES 108

FRUIT CONSERVES & GARNISHES 108

JELLIES & JAMS 108

JELLIES FOR MEATS 108

MEATS
    Beef 108
    Corned Beef 109
    Ground Beef 110
    Ham 110
    Heart 110
    Kidneys 110
    Lamb 110
    Liver 110
    Oxtails 110
    Pork 110
    Spareribs 111

MEATS (continued)
    Sweetbreads 111
    Tongue 111
    Tripe 111
    Veal 111

NUTS 112

PASTA 112

PIES (MAIN DISH) 112

POULTY
    Chicken 112
    Cornish Hen 113
    Squab 113
    Turkey 113

RICE, OTHER GRAINS 113

SALADS 114

SALAD DRESSINGS 115

SANDWICHES 115

SAUCES, BASTES & MARINADES 115

SOUFFLES 116

SOUPS
    Bean 116
    Cheese 116
    Chicken 116
    Consomme 116
    Egg 116
    Fruit 116
    Garnish for Soups 116
    Meat 116
    Seafood 116
    Vegetable 117

STEWS 117

STUFFINGS AND DRESSINGS 117

VEGETABLES 117

WILD GAME
    Boar 119
    Dove 119
    Duck 119
    Goose 119
    Guinea Hen 119
    Pheasant 119
    Quail 119
    Rabbit 119
    Venison 119

APPETIZERS & HORS D'OEUVRE

CANAPES

    Blossom Hill Cannibal Canapé - Epicurean, 73
    Blue Cheddar Party Rolls - Favorite, 24
    Canapé Pierre - Menus, 100
    Canapés San Jose - Adventures, 21
    Caraway Cheese Log - Favorite, 19
    Caviar Cheesecake - Menus, 123
    Cheese Pastry Twirls - Gourmet, 24
    Chicken Liver Sandwich - Adventures, 25
    Chicken Piroshki - Adventures, 23
    Crabmeat Canapés, Santa Clara - Adventures, 25
    Curried Shrimp Canapés - Adventures, 23
    Easy Lobster Canapés - Favorite, 17
    Mini-Pizzas - Menus, 123
    Molded Crab Canapés - Favorite, 22
    Mushroom Canapé Belleview - Menus, 112
    Party Pâté - Favorite, 21
    Quiche Emily - Menus, 123
    Raisin Curry Slices - Gourmet, 24
    Rancher's Apple Canapés - Adventures, 22
    Rolled Chicken Sandwiches - Adventures, 26
    Savory Appetizer Pastries - Gourmet, 26
    Stuffed French Rolls - Easy, 21
    Surprise Puffs - Gourmet, 25

DIPS AND SPREADS

    Anchovy Cheese Spread - Gourmet, 26
    Anchovy Wine Cheese Spread - Favorite, 18
    Blue-Cheddar Party Rolls - Favorite, 24
    Blue Cheese Butter - Adventures, 27
    Blue Cheese Sauterne - Gourmet, 23
    Blue Cheese Wine Spread - Gourmet, 22
    Brandied Chicken Liver Pâté - Epicurean, 74
    Braunsweiger Pâté - Gourmet, 22
    Caraway Cheese Log - Favorite, 19
    Cheddar Dip - Easy, 23
    Cheddar Port - Gourmet, 23
    Cheese Fondue - Epicurean, 75
    Cheese Spread for Apple Pie - Favorite, 117
    Chicken Ham Pâté - Gourmet, 23
    Christmas Cheese Ball - Favorite, 19
    Crab Delight Dip - Epicurean, 75
    Crab Dip Elegante - Gourmet, 24
    Fresno Liverwurst Spread - Easy, 22
    Gouda Cheese and Port - Gourmet, 23
    Ham and Cheese Spread - Gourmet, 25
    Herbed Cheese Spread Chablis - Favorite, 20
    Hot Cheese and Sauterne Dip - Gourmet, 25
    Lodi Blue Cheese Dip - Favorite, 23
    Mock Pâté De Foie Gras - Gourmet, 26
    Modesto Cheese Masterpiece - Favorite, 20
    Nippy Wine Cheese Sauce - Favorite, 21
    No-Fuss Cocktail Spread - Favorite, 22
    Party Cheese Spread - Gourmet, 23
    Party Pâté - Easy, 21
    Party Pâté - Favorite, 21
    Sherried Chicken Liver Pâté - Gourmet, 22

    Sherried Clam-Cheese Dip - Favorite, 24
    Sherry Deviled Ham - Gourmet, 23
    Shrimp Mousse - Favorite, 21
    Sonoma Shrimp-Crab Dip - Favorite, 23
    Swiss Cheese-Ripe Olive Dip - Adventures, 23
    Swiss Dip Sonoma - Gourmet, 25
    The Tuna-Sherry Caper - Favorite, 23
    3-Cheese Ring with Fruit - Favorite, 19
    Tuna Rarebit Dip - Favorite, 23
    Valley Special Dip - Gourmet, 24
    Vintner's Cheese Spread - Easy, 21

HOT AND COLD HORS D'OEUVRES

    Alaska King Crab Platter - Easy, 23
    Anchovy Delight - Easy, 22
    Avocado and Grapefruit Cocktail - Adventures, 27
    Avocado Crabmeat Cocktail Salad - Menus, 106
    Bacon and Liver Tidbits - Easy, 22
    Bacon Crisps - Menus, 122
    Blue Cheese Meat Balls à la Lico - Adventures, 24
    Bobby's Franks - Easy, 23
    California Bounty Bowl - Favorite, 23
    California Fruit Cocktail - Gourmet, 26
    California Marinated Mushrooms - Gourmet, 21
    Caviar Eggs in Aspic - Menus, 116
    Celery Victor - Menus, 102
    Cheese-Frost French Bread - Adventures, 27
    Chicken Liver Pâté - Menus, 122
    Chopped Liver Moderne - Adventures, 25
    Chunky Slices of Frankfurter - Adventures, 24
    Deviled Eggs in Aspic - Adventures, 26
    Cocktail Biscuits - Favorite, 17
    Cocktail Meat Balls with Curry Sauce - Adventures, 26
    Cocktail Sausage Hibachi - Adventures, 24
    Cranberry Shrimp - Easy, 23
    Dipsy Noodles - Easy, 21
    Easy Cocktail Franks - Easy, 22
    Fruit and Wine Appetizer - Adventures, 27
    Gold Coast Nuggets - Favorite, 18
    Grapevine Chicken Livers - Adventures, 24
    Guacamole Molds - Menus, 120
    Gun Club Pheasant - Adventures, 24
    Hearts of Palm Victor - Menus, 102
    Hearts of Palm with Continental Dressing - Menus, 118
    Hot Crab Hors D'Oeuvre - Favorite, 22
    Hot Miniature Turnovers - Favorite, 20
    Hot Seafood Tartlets - Favorite, 20
    Hot Sherried Chicken Livers - Favorite, 17
    Hot Shrimp Appetizer - Favorite, 19
    Little Links Hawaiian - Gourmet, 22
    Lobster Rumaki - Epicurean, 73
    Lobster Tail Glacé à la Marguerey - Epicurean, 74
    Miniature Turkey Turnovers - Favorite, 20
    Mushrooms Bourguignon - Epicurean, 77
    Mushrooms Catalan - Epicurean, 77
    Mushrooms Magnifique - Favorite, 18
    Napa Celery - Adventures, 23
    Nutty Cheese Ball Cucamonga - Adventures, 22
    Oyster Appetizers - Epicurean, 74
    Oyster Stuffed Mushroom Caps - Epicurean, 75
    Oysters Henriette - Menus, 104
    Pâté Maison - Menus, 114
    Pickled Fish Madera - Favorite, 18
    Porky Pineapple - Easy, 22
    Quick Antipasto - Adventures, 22
    Ripe Olives - Favorite, 22
    Rumaki - Gourmet, 25
    San Jose Giblets - Epicurean, 76
    Saratoga Chicken Livers - Easy, 22

Sautéed Mushroom Caps - Adventures, 24
Savory Mushrooms Hors D'Oeuvre - Gourmet, 26
Savory Stuffed Mushrooms - Menus, 123
Seasoned Croutons - Easy, 20
Sherried Cheese Canapés - Adventures, 21
Sherried Olives - Adventures, 22
Sherried Pickled Mushrooms - Adventures, 26
Sherried Seafood Appetizer - Gourmet, 21
Sherried Walnuts - Easy, 20
Shrimp Appetizer Mold - Menus, 123
Shrimp Cheese Appetizer - Easy, 23
Shrimp Sauterne - Easy, 21
Sonoma Steak Pot - Favorite, 22
Sophisticated Liver Sausage - Adventures, 22
Stuffed Celery - Favorite, 19
Stuffed Mushroom Missouri - Epicurean, 76
Tiny Winey Pizza Pies - Adventures, 27
Toasted Mushroom Rolls - Favorite, 18
Tripe Hors D'Oeuvre - Adventures, 25
Tomato Shrimp Appetizer, Green Goddess - Menus, 110
Vienna Bites - Menus, 122
Winemaker Cocktail Burgers - Favorite, 17
Wine Olives - Epicurean, 77

BEVERAGES

AFTER DINNER DRINKS

After-Dinner Peachie - Favorite, 15
California Café Brûlot - Favorite, 15
Fruited Sherry - Gourmet, 13
Sherried Coffee Dessert - Favorite, 15
Café Brûlé - Easy, 14

BEFORE DINNER DRINKS

Ash Blonde - Favorite, 13
Bamboo Cocktail - Favorite, 14
Blossom Hill Pink Delight - Easy, 17
Blossom Hill Sherry Sour - Favorite, 13
Brandanis - Easy, 17
Brandini - Adventures, 18
Brandy Manhattan - Adventures, 15
California Port and Tonic - Gourmet, 19
California Sherry Fizz - Easy, 14
California Tomato Juice Cocktail - Gourmet, 17
Champagne à la San Francisco - Adventures, 15
Champagne Continental - Adventures, 13
Champagne Julep - Favorite, 13
Classic Champagne Cocktail - Favorite, 13
Delano Export - Adventures, 19
French 75 Pitcher - Favorite, 12
Frozen Brandy Sour - Adventures, 14
Hot Clam-Tomato Cocktail - Favorite, 14
Iced Cranberry Rosé - Gourmet, 14
Key to the Cellar - Adventures, 14
Ladies' Delight - Favorite, 13
Lemon Sherry - Easy, 14
Maharajah's Burra Peg - Favorite, 13
Modesto Cocktail - Adventures, 15
Montana Cocktail - Favorite, 14
Orange Blossom Flip - Adventures, 18
Nectar of the Sea - Epicurean, 80
Orange Brunch Sauterne - Adventures, 19
Port Cranberry Refresher - Gourmet, 17
Sherry Daiquiri - Adventures, 14
Sherry Daiquiri - Favorite, 13
Sherry Flip - Favorite, 15
Sherry Frappé - Favorite, 13
Sherry Manhattan - Favorite, 13
Sherry Sour (Sherry Shrub) - Favorite, 13

Sierra Sunrise - Adventures, 13
Spritzer - Favorite, 12
The Bamboo - Gourmet, 18
Trocadero Cocktail - Favorite, 14
Valley of the Moon Cocktail - Adventures, 13
Vermouth Cocktail - Favorite, 13
Vermouth Frost - Gourmet, 16
Vermouth Old-Fashioned - Favorite, 14
V.G.B. - Adventures, 13
Wine Collins - Favorite, 14

COLD DRINKS

A Lion's Kiss - Epicurean, 79
Apricot-Pineapple Cooler - Adventures, 15
Basil Bowler - Favorite, 12
California Burgundy Refresher - Gourmet, 18
Cranberry Sparkler - Gourmet, 13
Easy Wine Lemonade - Favorite, 14
Evergreen Delight - Epicurean, 79
Frappé Roshar - Easy, 13
Frosted Fruit Juice - Epicurean, 80
Frosty Orange Cooler - Gourmet, 16
Green Bird - Easy, 14
Ice Cream Eggnog - Easy, 15
Instant Sparkler - Favorite, 12
Mint Cooler - Adventures, 17
Morning Sherry Tang - Easy, 14
Orange Sherry Flip - Gourmet, 18
Peaches and Wine Cooler - Gourmet, 18
Ported Strawberry Freeze - Gourmet, 17
Refreshing Tall Beverage - Adventures, 19
Rosé Cream - Favorite, 12
Rosé Lemonade for A Party - Gourmet, 15
Sauterne Sparkle - Gourmet, 16
Sherried Apple Eggnog - Gourmet, 16
Sherried Mocha Chocolate - Gourmet, 17
Sherried Tea Flip - Gourmet, 19
Sherry and Pineapple Nog - Gourmet, 17
Sherry Banana Shake - Gourmet, 18
Sherry Banana Shake - Favorite, 15
Sherry Cooler - Adventures, 14
Sophisticated Strawberry Shake - Adventures, 17
Star Syllabub - Gourmet, 16
Strawberry Sangria - Gourmet, 17
Summer Cooler - Favorite, 12
Summer House Tea - Favorite, 11
Wine-and-Tonic - Favorite, 12
Wine Snow Cones - Favorite, 14

HOT DRINKS

Café Brûlé - Easy, 14
California Caudle - Adventures, 20
Delightful Cup - Easy, 15
Evergreen Delight - Epicurean, 79
Fisherman's Coffee - Easy, 14
Glog - Adventures, 19
Holiday Chocolate - Gourmet, 20
Hot Buttered Sherry - Adventures, 20
Hot Clam-Tomato Cocktail - Favorite, 14
Hot Cranberry-Wine Cup - Favorite, 16
Hot Lemon Swizzle Eggnog - Favorite, 16
Hot Mulled Wine - Favorite, 16
Hot Sangaree - Gourmet, 20
Hot Spiced Wine - Favorite, 16
Hot Wine Cranberry Cup - Gourmet, 19
Mulled Burgundy Punch - Gourmet, 19
Mulled Sauterne Cup - Adventures, 19
Sherried Spiced Tea - Gourmet, 19

Snappy Tomato Juice - Gourmet, 18
Spicy Hot Fruit Drink - Adventures, 19
Swedish Glog - Gourmet, 19
Winter Warm-Up - Gourmet, 20

PUNCHES

American Beauty Punch - Gourmet, 14
Apricot Pitcher Punch - Gourmet, 14
Baccari Festival Punch - Easy, 16
Berry Champagne Punch - Easy, 19
Blossom Hill Champagne - Favorite, 11
Bombay Punch - Epicurean, 80
Bowle - Favorite, 11
Bubbling Fruit Punch - Easy, 14
Burgundy Apple Punch - Gourmet, 15
California Champagne Punch - Gourmet, 13
California Punch - Easy, 19
Champagne Punch No. 1 - Adventures, 15
Champagne Sparkler - Gourmet, 14
Champagne Wedding Punch - Gourmet, 15
Citrus Champagne - Easy, 13
Country Syllabub - Adventures, 17
Delano Egg Nog - Adventures, 17
Diplomat Punch - Easy, 16
5-Star Final Punch - Favorite, 9
Fremont Fruit Bowl - Adventures, 14
Golden Punch - Adventures, 17
Grenache Punch - Easy, 18
Hawaiian Punch - Easy, 16
Holiday Punch - Easy, 18
Holiday Special - Adventures, 18
Hurricane Punch - Adventures, 16
Livermore Wine Punch - Adventures, 18
Mai Tai Punch - Easy, 18
May Wine - Favorite, 10
Mulled Burgundy Punch - Gourmet, 19
Old Fashioned Champagne Bowl - Adventures, 16
Orange-Frosted Champagne Punch - Favorite, 11
Pacific Punch - Adventures, 16
Party Punch - Easy, 15
Perfection Punch - Favorite, 10
Pineapple Punch - Easy, 15
Pink Parfait Punch - Easy, 19
Pink Treat - Adventures, 15
Pre-Breakfast Punch - Favorite, 10
Punch in the Pink - Favorite, 9
Raspberry Sparkle - Adventures, 18
Reception Punch - Easy, 15
Rosé Fruit Punch - Epicurean, 80
Rosé Bowl - Easy, 17
Royal Ruby Punch - Easy, 16
Ruby Punch Bowl - Adventures, 16
San Franciscan - Easy, 19
Sangria - Favorite, 10
Sauterne Sparkle - Gourmet, 16
Sauterne with Sherbet Punch - Gourmet, 13
Silver Champagne Punch - Easy, 17
Simple Champagne Punch - Easy, 17
Southland Champagne Punch - Favorite, 11
Sparkling Burgundy Cup - Favorite, 11
Special Occasion Punch - Easy, 18
Star Syllabub - Gourmet, 16
Strawberry Rosé Punch - Gourmet, 14
Strawberry Sangria - Gourmet, 17
Vineyard Punch - Adventures, 16
Waldmeister Riesling - Easy, 16
Wedding Punch - Easy, 19
Wine Lemonade Punch - Gourmet, 15

Wine Punch Hot or Cold - Gourmet, 15
Winemakers' Champagne Punch - Epicurean, 79
Winter Punch - Adventures, 19

BRANDY FLAMING

Apple Charlotte Flambé - Favorite, 113
Beef Burgundy Flambé - Gourmet, 37
Beef Stew, Flamed with Brandy - Favorite, 34
Blazing Chicken - Epicurean, 38
Blossom Hill Lamb with Wine - Adventures, 53
Brandied Fricassee Chicken - Favorite, 57
California Crêpes Suzette - Epicurean, 85
Cherries Jubilee - Easy, 115
Chicken Breasts Flambees - Adventures, 60
Classic Chicken in Wine - Favorite, 57
Crêpes Suzette - Gourmet, 118
Flambéed Apples - Adventures, 99
Flaming Beef Grenadine - Epicurean, 20
Flaming Brandy - Adventures, 11
Flaming Brandy - Favorite, 34, 113
Flaming Cornish Hens - Epicurean, 43
Flaming Raisin Sauce - Gourmet, 48
Napa Crêpes Suzette - Adventures, 110

BREADS

Biscuits in the Round - Gourmet, 85
Cardamom Loaf - Gourmet, 88
Casserole Corn Bread - Gourmet, 86
Cheddar Onion Muffins - Gourmet, 87
Cheese Crisps - Menus, 106
Country Supper Bread - Gourmet, 86
Cucamonga Wine Ring - Gourmet, 88
Dumplings for Poached Salmon - Favorite, 74
French Bread Venetia - Menus, 79
Golden Gate Date Bread - Adventures, 107
Herb Toasties - Menus, 108
Joaquin Valley Raisin Scones - Gourmet, 86
"My" French Bread - Menus, 90
Parmesan Sticks - Menus, 102
Parmesan Wine Bread - Favorite, 102
Patio Cheddar Bread - Menus, 64
Patio Cheese Bread - Gourmet, 87
Pimiento Biscuits - Gourmet, 87
Poppy Cheese Buns - Menus, 96
Sesame Bread Sticks - Menus, 92
Sherried French Breads - Gourmet, 87
Sherry Orange Muffins - Gourmet, 85
Toasted Cheese-Topped French Bread - Gourmet, 86
Yorkshire Pudding - Menus, 109
Zesty French Bread - Favorite, 102

CHEESE DISHES

American Style (Fondue) - Favorite, 104
Ann's Cheddar Fondue with Dunkers - Menus, 98
Bread Custard Chablis - Adventures, 81
California Rarebit - Favorite, 86
Cheese and Wine Quiche - Gourmet, 74
Cheese Chablis - Easy, 114
Cheese Fondue - Epicurean, 75
Cheese Medley - Easy, 31
Cheese Pudding - Menus, 86
Cheese Pudding Mexicano - Menus, 86
Cheese Rarebit - Gourmet, 74
Cheese Soufflé Chablis - Favorite, 87
Cheese-Stuffed Peppers Marinara - Menus, 78
Cheese Timbales with Chili - Menus, 86
Crusty Potato Cheese Casserole - Gourmet, 73

Delphine's Chili-Cheese Custard - Menus, 78
Lasagna Bahama - Easy, 29
Macaroni & Cheese with Wine - Favorite, 84
Party Fondue - Gourmet, 74
Sausage Sampling Fondue - Gourmet, 73
Sherried Shrimp Rarebit - Favorite, 87
Sherry Rarebit - Adventures, 82
Sour Cream and Tortilla Casserole - Easy, 30
Trio Cheese - Menus, 109
Victorian Sherried Crab Fondue - Adventures, 27
Winey Cheese Bake - Adventures, 81
Wine Cheese Fondue - Favorite, 86

CREPES, PANCAKES, TOAST, WAFFLES

California Crêpes Suzette - Epicurean, 85
Chicken Pancakes au Gratin - Menus, 95
Crab Curry Crêpes - Adventures, 78
Crêpes Suzette - Gourmet, 118
Mexican Beef Pancakes - Menus, 35
Mincemeat Crêpes - Menus, 121
Napa Crêpes Suzette - Adventures, 110
Sherried French Toast - Adventures, 84
Sherry Snack Toast - Favorite, 103
Valley Fig Waffles - Favorite, 103
Waffles with Cheese-Bacon Sauce - Gourmet, 87
Wine-Cherry Pancakes - Adventures, 83

CURRIES

Chicken Curry in a Hurry - Gourmet, 54
Crab Curry Crêpes - Adventures, 78
Curried Rice and Chicken Livers - Gourmet, 77
Curried Lamb or Beef - Adventures, 51
Curried Lamb Shanks - Favorite, 50
Crabmeat or Shrimp Curry - Menus, 60
Curried Chicken - Menus, 45
Curried Veal Stew - Menus, 18
Fruit Curry - Easy, 32
Lamb Curry Calcutta - Menus, 23

DESSERTS

CAKES

Angel Dream Cake - Menus, 32
Apple Brandy Cake - Epicurean, 88
Bab's Baba - Favorite, 116
Bacchanalian Yule Cake - Adventures, 107
Banana Cream Crunch - Gourmet, 103
Brandied Layer Cake - Favorite, 113
Brandied Orange Cake - Gourmet, 101
Brandy Cheese Cake - Easy, 122
Cake with Jelly or Jam Sauce - Favorite, 114
Candy Cake - Easy, 121
Cherry Cake - Easy, 122
Chocolate Angel Refrigerator Cake - Menus, 107
Chocolate Cake - Easy, 119
Classic Zuppa Inglese - Epciurean, 83
Creamy Refrigerator Cake - Favorite, 114
Dark Raisin Cake - Gourmet, 100
Deluxe Cheese Cake - Gourmet 101
Dessert Wine Dumplings - Favorite, 116
Easy Egg Surprise - Adventures, 104
Easy Rum Cake - Menus, 68
Epicurean Peach Cobbler - Adventures, 98
Filbert Wine Cake - Gourmet, 99
Fudge Pound Cake - Menus, 95
Gingerbread - Gourmet, 104
Gingerbread with Sherry-Lemon Sauce - Gourmet, 104
Golden Gate Date Bread - Adventures, 107
Heaven Cake - Menus, 93
Heavenly Torte - Menus, 111
Holiday Fruit Cake - Adventures, 106
Ice Box Wine Cake - Adventures, 105
Jeans No-Bake Fruit Cake - Easy, 120
Lemon Ice Box Cake - Easy, 120
Marshmallow Fruit Cake - Gourmet, 112
Mincemeat Cake - Adventures, 111
Napa Valley Cake - Gourmet, 104
Pastel Wine Cake - Gourmet, 103
Peach Cake - Easy, 121
Peach Lemon Dream Cake - Gourmet, 99
Peach Upside Down Cake - Gourmet, 102
Persimmon Fruit Cake - Adventures, 107
Poor Man's Fruitcake - Easy, 122
Port-Pineapple Fruit Cake - Favorite, 114
Prune Cake with Penuche Frosting - Gourmet, 102
Quick Cake Dessert - Favorite, 114
Quick Cheese Cake - Gourmet, 100
Quick Easy Wine Cake - Favorite, 114
Refrigerator Cake - Easy, 109
Royal Wine Torte - Favorite, 113
Saint's Delight - Easy, 121
Sauterne Delight - Epicurean, 87
Sherry Cheesecake Modesto - Adventures, 106
Sherry Chiffon Cake - Gourmet, 101
Sherry Orange Cake - Easy, 119
Sherry Savarin - Epicurean, 85
Superb Chocolate Torte - Gourmet, 107
Thirsty Torte - Favorite, 113
Toasted Pound Cake - Menus, 17
Toddy Gingerbread - Gourmet, 101
Vanilla Wafer Cake - Easy, 109
Wine Cream Angel Cake - Adventures, 106
Wine Festival Angel Food Cake - Adventures, 108

CANDIES

Brandy Candy Cookies - Adventures, 107
Pecan Candy - Easy, 115
Prissy Pecans - Adventures, 109
Sherry Pralines - Gourmet, 117
University Dates - Adventures, 110

COOKIES AND BARS

Almond Sherry Cookies - Favorite, 115
Anise Cookies - Easy, 123
Apricot-Wine Cookies - Favorite, 115
Biscote - Epicurean, 88
Brandy Balls - Favorite, 115
Brandy Candy Cookies - Adventures, 107
Brandy Cookies - Adventures, 110
Cenci - Epicurean, 84
Cherry Wine Bars - Menus, 77
Chocolate Graham-Nut Bars - Menus, 54
Chocolate Sherry Cookies - Gourmet, 118
Davis Date Bars - Favorite, 116
Filled Ladyfingers - Menus, 23
Frosted Date Brownies - Menus, 71
Hungarian Tea Cakes - Menus, 24
Jelly-Filled Nut Balls - Menus, 40
Lebkuchen - Easy, 123
Mendocino Nut Drops - Favorite, 115
Mocha Sherry Brownie Squares - Gourmet, 118
Mystery Chocolate Balls - Menus, 10
Nutmeg Cookies - Easy, 123
Port-Date Pinwheels - Favorite, 116
Port Wine Bon Bons - Gourmet, 117

Port Wine Zwieback - Adventures, 109
Prissy Pecans - Adventures, 109
Sherried Raisin Bars - Adventures, 108
Sherry Balls - Favorite, 115
Vineyard Hermits - Adventures, 109
Wine Vinegar Cookies - Epicurean, 91

DESSERT PANCAKES

California Crêpes Suzette - Epicurean, 85
Crêpes Suzette - Gourmet, 118
Mincemeat Crêpes - Menus, 121
Napa Crêpes Suzette - Adventures, 110
Wine-Cherry Pancakes - Adventures, 83

DESSERT TOPPINGS AND FILLINGS

Almond Butterscotch Sauce - Menus, 113
Bacchus Apricot Sauce - Adventures, 111
Brandy Mince Meat - Epicurean, 86
Chocolate Sherry Frosting - Easy, 119
Chocolate Wine Sauce - Gourmet, 107
Coconut Cream - Menus, 11
Cranberry Sundae Sauce - Menus, 63
Dress-Up Sauce for Custard and Pudding - Gourmet, 100
Flaming Raisin Sauce - Gourmet, 48
Gala Dessert Topping - Favorite, 119
Jam & Brandy Topping - Adventures, 112
Marsala Orange Sauce - Easy, 114
Nectar for Fruits - Favorite, 119
Orange Icing - Menus, 71
Pineapple Port Sauce - Adventures, 112
Plum-Port Sauce - Adventures, 111
Port Wine Sundae Sauce - Favorite, 118
Raspberry White Wine Sauce - Adventures, 111
Rum-Butterscotch Sauce - Menus, 37
Seafoam Pudding Sauce - Favorite, 118
Sherried Chocolate Sauce - Adventures, 112
Sherried Pancake or Waffle Syrup - Gourmet, 87
Sherried Prune Sauce - Gourmet, 119
Sherry Butter-Nut Sauce - Adventures, 112
Sherry Nutmeg Whip Topping - Gourmet, 105
Sherry Pecan Sauce - Gourmet, 119
Sherry Spice Sauce for Apple Pie - Adventures, 111
Spicy Burgundy Sauce - Gourmet, 119
Strawberry Cardinal Topping - Epicurean, 86
Toffee Topping for Cake - Menus, 47
Topping for Sundaes - Easy, 122
Tutti Fruitti - Epicurean, 91
Wine Cranberry Sundae Topping - Gourmet, 116

FRUIT DESSERTS

Almond Stuffed Peaches - Easy, 117
Apple Charlotte Flambé - Favorite, 113
Applesauce - Easy, 112
Apples for Baking, Stuffing - Adventures, 99
Baked Apples Delano - Easy, 112
Baked Apples Piedmont - Easy, 111
Baked Apricots Paysanne - Adventures, 98
Baked Marmalade Pears - Menus, 42
Baked Pears San Gabriel - Favorite, 107
Banana Coconut Rolls - Gourmet, 107
Bananas Tropical with Coconut Cream - Menus, 11
Berries à la Muscatel - Easy, 122
Blossom Hill Baked Apples, I & II - Easy, 112
Brandied Cherries - Favorite, 113
Brandied Fruit and Sherbet Cup - Menus, 86
Brandied Prunes - Favorite, 113
Bulgarian Brandied Fruit - Epicurean, 89

California Cocktail - Easy, 114
California Orange Soufflé - Adventures, 101
Canned Figs with Sherry - Favorite, 106
Cantaloupe and Port - Easy, 116
Champagne Over Fruits - Favorite, 106
Cherries Brandianne - Easy, 110
Cherries Jubilee - Easy, 115
Chocolate Muscatel Peaches - Epicurean, 89
Crunchy Fruit Cobbler - Easy, 119
Crusty Baked Bananas - Menus, 48
Curried Fruit Compote - Epicurean, 89
Delano Peach Delight - Favorite, 106
Epicurean Baked Apples - Favorite, 109
Figs and Cream Sherry - Adventures, 100
Figs Continental - Gourmet, 116
Flambéed Apples - Adventures, 99
Fresh Peach-Strawberry Bowl - Menus, 20
Fruit Medley - Menus, 72
Fruits in Champagne - Gourmet, 114
Fruits in Wine Sauce - Gourmet, 116
Frutta Amabile (Pineapple) - Favorite, 109
Gina Fruit Cup - Easy, 117
Glazed Apples Rosé - Gourmet, 113
Grapefruit au Cointreau - Menus, 58
Grapefruit Alaska - Favorite, 108
Grapes - Favorite, 106
Honey Apple Crisp - Adventures, 99
Honeyed Green Grapes - Favorite, 109
Hot Canned Peaches - Favorite, 108
Hot Fruit Compote - Adventures, 100
Hot Fruit Compote with Port - Gourmet, 114
Lemon Honey Bananas - Easy, 116
Lemon Prune Delight - Easy, 117
Lisa Fruit Cup - Favorite, 108
Meringues with Mincemeat Wine Sauce - Gourmet, 119
Olympian Oranges - Adventures, 100
Orange and Grapefruit Sections - Adventures, 100
Orange-Pineapple Cup - Menus, 78
Orange Wine Charlotte - Gourmet, 115
Peaches Diane - Gourmet, 116
Peaches en Gelée - Easy, 120
Peaches in Cream - Easy, 118
Peaches in Honey and Wine - Gourmet, 114
Peaches in Wine - Favorite, 110
Peaches with Muscatel - Favorite, 111
Pear Crisp - Easy, 111
Pears au Vin - Easy, 114
Pears Elwood - Easy, 111
Pears Gertrude - Easy, 110
Pears in Port - Easy, 108
Pears Poached in White Wine - Gourmet, 100
Pears Sabayon - Adventures, 98
Pears with Chocolate Sauce - Easy, 113
Pineapple de Menthe - Menus, 44
Pink Pears Rosé - Adventures, 100
Plum Fluff - Favorite, 110
Plum Wine Jelly - Epicurean, 87
Ported Fruit Medley - Gourmet, 115
Prune Betty - Easy, 113
Prune Crisp - Easy, 113
Prunes in California Claret or Burgundy - Gourmet, 116
Prunes in California Port - Gourmet, 116
Prunes in California Sherry - Gourmet, 116
Raisins, Softened or Plumped - Favorite, 118
Rhubarb Wine Soup - Easy, 113
Rhubarb Zinfandel - Easy, 113
Ripon Cherry Delight - Adventures, 110
St. Helena Fruit Cup - Gourmet, 116
Saratoga Fruit Cup - Favorite, 106

Sauterne Fruit Compote - Favorite, 108
Sherried Grapefruit - Favorite, 110
Sherried Oranges - Favorite, 107
Sherried Watermelon - Adventures, 97
Sparkling Champagne Strawberries - Epicurean, 90
Special Apple Crisp - Menus, 59
Spiced Peach Champagne Cup - Gourmet, 115
Strawberries à l'Impératrice - Gourmet, 111
Strawberries Americo - Favorite, 107
Strawberries in Champagne - Favorite, 107
Strawberries Marsala - Easy, 115
Strawberries Merriann - Menus, 57
Strawberries Romanoff - Easy, 110
Strawberries with Port & Brown Sugar - Favorite, 107
Stuffed Peaches Piemontese - Favorite, 109
Stuffed Pears Milanese - Adventures, 99
Summer Peaches Sabayon - Adventures, 97
Swedish Applesauce Torte - Menus, 16
University Dates - Adventures, 110
Wine-Spiced Prunes - Favorite, 109
Wine Taster's Bananas - Favorite, 108

ICE CREAM DESSERTS

Angel Nectar Dessert - Easy, 115
Coffee-Flavored Sundae - Easy, 118
Cranberry Peach Melba - Menus, 63
Crème De Menthe Mousse - Menus, 115
Delano Peach Delight - Favorite, 106
Frozen Date-Pecan Delight - Menus, 119
Frozen Lemon Cream - Menus, 61
Frozen Sherry Cream Glacé - Gourmet, 109
Graham Cracker Ice Cream - Menus, 80
Grapefruit Alaska - Favorite, 108
Ice Cream Pudding - Easy, 118
Ice Cream with Coconut - Easy, 115
Mandarin Orange Sundae - Menus, 39
Maple-Peanut Sundae - Menus, 66
Marmalade Sundae - Menus, 90
Peach Supreme - Menus, 33
Port Volcano - Favorite, 107
Ported Cherry Sundae - Gourmet, 119
Quick Peach Melba - Menus, 51
Rosé Strawberry Cream - Favorite, 111
"Rudy's Special" - Easy, 116
Rum-Butterscotch Ice Cream Sandwich - Menus, 37
Sauterne Ice - Easy, 117
Surprise Marshmallow Sundae - Menus, 55
Tutti-Frutti Bombe - Easy, 123

PIES, TARTS

Al's Favorite Rhubarb Pie - Adventures, 106
Apple Cobbler - Gourmet, 105
Apple Pie with Port - Gourmet, 105
Apple Strudel - Menus, 28
California Berry Pie - Easy, 110
California Raisin Tartlets - Gourmet, 107
Cheese Spread for Apple Pie - Favorite, 117
Cheesecake Pie - Menus, 91
Cranberry Wine Chiffon Pie - Gourmet, 105
Cream Fruit Cocktail Pie - Gourmet, 103
Delicious Sherry Cream Pie - Epicurean, 91
Elk Grove Turnovers - Adventures, 109
Frozen Brandy Pie - Favorite, 117
Glazed Cherry Port Tarts - Menus, 101
Graham Cracker Torte - Menus, 30
Grape Tart - Adventures, 100
Honey Sherried Crunch Pie - Gourmet, 106
Lemon-Glazed Cheese Pie - Adventures, 105

Lemon Velvet Pie - Menus, 13
Lemony Angel Pie - Menus, 74
Masquerade Pie - Menus, 105
Mincemeat Chiffon Pie - Menus, 41
Mincemeat Tarts - Adventures, 108
Mocha Chiffon Pie - Menus, 84
Nectar-Glazed Strawberry Tarts - Menus, 60
Parfait Pie Chablis - Adventures, 105
Port Berry Pie - Adventures, 108
Pumpkin Chiffon Pie - Menus, 34
Sherried Fresh Peach Pie - Favorite, 117
Sherry Apple Pie - Easy, 120
Sherry Chiffon Pie - Gourmet, 104
Sherry Cream Pie - Favorite, 117
Sherry-Glazed Apple Pie - Gourmet, 106
Sherry in Apple Pie Filling - Favorite, 117
Sour Cream Mincemeat Pie - Menus, 82
Strawberry Port Pie - Gourmet, 106
Tangy Lemon-Raisin Pie - Favorite, 118
Wonderful Chocolate Pie - Menus, 87
Valley Mince Pie - Favorite, 118
Vineyard Holiday Pie - Favorite, 117
Vintner's Chiffon Pie - Easy, 112

PUDDINGS, GELATIN DESSERTS

Almond Bavarian - Easy, 114
Angel Parfait - Gourmet, 112
Apple Charlotte Flambé - Favorite, 113
Banana Nut Trifle - Gourmet, 109
Biscuit Tortoni - Adventures, 103
Bonet - Adventures, 102
Brandied Coffee Jelly - Menus, 43
Brandied Peach Pudding - Menus, 96
Brandy Pudding - Easy, 118
Brandy Pudding Selma - Favorite, 112
Broiled Coconut Cream Pudding - Gourmet, 108
Butterscotch Pecan Pudding - Menus, 27
Chadeau en Tasse Wein - Epicurean, 88
Champagne Jelly - Favorite, 111
Chantilly Rice Pudding - Gourmet, 118
Cheese Chablis - Easy, 114
Cherries in Wine Gelatin - Gourmet, 113
Chocolate Cloud Soufflé - Menus, 49
Chocolate Moussette - Menus, 15
Coconut Bavarian Cream - Menus, 113
Cranberry Wine Marlow - Gourmet, 111
Cranberry Wine Dessert Mold - Gourmet, 113
Cream Puff Fantasy - Gourmet, 106
Crème au Vin - Adventures, 101
Crème Brûlée - Gourmet, 117
Crème d'Orange - Menus, 103
Custard Favorite - Adventures, 102
Custard's Last Stand - Adventures, 103
Danish Strawberry Mousse - Adventures, 103
Dessert Cream Cheese - Epicurean, 90
Easy Zabaglione - Favorite, 112
English Trifle Livermore - Adventures, 104
Flavored Chocolate Pudding - Adventures, 118
Food for the Gods - Favorite, 112
Frozen Fruit Crème - Gourmet, 112
Frozen Raisin Tortoni - Gourmet, 108
Fruit Cocktail Pudding-Cake - Menus, 70
Fruited Lemon Dessert Ring - Menus, 62
Gingerbread Pear Pudding - Easy, 111
Golden State Rice Pudding - Gourmet, 111
Grand Sherry Chocolate Mousse - Epicurean, 87
Instant Vanilla Pudding - Favorite, 120
Jellied Orange Delight - Menus, 56
Macaroon Trifle - Epicurean, 84

Minted Lemon Jelly - Menus, 26
Mocha Moussette - Menus, 15
Muscatel Pudding - Adventures, 104
Orange Dessert Ring with Fruit - Menus, 72
Orange Sherry Cream - Adventures, 101
Orange Tapioca Cream - Easy, 116
Peach and Cream Pudding - Easy, 116
Pesche Bourdalone - Adventures, 98
Port of Napa Gelatin - Favorite, 111
Port Pudding - Epicurean, 90
Pot de Crème Parfaits - Easy, 109
Pudding-in-a-Hurry - Favorite, 110
Pudding Shortcakes - Menus, 98
Raisin Angel Pudding - Gourmet, 110
Raspberry Parfait Pudding - Menus, 92
Rhine Foam Lemon Cream - Favorite, 110
Rich Sherry Trifle - Gourmet, 109
Rocky Road Pudding - Gourmet, 113
Rosé Strawberry Cream - Favorite, 111
Rosy Red Peach Rice Cream - Gourmet, 109
Sabayon Pudding - Menus, 38
San Martin Sherry-Mallow - Adventures, 102
Saratoga Trifle - Easy, 118
Sherried Caramel Custard - Favorite, 111
Sherried Gelatin Dessert - Epicurean, 90
Sherried Peach Bavarian - Gourmet, 114
Sherried Pots de Crème - Gourmet, 117
Sherry Cherry Cream - Gourmet, 110
Sherry Coconut Mousse - Gourmet, 115
Sherry Trifle Anglais - Adventures, 104
Spanish Wine Cream - Adventures, 102
Squire's Pudding - Gourmet, 112
Steamed Raisin Pudding - Easy, 108
Strawberry Mousse - Gourmet, 110
Strawberry Red Wine Parfait - Adventures, 103
Strawberry Wine Cream - Gourmet, 111
Strawberry Wine Fluff - Adventures, 101
Upside-Down Boysenberry Pudding - Menus, 12
Vintner's Date Pudding - Adventures, 99
Wine Milk Chocolate Mousse - Gourmet, 110
Zabaglione - Gourmet, 108
Zabaglione Classic - Favorite, 112
Zabaglione Ring with Fruit - Menus, 117
Zuppa Inglese - Adventures, 105

EGG DISHES

Bacon and Egg Pie - Menus, 68
Baked Deviled Eggs with Sprimp Sauce - Menus, 81
Baked Eggs Florentine - Menus, 82
Celery-Egg Timbales with Lobster Sauce - Menus, 62
Crab Omelette Supreme - Epicurean, 51
Delphine's Chili-Cheese Custard - Adventures, 78
Deviled Egg Ring with Shellfish - Menus, 63
Eggs à la Monsignor Gerald Cox - Epicurean - 55
Eggs Baked in Spinach Nests - Favorite, 86
Eggs in Sauterne Aspic - Gourmet, 75
Eggs Poached in White Wine - Adventures, 83
Eggs with Cream Cheese - Adventures, 83
Ethelwyn's Egg Delicacy - Easy, 27
Hash with Eggs Hollandaise - Menus, 90
Imaginative Omelet - Easy, 30
Mushroom-Stuffed Eggs Parisienne - Menus, 81
Mushrooms Benedict - Easy, 32
Omelet with Artichokes - Epicurean, 57
Parmesan Eggs - Adventures, 84
Pickled Eggs - Gourmet, 74
Poached Eggs with Sherried Cream Sauce - Gourmet, 74
Poached or Fried Eggs - Favorite, 84
Regina Fritata - Epicurean, 55
Scrambled Eggs Chablis - Gourmet, 75
Scrambled Eggs Sauterne - Favorite, 88
Scrambled Eggs with Lox - Adventures, 83
Sherried Eggs - Favorite, 88
Spanish Omelet - Easy, 27
Stuffed Eggs Gourmet - Favorite, 86
Valley Royal Eggs - Epicurean, 57
Wine Country Parmesan Omelet - Favorite, 87

FISH AND SHELLFISH

FISH

Baked Fish au Chablis - Adventures, 73
Baked Fish Cucamonga - Favorite, 69
Baked Fish Fillets Piquant - Gourmet, 68
Baked Fish Fillets Tartar - Menus, 56
Baked Fish Louisiana - Menus, 53
Baked Fish Pimiento - Favorite, 73
Baked Fish with Chablis - Gourmet, 68
Baked Pike with Herbs - Easy, 54
Baked Rock Cod with Potatoes - Favorite, 73
Baked Salmon with Sour Cream - Menus, 56
Baked Sole in Oyster-Cheese Sauce - Menus, 52
Baked Sole Paprika - Adventures, 74
Baked Sole with Clam Sauce - Menus, 53
Baked Sole with Salmon - Easy, 50
Baked Striped Bass Fillets - Epicurean, 49
Baked Trout St. Helena - Adventures, 71
Barbecued or Grilled Salmon - Favorite, 73
Barbecued Salmon Steaks, Vermouth - Gourmet, 69
Barbecued Trout - Easy, 63
Broiled Fish North Coast - Favorite, 72
Broiled Trout Santa Rosa - Adventures, 75
Buffet Pickled Fish - Adventures, 78
Ciaravino Sole - Easy, 57
Cod Auvergne - Easy, 59
Crisp Baked Fish Fillets - Menus, 55
Emily's Tuna Mousse - Menus, 64
Fiesta Fish Casseroles - Favorite, 74
Fillet of Sole Florentine - Epicurean, 47
Fillet of Sole Monterey - Favorite, 70
Fillet of Sole San Joaquin - Adventures, 73
Fish and Tomato Bake - Gourmet, 67
Fish Angeles - Easy, 51
Fish au Vin Rouge - Easy, 58
Fish Barbecue - Adventures, 33
Fish Fillets Florentine - Menus, 54
Fish Fillets Marguerite - Menus, 58
Fish Fillets with Shrimp Sauce - Gourmet, 65
Fish Poached in White Wine - Gourmet, 66
Fish Steaks Burgundy Sauce - Gourmet, 67
Fish Sticks Piquant - Gourmet, 68
Fisherman's Delight - Easy, 55
Fisherman's Soup - Epicurean, 56
Fisherman's Stew - Adventures, 70
Fish Fillets Baked in Wine-Mushroom Sauce - Adventures, 7
Fish in Wine Sauce - Adventures, 74
Frog Legs Gourmet - Easy, 59
Frog Legs in Wine - Adventures, 77
Frog Legs Pinot Blanc - Adventures, 77
Frozen Fish Sticks - Favorite, 71
Frying Fish (Wine in Drippings) - Favorite, 120
Halibut Portuguesa - Adventures, 70
Halibut Veronique - Easy, 56
Halibut with Shrimp Sauce - Gourmet, 67
Herbed Fish Sauterne - Favorite, 70
Japanese Charcoal-Broiled Fish - Adventures, 72

La Darne de Saumon de Gaspé, Frontenac - Adventures, 72
Ling Cod Marguery - Adventures, 71
Neapolitan Tuna-Tomato Pie - Menus, 70
Oven-Fried Fish - Favorite, 71
Poached Frozen Trout - Favorite, 73
Poached Halibut Florentine - Gourmet, 66
Poached Salmon Fremont - Favorite, 74
Poached Salmon or Halibut - Menus, 59
Poached Sole with Grapes - Favorite, 69
Poached Trout - Gourmet, 69
Pompano en Papillotte - Favorite, 72
Quick Friday Special - Adventures, 72
Russian River Steelhead - Favorite, 71
St. Helena Sole - Favorite, 70
Salmon à la Marsala - Adventures, 73
Salmon Court Bouillon - Favorite, 74
Salmon Mold Sauterne - Gourmet, 68
Salmon Mousse - Epicurean, 46
Salmon Snack Chablis - Favorite, 74
Salmon with Water Chestnut Dressing - Adventures, 71
San Francisco Sole - Easy, 56
Saratoga Sole - Adventures, 72
Sherry Almond Sole - Favorite, 70
Smoked Salmon and Sole - Easy; 57
Sole Angelique - Menus, 52
Sole Bonne Femme - Gourmet, 66
Sole Calypso - Menus, 51
Sole Casserole - Easy, 57
Sole Golda - Easy, 57
Sole Marguery - Easy, 57
Sole Sauté with Avocado Sauce - Menus, 51
Sole Veronica - Menus, 57
Sole with Crabmeat Mephisto - Menus, 112
Sole with Mushroom Sauce - Gourmet, 65
Sole with Shell Fish - Favorite, 71
Sole with Shrimp and Crab Filling - Epicurean, 45
Sole with Shrimp, Hollandaise - Menus, 56
Sole with Shrimp Pronto - Menus, 52
Sole with Wheat Germ - Easy, 58
Spanish Baked Fish - Adventures, 73
Striped Bass au vin Blanc - Favorite, 72
Stuffed Fish Rolls - Epicurean, 47
Stuffed Sole New Orleans - Menus, 53
Superb Sole - Easy, 56
Trout in Wine - Favorite, 73
Tuna Casserole - Gourmet, 68
Tuna Cho-Cho-San - Favorite, 78
Tuna in Mushroom Sauce - Easy, 56
Tuna-Like-Beef Casserole - Adventures, 75
Tuna Noodle Special - Menus, 85
Tuna Tetrazzini - Favorite, 78
Walnut-Crusted Sole, Meunière - Menus
Wine Baked Fish - Epicurean, 49
Winemasters' Swordfish - Epicurean, 47

SHELLFISH

Abalone Livermore - Favorite, 76
Artichoke and Shrimp Casserole - Epicurean, 48
Baked Clams au Gratin - Easy, 58
Barbecue Shrimp Supreme - Easy, 54
Braised Prawns - Gourmet, 72
Clammers' Delight - Easy, 58
Cioppino - Gourmet, 67
Coquille St. Jacques - Favorite, 76
Crab Acapulco - Favorite, 77
Crab-Artichoke Casserole - Favorite, 77
Crab Casserole - Easy, 52
Crab Coquille - Epicurean, 48
Crab Curry Crêpes - Adventures, 78
Crab Delight - Easy, 51
Crab Newburg - Easy, 50
Crab Omelette Supreme - Epicurean, 51
Crab Pie with Almonds - Epicurean, 50
Crab Quiche - Easy, 51
Crab Rio - Menus, 58
Crab Toast - Easy, 51
Crabmeat and Artichoke Casserole - Menus, 97
Crabmeat or Shrimp Curry - Menus, 60
Crabmeat or Shrimp Jacques - Menus, 61
Crabmeat Sandwich Puff - Menus, 87
Crustacean Casserole - Easy, 52
Deviled Clams Morro Bay - Favorite, 78
Easy Deviled Crab - Favorite, 77
Feathery Shrimp - Easy, 53
Fiesta Fish Casseroles - Favorite, 74
Last Minute Shrimp Newburg - Gourmet, 69
Lemon Flavored Crab or Shrimp Gelatin - Adventures, 71
Lobster Casserole - Easy, 53
Lobster Newburg - Favorite, 76
Lobster Puffs - Easy, 53
Lobster Special - Gourmet, 70
Lobster Tarts Diablo - Menus, 62
Lobster Thermidor - Easy, 53
Lucious Crab Casserole - Adventures, 75
Milanese Crab Casserole - Easy, 52
Mt. Tivy Crab - Easy, 52
Old Rancho Shrimp Creole - Epicurean, 51
Oyster Loaf - Easy, 55
Oyster Stew and White Wine - Gourmet, 72
Oysters Henriette - Menus, 104
Oysters in Champagne - Adventures, 78
Oysters Provençales - Epicurean, 46
Pickled Shrimp - Gourmet, 70
Prawns and Asparagus - Adventures, 77
Prawns on Skewers - Easy, 59
Prawns Sarapico - Gourmet, 70
Quick Clam-Corn Dinner - Favorite, 78
Quick Seafood Maryland - Adventures, 74
Riesling Seafood Shells - Favorite, 75
Saratoga Shrimp - Adventures, 76
Scallops à la Pierre - Adventures, 75
Scallops in Wine Cream Sauce - Epicurean, 53
Scallops in Wine Sauce - Gourmet, 71
Scallops Sonoma - Easy, 59
Scampi - Gourmet, 71
Scampi Delectable - Epicurean, 49
Scampi Trecate - Favorite, 76
Seafood and Rice Casserole Delecta - Menus, 85
Seafood en Coquille - Gourmet, 71
Seafood Nicholas - Gourmet, 65
Seafood the Vintner's Way - Adventures, 78
Shellfish Thermidor - Epicurean, 50
Sherried Shrimp - Favorite, 75
Sherried Shrimp Rarebit - Favorite, 87
Sherry and Parmesan Scampi - Epicurean, 53
Sherry Crab Soufflé - Adventures, 79
Shrimp à la Newburg - Gourmet, 69
Shrimp Amandine - Adventures, 76
Shrimp and Asparagus Casserole - Adventures, 76
Shrimp and Crabmeat Mold Supreme - Menus, 63
Shrimp Casserole Harpin - Adventures, 77
Shrimp Creole - Easy, 55
Shrimp In White Sauce - Easy, 55
Shrimp, Italian Style - Easy, 54
Shrimp Newburg - Favorite, 75
Shrimp or Lobster Chunks, Cooked - Adventures, 118

Shrimp Pimiento - Easy, 54
Shrimp Richert - Adventures, 79
Shrimp Tiffany - Epicurean, 52
Skewered Shrimp in White Wine - Epicurean, 52
Southern Clam Casserole - Gourmet, 68
Valley Lobster Tails - Adventures, 76
Wine Land Crabmeat - Favorite, 77
Winemaker's Shrimp - Favorite, 75
Wine Marinated Cracked Crab - Epicurean, 51

FONDUES

American Style (Fondue) - Favorite, 104
Ann's Cheddar Fondue with Dunkers - Menus, 98
Cheese Fondue - Epicurean, 75
Party Fondue - Gourmet, 74
Sausage Sampling Fondue - Gourmet, 73
Victorian Sherried Crab Fondue - Adventures, 27
Wine Cheese Fondue - Favorite, 86

FRUIT CONSERVES & GARNISHES

Baked Peaches (garnish) - Menus, 90
Basic Syrup for Quick Spiced Fruits - Gourmet, 53
Burgundy Pear Poultry Garnish - Gourmet, 55
Easy Ported Fruits - Favorite, 104
Garnish with Lemon Cups - Gourmet, 66
Grape Garnish - Favorite, 104
Wine Land Prunes - Favorite, 105

JELLIES & JAMS

Basic Wine Jelly - Favorite, 104
Harvest Pear Jam - Favorite, 105
Cranberry-Claret Jelly - Adventures, 117
Jelly or Jam as Cake Sauce - Favorite, 120
Light Muscat Jelly - Favorite, 104
Minted Wine Jelly - Favorite, 105
Orange and Port Jelly - Gourmet, 103
Port-Herb Jelly - Favorite, 104
Wine Jelly - Menus, 40
Vineyard Apple Butter - Favorite, 105

JELLIES FOR MEATS

Claret Cranberry Jelly - Gourmet, 36
Cranberry Apple Wine Sherbet - Gourmet, 38
Jelly and Wine for Pork Chops - Gourmet, 51
Minted Wine Jelly - Gourmet, 48

MEATS

BEEF

Baked Chuck Roast - Easy, 71
Baked Short Ribs - Favorite, 36
Baked Swiss Steak with Rice - Menus, 11
Barbara's Beef Stew - Easy, 76
Barbecue Flank Steak - Easy, 69
Barbecued Chuck Roast - Gourmet, 35
Barbecued Pot Roast - Favorite, 39
B.B.Q. Steak Special - Adventures, 36
Beef and Pork Ragoût - Menus, 13
Beef Berenice - Easy, 69
Beef Burgundy - Epicurean, 18
Beef Burgundy Flambé - Gourmet, 37
Beef in Herb Sauce - Easy, 67
Beef in Sour Cream - Adventures, 35
Beef Magnifique - Favorite, 35
Beef Pinot Noir - Easy, 66

Beef Pot Pie, Parmesan Biscuit Crust - Favorite, 35
Beef Ragoût - Epicurean, 15
Beef Roll-Ups, Milanese - Favorite, 42
Beef Romanoff - Menus, 106
Beef Roulades in Red Wine - Favorite, 42
Beef San Joaquin - Menus, 10
Beef Stew Burgundy - Favorite, 33
Beef Stew Filice - Easy, 80
Beef Stew, Flamed with Brandy - Favorite, 34
Beef Stroganoff - Favorite, 40
Beef Stroganoff Nerelli - Easy, 66
Beef Sukiyaki - Adventures, 39
Beef Suzanna - Easy, 72
Beef with Horseradish Sauce - Favorite, 33
Berkeley Goulash - Easy, 76
Boeuf à la Bourguignonne - Epicurean, 20
Boeuf à la Mode - Easy, 73
Boeuf en Daube - Adventures, 36
Boeuf Mironton - Favorite, 34
Boeuf Salmi - Favorite, 41
Bourbonnais Beef Stew - Easy, 80
Braised Beef Italienne - Menus, 14
Braised Beef with Olives - Menus, 12
Braised Stuffed Flank Steaks - Epicurean, 16
Burgundy Meat Rolls - Easy, 67
California Beef Stew - Gourmet, 36
California Beef Sukiyaki - Gourmet, 42
Canned Beef Stew - Favorite, 33, 120
Casserole Maddalena - Easy, 71
Contra Costa Flank Steak - Adventures, 36
Curried Lamb or Beef - Adventures, 51
Davis Teriyaki - Adventures, 38
Delicious and Easy Pot Roast - Gourmet, 34
Deviled Swiss Steak - Easy, 65
Dodie's Chipped Beef - Easy, 66
Easy Baked Stew - Favorite, 34
Easy Cabernet Pot Roast - Favorite, 38
Easy-Do Beef Stew - Menus, 13
Easy Oven Pot Roast - Favorite, 35
Easy Stroganoff - Gourmet, 38
Entrecôte with Watercress - Epicurean, 19
Epicurean Beef Casserole - Gourmet, 37
Ernie's Tenderloin Brochette with Bordelaise Sauce -
    Epicurean, 22
Estofado de Vaco Española - Gourmet, 38
Five Hour Stew - Easy, 81
Flaming Beef Grenadine - Epicurean, 20
Franks & Peppers - Easy, 73
Fresno Hash - Adventures, 39
Golfer's Beef Stew - Easy, 65
Great Gravy Pot Roast - Adventures, 34
Green Pepper Steak Gilroy - Adventures, 37
Gribelis Noodles - Easy, 69
Guerneville Goulash - Easy, 69
Hash with Eggs Hollandaise - Menus, 90
Healdsburg Stroganoff - Easy, 67
International Angus Steak - Epicurean, 17
Janey's Stew - Easy, 75
Jiffy Beef Bourguignonne - Gourmet, 34
Jiffy Beef Stew - Adventures, 118
Korean Steaks - Epicurean, 17
Lazy Bones - Menus, 15
Lazy Stew - Menus, 15
Lazy Sunday Oven Dinner - Favorite, 39
L'il Ole Winemaker Pot Roast - Adventures, 35
London Broil - Gourmet, 37
London Broil à la Emily - Menus, 16
Low Budget T-Bone Steak - Favorite, 37
Marinated Roast Beef - Gourmet, 34
Marinated Rump Roast - Easy, 72

Mexican Beef and Bean Stew - Menus, 12
Modesto Beef - Easy, 74
Mushroom Braised Beef - Menus, 11
Napa Valley Meat Roll - Epicurean, 18
Pacific Flank Steak - Adventures, 38
Paper-Thin Steaks Poivrade - Favorite, 41
Pepper Steak Barbecued - Favorite, 41
Pepper Steaks with Sherried Sauce - Gourmet, 35
Portuguese Soup - Easy, 73
Pot Roast Monterey - Menus, 17
Pot Roast Piemontese - Favorite, 39
Pot Roast Schwaltzburg - Easy, 72
Pot Roast Superior - Gourmet, 41
Puchero Chollo - Epicurean, 24
Rancher's Beef Short Ribs - Gourmet, 41
Red Wine Pot Roast - Adventures, 37
Roast Beef Mañana - Favorite, 38
Roast Prime Ribs of Beef - Menus, 108
Rolatini - Adventures, 39
Rollatini Italia - Easy, 70
Rolled Steaks Livermore - Adventures, 38
Round of Beef with Sherry - Favorite, 36
Ruladini - Favorite, 43
Rump Roast Stew - Easy, 76
Sanger Stew - Easy, 75
Sanger Style Steak Sandwiches - Adventures, 37
San Jose Steak - Easy, 68
Santa Clara Pot Roast - Gourmet, 33
Sauerbraten, Potato Pancakes - Favorite, 37
Savory Roast of Beef - Favorite, 38
Savory Soup Stew - Gourmet, 36
Savory Stew - Easy, 75
Savory Swiss Steak - Gourmet, 34
Sherried Beef Delight - Adventures, 35
Sherried Stroganoff - Gourmet, 40
Simple Swiss Steak - Gourmet, 36
Spanish Steak - Easy, 68
Steak au Poivre - Easy, 66
Steak Bordelaise, Vermouth - Epicurean, 19
Steak Casserole - Easy, 68
Steak Colbert with Rice - Gourmet, 38
Steak in Zinfandel Sauce - Easy, 70
Steak Lorraine - Easy, 71
Steak with Marinade - Easy, 70
Steaks Dianne - Epicurean, 16
Stew à la Grecque - Menus, 14
Stew Rosé - Easy, 74
Stew with Polenta - Favorite, 34
Stuffed Flank Steak Bohemia - Menus, 16
Sunday Chipped Beef - Menus, 98
Sweet and Sour Franks - Easy, 74
Swiss Steak Aguirre - Easy, 68
Swiss Steak Sauterne - Favorite, 36
Swiss Steak Supreme - Favorite, 36
Teriyaki Steak Strips - Adventures, 38
Teriyaki Steaks - Gourmet, 37
Valley Chateaubriand - Adventures, 37
Vineyard Beef Roast - Adventures, 35
Vintner's Stew - Favorite, 34
Wild West Beef Kabobs - Gourmet, 40
Wine Shortribs - Epicurean, 19
Winebraten - Favorite, 37

CORNED BEEF

Baked Corned Beef - Favorite, 42
Corned Beef and Cabbage - Adventures, 34
Gourmet Corned Beef - Gourmet, 35

GROUND BEEF

Barbarini Caliente - Easy, 78
Beefburger Pie - Menus, 66
Beef Casserole with Bulgur - Gourmet, 40
Beef Kiev - Adventures, 41
Beef Mousse - Menus, 30
Beef-Mushroom Casserole - Easy, 81
Beef-Rice Casserole - Favorite, 41
Buffet Meat Balls - Adventures, 40
Buffet Meat Balls - Gourmet, 39
Burgundy Hashburgers - Gourmet, 39
Burgundy Meatballs - Favorite, 42
California Beef Balls - Gourmet, 39
California Beef Patties - Easy, 78
California Meat Roll - Easy, 77
Cannelloni à la Emily - Menus, 75
Chili-Beef Muffins - Menus, 30
Chili Burgundies - Gourmet, 33
Copenhagen Meat Balls - Easy, 78
Creole Burgers - Easy, 76
Crusty French Meat Loaf - Menus, 32
Delano Stroganoff - Adventures, 41
Devonshire Beef Pie - Menus, 67
Elegant Hamburgers - Menus, 26
Enchilada Casserole - Easy, 75
Green Pepper Hamburgers - Gourmet, 35
Ground Beef with Glamour - Favorite, 40
Hambolognas - Menus, 28
Hamburger Mignon - Menus, 26
Hamburger-Mushroom Casserole - Menus, 33
Hamburger-Spinach Special - Menus, 31
Hamburger Stroganoff - Menus, 29
Hamburger-Stuffed Mushrooms - Menus, 33
Hamburgers Hollandaise - Menus, 27
Hamburgers with Chili Rabbit - Adventures, 40
Hash Pasties - Menus, 67
Hawaiian Meat Balls - Easy, 79
Italian Ground Beef - Easy, 79
Italian Noodle Casserole - Menus, 76
Jiffy Meat Balls - Easy, 77
Lodi Stuffed Cabbage - Easy, 77
Macaroni Goulash - Easy, 79
Macaroni Marinara - Menus, 92
Mario's Baked Spaghetti - Menus, 92
Mariposa Meat Balls - Menus, 29
Meat Ball Stroganoff - Easy, 80
Meat Balls in Caper Sauce (Klopse) - Adventures, 40
Meat Balls Marinara - Menus, 89
Mexican Beef Pancakes - Menus, 35
Mexican Meat Balls - Menus, 89
More!! - Easy, 80
One Dish Dinner - Easy, 74
Parmesan Meat Balls - Gourmet, 40
Pastetseo - Menus, 74
Pepper Steak Patties - Menus, 27
Quick Spicy Casserole - Adventures, 41
Savory Steak Patties - Easy, 81
Sherried Cheeseburgers - Gourmet, 41
Skillet Special - Adventures, 40
Soy-Broiled Hamburgers - Easy, 79
Special of the Kitchen - Gourmet, 41
Steak au Poivre - Easy, 66
Steakies - Menus, 28
Stuffed Cabbage Rolls - Adventures, 39
Stuffed Meat Loaf - Menus, 31
Stuffed Peppers Lomita - Menus, 34
Stuffed Zucchini with Tomato Sauce - Menus, 79
Sunday Night Casserole - Menus, 76
Super Roast Beef Hash - Menus, 90

Tomato Meat Loaf - Menus, 31
Wild Rice Chuckballs - Adventures, 41
Winederful Meat Loaf - Favorite, 40
Zucchini Casserole - Easy, 77

HAM

Apricot Ham Steak - Adventures, 43
Artichoke and Ham Casserole - Gourmet, 49
Baked Ham Slice Sauterne - Favorite, 45
Baked Ham Steak - Epicurean, 26
Braised Ham Financière - Favorite, 46
Cherry-Sherry Baked Ham - Favorite, 46
Ham and Celery Rolls au Gratin - Menus, 93
Ham and Cheese Pie - Menus, 72
Ham and Cheese Tarts - Menus, 72
Ham in A Pastry Crust - Adventures, 118
Ham in Champagne - Easy, 83
Ham Mardi Gras - Easy, 85
Ham-Mushroom Pie - Menus, 71
Ham Portuguese Style - Favorite, 47
Ham with Oranges - Favorite, 46
Holiday Ham - Gourmet, 49
Marmalade-Glazed Ham - Menus, 77
Mushroom Ham Loaf - Menus, 77
Napa Macaroni-Ham Bake - Adventures, 46
Sherry-Glazed Ham - Favorite, 46
Sherry Walnut Ham - Gourmet, 50
Spicy Peach Ham Ring - Adventures, 45
Tart Ham Chablis - Easy, 85
Tropical Ham - Adventures, 45
Tropical Sherried Ham - Adventures, 45
Wine Glazed Ham - Gourmet, 50
Wine Wonderland Ham - Adventures, 46

HEART

Beef Heart Pinot Blanc - Epicurean, 23

KIDNEYS

Grand Mixed Grill - Easy, 95
Kidneys and Heart in Wine - Easy, 95
Kidneys Burgundy - Adventures, 55
Kidneys Hunter Style - Epicurean, 23
Kidneys in Sherry - Adventures, 55
Kidneys Sauté - Favorite, 52
Sautéed Veal Kidneys - Easy, 95
Stewed Kidneys - Easy, 96

LAMB

Baked Stuffed Lamb Chops - Menus, 102
Barbecued Lamb Chops Vermouth - Adventures, 50
Barbecued Leg of Lamb - Favorite, 50
Blossom Hill Lamb with Wine - Adventures, 53
Braised Lamb Burgundy - Favorite, 49
Braised Lamb Chops - Easy, 93
Braised Leg of Lamb - Gourmet, 46
Breast of Lamb Mendocino - Favorite, 51
Butterfly Leg of Lamb - Gourmet, 49
Chicken, Turkey or Lamb Barbecue - Adventures, 33
Curried Lamb or Beef - Adventures, 51
Curried Lamb Shanks - Favorite, 50
Fresno Lamb Shanks - Adventures, 53
Gourmet Lamb Chops - Easy, 93
Lamb and Prunes Armenian - Gourmet, 46
Lamb Chops Baked in White Wine - Adventures, 50
Lamb Chops Cathy - Adventures, 51
Lamb Chops in Potato Cheese Sauce - Gourmet, 47

Lamb Curry Calcutta - Menus, 23
Lamb Blocks with Potatoes - Adventures, 52
Lamb Fricassee - Easy, 92
Lamb Goulash - Easy, 93
Lamb Rack Burgundy - Adventures, 50
Lamb Shanks Canterbury - Gourmet, 47
Lamb Shanks in Mushroom Sauce - Menus, 21
Lamb Shanks in Red Sauce - Easy, 92
Lamb Shanks in Wine - Gourmet, 48
Lamb Shanks Marino - Menus, 21
Lamb Stew Santa Clara - Favorite, 49
Lamb with Lima Beans - Easy, 91
Leg of Lamb - Adventures, 51
Leg of Lamb Marsala - Adventures, 49
Leg of Lamb Mexican - Adventures, 52
Leg of Lamb Saratoga - Easy, 91
Melt-In-Your-Mouth Lamb - Adventures, 52
Mib's Lamb Shanks - Epicurean, 26
Mint-Stuffed Leg of Lamb - Favorite, 50
Roasted Lamb Shanks with Potatoes - Epicurean, 27
Roast Rack of Lamb - Menus, 104
Santa Clara Valley Shanks - Adventures, 53
Savory Braised Lamb - Menus, 22
Savory Lamb Shoulder Chops - Gourmet, 47
Sesame Lamb Rack - Gourmet, 47
Sherried Lamb Hawaii - Adventures, 51
Sherried Lamb in Patty Shells - Epicurean, 28
Shish Kabab Sauterne - Gourmet, 46
Shish Kebob San Joaquin - Favorite, 51
Simple Lamb Stew - Easy, 92
Spanish Lamb - Epicurean, 27
Stuffed Leg of Lamb Royale - Adventures, 52
Vineyard Lamb Shanks - Favorite, 50
Wine Marinated Barbecued Lamb - Gourmet, 48

LIVER

Italian Liver Lodi - Adventures, 54
Liver and Macaroni Shells - Easy, 96
Liver and Mushrooms - Easy, 95
Liver Santa Rosa - Easy, 96
Liver Vino Blanco - Favorite, 51
Liver William - Favorite, 51
New Baked Liver - Easy, 94

OXTAILS

Oxtail Stew with Red Wine - Favorite, 53
Oxtails in Savory Sauce - Adventures, 54

PORK

Apple-Stuffed Crown Roast of Pork - Adventures, 42
Bacon and Egg Pie - Menus, 68
Bacon Curlicues - Menus, 86
Bacon-Mushroom Pie - Menus, 71
Bacon-Onion Pie - Menus, 71
Baked Pork Chops - Easy, 82
Baked Pork Chops with Rice - Menus, 24
Beans and Frankfurters - Adventures, 43
Beef and Pork Ragoût - Menus, 13
Boston Butt Roast - Easy, 83
Braised Stuffed Pork Chops - Menus, 110
Brunch Treat Pork Sausage - Adventures, 118
Cream Sherry Porkchops - Epicurean, 25
Easy Wine Pork Chops - Favorite, 47
Favorite Braised Pork Chops - Menus, 24
French Pork Birds - Gourmet, 51
French Sauerkraut - Easy, 85
Fruit-Sherry Pork Chops - Favorite, 47

German Meat Pie - Favorite, 49
German Sausage Burgundy - Easy, 84
Gourmet Pork Chops - Adventures, 42
Hearty Pork-and-Sauerkraut Casserole - Adventures, 44
La Choucroute Garnie - Adventures, 44
Leg of Pork - Adventures, 42
Lodi Jambalaya - Favorite, 48
Loin of Pork, Larkmead - Epicurean, 25
Morgan Hill Pork Sausages - Favorite, 48
Peas and Pork Oriental - Favorite, 48
Pork Barbecue - Adventures, 33
Pork Chops and Apples - Easy, 83
Pork Chops in Winey Plum Sauce - Adventures, 42
Pork Chops St. Helena - Easy, 84
Pork Chops Supreme - Easy, 84
Pork Chops with Piquant Sauce - Gourmet, 52
Pork San Joaquin - Adventures, 43
Pork Scalloppini - Adventures, 43
Pork Tenderloin in Wine - Favorite, 48
Roast Pork Rosemary - Favorite, 47
Roast Suckling Pig - Epicurean, 31
Sausage and Zucchini Torta - Menus, 79
Sausage Vermouth - Easy, 84
Sausages and Cabbage - Easy, 83
Sherry Pork Chops and Apples - Adventures, 43
Smoked Bratwurst in Sauterne - Adventures, 45
Smoked Sausages - Favorite, 120
Sauterne Pork Chop Bake - Gourmet, 50
Stuffed Chops au Vin - Easy, 82
Sunday Morning Sausage - Adventures, 45
Veal and Pork Drumsticks - Menus, 19
Wine Glazed Corned Pork - Gourmet, 51
Yorkshire Sausage Pudding - Menus, 80

SPARERIBS

Burgundy Grilled Spareribs - Adventures, 44
Chinese Spareribs - Easy, 85
Greek Spareribs - Easy, 85
Morgan Hill Spareribs - Easy, 83
Oven Barbecued Spareribs - Adventures, 44
Sherry-Glazed Spareribs - Favorite, 49
Spareribs in B.B.Q. Sauce - Easy, 84
Spareribs Pacifica - Gourmet, 50

SWEETBREADS

Sweetbreads à la King - Favorite, 52
Sweetbreads Breaded, Marsala - Favorite, 52
Sweetbreads Vermouth - Epicurean, 21
Veal Sweetbreads Los Gatos - Favorite, 52

TONGUE

Beef Tongue in Port Wine Sauce - Adventures, 54
Boiled Tongue Dante - Adventures, 54
La Lunga - Epicurean, 21
Lamb Tongue Bon Vin - Favorite, 53
Pickled Tongue - Easy, 94
Sweet-Sour Tongue - Favorite, 53
Tongue in White Wine Aspic - Adventures, 55
Tongue Napa Valley - Favorite, 53

TRIPE

Savona Tripe Stew - Adventures, 55
Tripe Burgundian - Easy, 96

Tripe Parisienne - Favorite, 54
Trippa Novarese - Favorite, 54

VEAL

Baked Veal Chops - Gourmet, 42
Baked Scallopini - Favorite, 43
Braised Veal Chops with Mushroom Sauce - Gourmet, 43
Braised Veal Chops Amelia - Menus, 19
Braised Veal Modesto - Adventures, 48
Braised Veal Roast - Epicurean, 31
Breaded Roast Veal - Easy, 88
Breaded Veal - Gourmet, 45
Breast of Veal Genovese - Adventures, 49
Curried Veal Stew - Menus, 18
German Chow Mein - Easy, 87
Gourmet Veal Birds - Favorite, 44
Jellied Veal and Ham Loaf - Menus, 20
Joaquin Veal Parmigiana - Easy, 90
Joe's Veal Croquettes au Vin - Favorite, 44
Lodi Veal Sauté - Adventures, 47
Luncheon Casserole - Favorite, 45
Meat Birds San Rafael - Easy, 87
Mock Partridges - Easy, 88
Mountain View Veal with Eggplant - Adventures, 47
Niçoise Veal Scallops - Adventures, 47
Pan Roasted Veal - Easy, 87
Provolone Veal - Easy, 86
Roman Veal Rolls - Gourmet, 43
Saltimbocca - Favorite, 44
San Mateo Casserole - Easy, 90
Spanish Veal Roast - Easy, 88
Spicy Pot Roast of Veal - Favorite, 39
Stuffed Veal Birds in Sour Cream Gravy - Gourmet, 43
Veal and Ham Pie - Menus, 68
Veal and Pimiento - Gourmet, 43
Veal and Pork Drumsticks - Menus, 19
Veal and Rice Buffet - Gourmet, 44
Veal Capri - Menus, 100
Veal Casserole à la Swiss - Adventures, 50
Veal Chops and Rice Chablis - Gourmet, 44
Veal Chops Geneva - Easy, 90
Veal Chops Parmesan - Adventures, 47
Veal Chops St. Helena, Herb - Adventures, 48
Veal Chops Tarragon - Favorite, 44
Veal Cream Stew - Menus, 18
Veal Elegant - Easy, 89
Veal Francisco - Gourmet, 45
Veal, Ham and Eggplant - Easy, 89
Veal in White Wine Sauce - Gourmet, 42
Veal Marengo - Gourmet, 44
Veal - Noodle Casserole with Wine - Gourmet, 42
Veal Paprika - Favorite, 45
Veal Piccante - Adventures, 46
Veal Pocket - Adventures, 49
Veal Roast Moutarde - Easy, 89
Veal Roast with Wine Sauce - Adventures, 48
Veal Sauté - Epicurean, 30
Veal Sauterne - Gourmet, 45
Veal Scallopini Marsala - Favorite, 43
Veal Scallopini Zucchini - Easy, 87
Veal Scallops, Roman Style - Epicurean, 24
Veal Steaks, Sauterne - Epicurean, 29
Veal Stew - Easy, 86
Veal Supreme - Favorite, 45
Veal Vermouth - Epicurean, 29
Veal Viennese - Adventures, 46
Veal with Artichokes - Favorite, 43
Veal with Peas - Epicurean, 30
Velvety Veal - Adventures, 48

NUTS

Sherried Walnuts - Easy, 20
Sherry-Spiced Nuts - Favorite, 105

PASTA

Baked Spaghetti Ukiah - Favorite, 84
Burgundy Lasagne - Adventures, 82
Cannelloni à la Emily - Menus, 75
Canneloni with Spinach Soufflé Filling - Epicurean, 65
Chicken Tortilla - Epicurean, 34
Continental Lasagna - Gourmet, 76
Crabmeat and Spaghetti au Gratin - Gourmet, 76
Creamy Noodle Casserole - Menus, 107
Five Minute Spaghetti - Easy, 29
Individual Tamale Pies - Gourmet, 75
Italian Noodle Casserole - Menus, 76
Lasagna Bahama - Easy, 29
Livermore Spaghetti - Favorite, 85
Macaroni and Cheese Torta - Menus, 93
Macaroni and Cheese with Wine - Favorite, 84
Macaroni Marinara - Menus, 92
Macaroni Ring - Menus, 46
Manicotti Healdsburg - Easy, 31
Mario's Baked Spaghetti - Menus, 92
Mock Ravioli - Adventures, 82
Noodles O'Brien - Menus, 18
Pasta with Clam Sauce - Adventures, 84
Pastetseo - Menus, 74
Shell Macaroni in Curried Clam Sauce - Epicurean, 58
Spaghetti - Favorite, 120
Spaghetti Carbonara - Easy, 29
Spaghetti in Wine - Adventures, 82
Spaghetti Réchauffé - Adventures, 81
Sour Cream and Tortila Casserole - Easy, 30
Sunday Night Casserole - Menus, 76
Tuna Noodle Special - Menus, 85
Two-Minute Enchilada Casserole - Menus, 91

PIES (MAIN DISH)

Bacon and Egg Pie - Menus, 68
Bacon-Mushroom Pie - Menus, 71
Bacon-Onion Pie - Menus, 71
Beefburger Pie - Menus, 66
Beef Pot Pie, Parmesan Biscuit Crust - Favorite, 35
Cheese and Wine Quiche - Gourmet, 74
Chicken à la King Pie - Menus, 69
Crab Pie with Almonds - Epicurean, 50
Crab Quiche - Easy, 51
Cracker Pie Shell - Menus, 66
Devonshire Beef Pie - Menus, 67
Ham and Cheese Pie - Menus, 72
Ham-Mushroom Pie - Menus, 71
Hash Pasties - Menus, 67
Individual Tamale Pies - Gourmet, 75
Neapolitan Tuna-Tomato Pie - Menus, 70
Veal and Ham Pie - Menus, 68
Viennese Chicken Pie - Menus, 69

POULTRY

CHICKEN

Alice's Chicken Casserole - Easy, 99
Amandine Chicken - Easy, 99
Artichokes and Chicken à la Crème - Gourmet, 55
Baked Chicken Red-and-White - Adventures, 62
Baked Chicken Rosé - Favorite, 56
Baked Chicken with Red Wine - Menus, 43
Baked Stuffed Mushrooms Lundi - Menus, 87
Barbecue Basted Chicken - Easy, 100
Barbecued Chicken - Favorite, 55
Barbecued Chicken Legs - Gourmet, 54
Blazing Chicken - Epicurean, 38
Brandied Fricassee Chicken - Favorite, 57
Brandy & Dry Vermouth Chicken - Favorite, 57
Breasts of Chicken au Porto - Favorite, 61
Breast of Chicken Eugenie - Gourmet, 58
Breast of Chicken Sans Souci - Menus, 116
Breast of Chicken Supreme - Easy, 107
Broiled Chicken - Gourmet, 59
Broilers California - Easy, 98
Budget Bake - Easy, 101
California Chicken - Easy, 103
California Style Brunswick Stew - Adventures, 61
Californian Baked Chicken - Favorite, 56
Chicken à la Gallo - Adventures, 56
Chicken à la King - Easy, 102
Chicken à la King Pie - Menus, 69
Chicken à la Sophie - Menus, 42
Chicken à la Waleski - Epicurean, 38
Chicken Almond - Favorite, 59
Chicken and Ham Delancey - Menus, 48
Chicken and Lobster with Sherry - Gourmet, 57
Chicken and Mushrooms - Gourmet, 56
Chicken & Rice Creole - Favorite, 59
Chicken and Riesling - Gourmet, 59
Chicken and Stuffing Casserole - Menus, 94
Chicken and Wild Rice - Easy, 98
Chicken Atherton - Easy, 104
Chicken Breasts Flambées - Adventures, 60
Chicken Breasts in Sour Cream - Gourmet, 54
Chicken Breasts Mandarin - Epicurean, 39
Chicken Brittany - Menus, 39
Chicken Cacciatore - Favorite, 58
Chicken Castillo with Saffron Rice - Menus, 41
Chicken Chablis - Gourmet, 60
Chicken Curry in a Hurry - Gourmet, 54
Chicken Hearts in Sour Cream - Epicurean, 35
Chicken Hunter Style - Favorite, 58
Chicken in Sour Cream - Adventures, 57
Chicken-in-the-Pot - Favorite, 29
Chicken in the Vine - Favorite, 60
Chicken Jerusalem - Menus, 37
Chicken Jubilee - Favorite, 60
Chicken Kiev - Adventures, 60
Chicken Livers and Bacon - Easy, 106
Chicken Livers in Port - Favorite, 61
Chicken Livers in Wine Sauce - Menus, 86
Chicken Livers Sauté - Gourmet, 56
Chicken Marengo Style - Adventures, 58
Chicken Marengo with Sauterne - Gourmet, 57
Chicken Marengo with Sherry - Gourmet, 58
Chicken Marsala - Favorite, 60
Chicken Mascotte - Menus, 37
Chicken Napa - Easy, 98
Chicken Napa Valley - Adventures, 59
Chicken Napoli - Menus, 42
Chicken or Tuna à la King - Menus, 93
Chicken Oriental - Adventures, 58
Chicken Parisienne - Favorite, 58
Chicken Provence - Menus, 39
Chicken Raphael Weill - Favorite, 58
Chicken Rice Torta - Menus, 83
Chicken Sauté Mayonnaise - Menus, 40
Chicken Sauterne - Adventures, 59
Chicken Stroganoff - Epicurean, 37
Chicken Supreme - Menus, 46

Chicken Tarragon - Easy, 105
Chicken Tetrazzini - Gourmet, 56
Chicken Timbales Golden Gate - Menus, 47
Chicken Tortilla - Epicurean, 34
Chicken Vermouth - Adventures, 57
Chicken with Artichokes - Adventures, 58
Chicken with Avocado - Gourmet, 58
Chicken with Burgundy and Black Cherry Sauce - Epicurean, 36
Chicken Zellerbach - Favorite, 55
Chopped Chicken Casserole - Easy, 103
Classic Chicken in Wine - Favorite, 57
Company Chicken - Gourmet, 59
Coq au Vin - Easy, 102
Creamed Artichokes with Chicken au Gratin - Menus, 84
Creamed Chicken and Ham Gourmet - Menus, 45
Crunchy Creamed Chicken - Gourmet, 53
Curried Chicken - Menus, 45
Delano Chicken - Easy, 100
Delicious Chicken Casserole - Epicurean, 37
Della Robia Chicken - Gourmet, 53
Easy Roast Chicken - Favorite, 56
Epicurean Chicken Livers - Epicurean, 34
Favorite Chicken Salad - Menus, 46
Franzia Baked Chicken - Epicurean, 35
Giblet Stew - Easy, 106
Ginger Chicken - Adventures, 57
Gold Rush Chicken Livers - Favorite, 61
Golden Gate Chicken on Rice - Gourmet, 56
Herbed Chicken - Easy, 100
Honolulu Chicken - Epicurean, 36
Huntington Chicken - Adventures, 61
Hurried Broiled Chicken - Easy, 104
Italian Chicken in Foil - Gourmet, 57
Italian Chicken Sauté - Menus, 38
Jeanne's Chicken Mousse - Menus, 96
Joella Chicken - Easy, 101
Lazy Sunday Chicken - Easy, 102
Limed Chicken with Sherry - Adventures, 57
Lodi Chicken - Favorite, 59
Los Gatos Chicken - Easy, 98
Mahogany Chicken - Gourmet, 55
Meat Pie Elegant - Easy, 100
Mexican Chicken - Easy, 105
Mission San Jose Chicken - Gourmet, 59
Mock Turtle Stew - Easy, 107
Oven-Barbecued Chicken - Menus, 44
Oven-Crisp Chicken - Menus, 44
Petite Poulette au Vin - Epicurean, 40
Pilaf and Chicken - Easy, 105
Pollo Engrappa - Adventures, 61
Pollo Fiorentino - Easy, 103
Pollo Schiacciato - Adventures, 59
Pollo Supreme - Easy, 98
Poulet au Moment Même - Adventures, 60
Poulet Avec Raisins Blancs - Easy, 101
Quick Cacciatore - Easy, 104
Quick Chicken - Easy, 102
Roast Halves of Chicken - Easy, 104
Roasted Chicken Calabrian - Favorite, 55
Rolled Chicken Breasts - Menus, 120
Rosemary Chicken - Easy, 103
Sanger Fryers - Easy, 105
Sautéed Chicken in Cream - Favorite, 60
Scalloped Chicken and Noodles - Menus, 94
Sherried Chicken Livers - Adventures, 63
Sherried Supper Special - Gourmet, 57
Sherry Chicken - Adventures, 58
Smothered Chicken - Adventures, 59

Smothered Chicken - Favorite, 59
Spanish Padre Chicken - Gourmet, 60
Special Creamed Chicken or Seafood - Menus, 93
Stuffed Chicken Bigarade - Gourmet, 55
Summer Chicken Loaf - Adventures, 60
Superb Barbecued Chicken - Favorite, 57
Supreme Deviled Chicken - Favorite, 61
Sweet - Sour Chicken - Easy, 97
Theresa's Sherry-Flavored Chicken - Epicurean, 42
Thyme Flavored Chicken - Easy, 99
Vermouth Baked Chicken - Easy, 100
Viennese Chicken Pie - Menus, 69
Wine Baked Chicken Quarters - Gourmet, 60
Wine-Mushroom Chicken Mix - Adventures, 61

CORNISH HENS

Breasts of Cornish Game Hen - Favorite, 63
Cornish Hen Baked in Wine - Adventures, 64
Cornish Hens with Herb Dressing - Gourmet, 64
Festive Cornish Hens - Easy, 101
Flaming Cornish Hens - Epicurean, 43
Ported Game Hens - Adventures, 63
Roast Rock Cornish Game Hens - Menus, 115

SQUAB

Squab and Weinkraut - Easy, 106
Squab Casserole - Easy, 107
Squabs in Red Wine - Favorite, 62
Squabs in White Wine - Epicurean, 39
Squabs Sautéed in White Wine - Adventures, 56
Stuffed Roasted Squabs - Favorite, 62

TURKEY

Baked Turkey Sandwiches - Adventures, 62
Barbecued Turkey - Favorite, 63
Glazed Turkey - Gourmet, 62
Gourmet Turkey Bits - Gourmet, 61
Grilled Young Turkey Halves - Gourmet, 61
Modesto Turkey with Waffles - Gourmet, 63
Quick Roast Turkey Chablis - Favorite, 62
Roast Turkey Hickory Hill - Menus, 118
Roast Turkey Rosé - Favorite, 63
Sherried Turkey with Stuffing - Gourmet, 60
Skewered Turkey - Gourmet, 61
Turkey à la King - Gourmet, 61
Turkey Lodi - Easy, 106
Turkey Nero Sandwiches - Gourmet, 61
Turkey on Rye - Gourmet, 62
Turkey Sandwiches Davis - Favorite, 101
Turkey Thermidor - Gourmet, 62
Turkey Timbales with Sherry Mushroom Sauce - Gourmet, 63
Turkey with Wine Sauce - Gourmet, 62
Turkeyaki - Adventures, 62
Young Turkey in its Juices - Adventures, 63

RICE, OTHER GRAINS

Baked Barley with Mushrooms - Menus, 105
Baked Rice with Shrimp - Easy, 28
Baked Spanish Rice with Chili Con Carne - Menus, 91
Brown Risotto with Wine - Adventures, 80
Chicken-Noodle Rice - Menus, 49
Chili-Cheese Rice - Menus, 89
Consommé Rice with Ham - Gourmet, 78
Corn-Rice Pilaf - Menus, 53
Curried Rice & Chicken Livers - Gourmet, 77

Epicurean Risotto - Easy, 31
Farina Mia - Menus, 89
Five-Minute Pilaf - Adventures, 118
Fruit Curry - Easy, 32
Gnocchi - Menus, 39
Gnocchi Parmesan - Menus, 111
Hawaiian Rice Molds - Menus, 60
Hoppin' John - Favorite, 87
Kasha - Menus, 22
Mushroom Pilaf - Adventures, 81
Mushroom Rice - Menus, 115
Mushroom Tuna Casserole - Easy, 32
Mushroom-Wild Rice Casserole - Adventures, 80
Noodle-Rice Medley - Easy, 29
Paul's Pilaf - Easy, 30
Peasant Pilaf - Menus, 103
Perfect Pilaf - Menus, 29
Polenta - Menus, 14
Polenta Parmesan - Menus, 38
Raisin Rice - Menus, 23
Raisins in Pilaf or Rice - Favorite, 85
Rice and Spinach Torta - Menus, 13
Rice Dressing for Turkey - Easy, 28
Rice with Mushrooms - Epicurean, 57
Risotto Alla Cucamonga - Favorite, 85
Risotto Italiene - Epicurean, 56
Risotto Milanese - Favorite, 85
Risotto Rialto - Menus, 121
Risotto with Chicken Livers - Adventures, 84
Risotto with Pesto - Easy, 28
Saffron Rice - Gourmet, 78
Sauterne Rice - Gourmet, 77
Savory Barbecue Rice - Favorite, 85
Sherried Orange Rice - Gourmet, 76
Skillet Parmesan Rice - Gourmet, 77
Summer Rice Mold - Gourmet, 76
Tired Rice? - Easy, 30
Toasty Pilaf - Menus, 44
Wine Baked Pilaf - Gourmet, 77
Zucchini and Rice Torta - Menus, 101

SALADS

Apple-Raisin Slaw - Adventures, 87
Avocado Crabmeat Cocktail Salad - Menus, 106
Avocado-Lime Mousse - Adventures, 86
Avocado Mousse--Party Size - Gourmet, 91
Avocado with Jellied Madrilene - Gourmet, 92
Baked Fish Salad - Adventures, 74
Bean Salad Escalon - Favorite, 97
Beet Salad Ring - Menus, 66
Bing Cherry and Port Mold - Gourmet, 91
Black Cherry Salad - Easy, 41
Buffet Vegetable Salad - Menus, 35
Celery Heart and Tomato Salad - Menus, 72
Celery or Asparagus Vinaigrette - Menus, 94
Celery Victor - Menus, 102
Cherry-Pineapple Salad Mold - Adventures, 86
Chilled Broccoli with Mustard Mayonnaise - Menus, 67
Cinnamon Gelatin - Easy, 39
Cleo's Christmas Salad - Easy, 36
Cole Slaw - Menus, 55
Cranberry Burgundy Salad - Gourmet, 92
Cranberry Fruit Mold - Easy, 41
Cranberry-Orange-Grapefruit Salad - Menus, 47
Cranberry-Orange Salad Molds - Menus, 68
Cranberry-Port Salad - Favorite, 99
Cranberry Salad - Easy, 39
Cucamonga Artichoke Hearts - Adventures, 85
Deviled Egg Ring with Shellfish - Menus, 63
Dilly Potato Salad - Menus, 20
Easy Chicken Salad - Easy, 37
Emily's Tuna Mousse - Menus, 64
Favorite Chicken Salad - Menus, 46
Fruit or Melon, Molded - Favorite, 120
Fruit Salad au Nature - Adventures, 87
Fruit Wine Compote - Epicurean, 70
Gelatin Mold - Easy, 39
Grapefruit Avocado Salad - Menus, 83
Green Bean Salad - Menus, 80
Green Salad with Artichoke Hearts & Mushrooms - Menus, 91
Guacamole Molds - Menus, 120
Hasty Tasty Tomato Molds - Menus, 98
Hearts of Palm Victor - Menus, 102
Hearts of Palm with Continental Dressing - Menus, 118
Jeanne's Chicken Mousse - Menus, 96
Jellied Fruit Salad - Easy, 37
Lemon-Flavored Crab or Shrimp Gelatin - Adventures, 71
Lime Gelatin Salad - Easy, 38
Luncheon Salad with Wine-Cheese Dressing - Adventures, 87
Macaroni Salad - Easy, 40
Mandarin Orange Molds with Pineapple - Menus, 87
Molded Fruit Medley - Favorite, 99
Molded Waldorf Salad Muscatel - Gourmet, 92
Old-Fashioned Hot Potato Salad - Favorite, 98
Out-of-this-World Salad - Easy, 38
Pacific Crab Salad - Favorite, 97
Pear and Orange Salad - Menus, 95
Pineapple Cucumber Salad Molds - Menus, 85
Port-Cherry Salad Molds - Favorite, 98
Port Pear Salad - Easy, 40
Potato Salad Sauterne - Favorite, 97
Rancher's Turkey Salad - Favorite, 98
Raspberry Gelatin Salad - Easy, 37
Raspberry Pear Salad - Easy, 39
Red Cabbage Slaw - Easy, 40
Relish-Salad Platter - Menus, 76
Rosé-Strawberry Salad Mold - Adventures, 86
Rosy Applesauce Mold - Gourmet, 92
Ruby Cranberry Ring - Easy, 38
Salade Niçoise - Easy, 41
Salmon Sauterne Mold - Favorite, 99
Shrimp and Crabmeat Mold Supreme - Menus, 63
Shrimp Rémoulade - Gourmet, 90
Sliced Tomatoes with Watercress Dressing - Menus, 32
Sour Cream Potato Salad - Gourmet, 89
Spinach Salad & Dressing - Favorite, 98
Spring Salad Buffet Molds - Favorite, 99
Stuffed Cherry Tomatoes - Easy, 37
Tangy Tomato-Avocado Aspic - Menus, 69
Tangy Tuna Mold - Epicurean, 69
Tart Burgundy Gelatin Salad - Adventures, 85
Tomato Aspic - Epicurean, 69
Tomato Aspic and Green Bean Salad - Menus, 92
Tomato Shrimp Appetizer, Green Goddess - Menus, 110
Tomato-Shrimp Aspic, Sherried - Adventures, 86
Tomatoes Rosé - Gourmet, 90
Toss-with-A-Flourish Red Wine Salad - Adventures, 88
Tuna Louis - Gourmet, 89
Two-Bean Salad - Menus, 89
Under-the-Sea Salad - Easy, 38
Varied Fruit Salad - Easy, 41
Vegetable Bouquet Salad - Menus, 74
Vegetable Consommé Molds - Menus, 82
Vegetable Kabobs - Menus, 75
Vegetable Salad Mold - Gourmet, 90
Vermicelli Salad - Menus, 64

Vintage Aspic - Favorite, 99
Warm or Cold Potato Salad - Adventures, 87
Wine Marinated Vegetables - Gourmet, 91
Zucchini and Tomato Salad - Menus, 84
Zucchini Vinaigrette - Gourmet, 90

SALAD DRESSINGS

Apricot Sherry Dressing - Gourmet, 93
Avocado Dressing Livermore - Favorite, 100
Blue Cheese Salad Dressing - Adventures, 88
Bohemian French Dressing - Menus, 70
Burgundy Salad Dressing - Adventures, 88
Canapé Dressing - Menus, 100
Continental Dressing - Menus, 118
Cosmopolitan Salad Dressing - Adventures, 88
De Luxe Parmesan Dressing - Favorite, 100
Dressing for Fruit Salad - Easy, 41
Favorite Salad Dressing - Gourmet, 94
French Dressing Aurora - Menus, 28
Fruit Dressing - Easy, 41
Fruit-Flavored Salad Dressing - Gourmet, 93
Fruit Salad Dressing - Epicurean, 70
Golden Dressing - Gourmet, 93
Gourmet Salad Dressing - Epicurean, 68
Hanna Fromm's Own Salad Dressing - Adventures, 88
Harlequin French Dressing - Menus, 54
Herb French Dressing - Menus, 21
Homemade Mayonnaise - Easy, 40
Honey Wine Dressing - Gourmet, 93
Lemon Cream Mayonnaise - Menus, 116
Linden Dressing - Menus, 48
Louis Dressing - Favorite, 97
Louis Dressing - Menus, 63
Lorraine Dressing - Menus, 83
Mushroom French Dressing - Menus, 84
Mustard Mayonnaise - Menus, 67
Pimiento Cheese Salad Dressing - Gourmet, 93
Poor Man's Salad Dressing - Favorite, 100
Poppy Seed Dressing - Menus, 47
Red Wine Salad Dressing - Adventures, 88
Riesling Salad Dressing - Favorite, 100
Rosé Fruit Salad Dressing - Gourmet, 91
Rosy Honey Dressing - Menus, 95
Seasoned Wine for Salad Dressing - Epicurean, 70
Sour Cream Dressing, Green Bean Salad - Menus, 80
Sour Cream Dressing, Jeanne's Chicken Mousse - Menus, 96
Tangy Blue Cheese Dressing - Favorite, 100
Tush Dressing - Favorite, 100
Vinaigrette Dressing - Menus, 94
Watercress Dressing - Menus, 32

SANDWICHES

Afternoon Refreshment - Favorite, 102
Avocado Club Sandwich - Adventures, 96
Baked Turkey Sandwiches - Adventures, 62
Buon Gusto Sandwiches - Favorite, 101
Chicken Liver Sandwich - Adventures, 25
Rolled Chicken Sandwiches - Adventures, 26
Sandwich Surprise - Favorite, 102
Sanger Style Steak Sandwiches - Adventures, 37
Turkey Nero Sandwiches - Gourmet, 61
Turkey on Rye - Gourmet, 62
Turkey Sandwiches Davis - Favorite, 101

SAUCES, BASTES & MARINADES

All Purpose Barbecue Sauce - Gourmet, 98
All-Purpose Sauce Amandine - Adventures, 116

Almond-Butter Sauce - Menus, 55
Applesauce - Favorite, 80
Avocado Sauce - Menus, 51
Barbecue Sauce - Adventures, 114
Barbecue Sauce - Easy, 35
Barbecued Poultry Pleaser - Favorite, 81
Basic Wine Sauce - Favorite, 80
Baste for Cornish Hens - Gourmet, 64
Beef or Veal Barbecue Sauce - Adventures, 33
Brown Gravy, Roast Prime Ribs of Beef - Menus, 108
Burgundy Basting Sauce - Gourmet, 97
Burgundy Wine Sauce - Adventures, 114
Buttery Mushroom Wine Sauce - Gourmet, 97
California Chutney - Adventures, 115
Canned Tomato Sauce - Adventures, 118
Caper-Sour Cream Sauce - Menus, 55
Cheese Sauce - Easy, 86
Chicken Barbecue Sauce - Easy, 35
Chicken Liver Pasta Sauce - Easy, 34
Clam Sauce Romano - Easy, 35
Clam Spaghetti Sauce - Gourmet, 75
Classic Cumberland Sauce - Favorite, 82
Cranberry Basting Sauce - Gourmet, 96
Cranberry-Rosé Ham Glaze - Adventures, 46
Cream Sauce, Cannelloni à la Emily - Menus, 75
Creamy Fish Sauce West Coast - Adventures, 117
Cucamonga Spaghetti Sauce - Favorite, 79
Cumberland Sauce - Easy, 63
Cumberland Sauce - Gourmet, 96
Currant Sauce Piquant, Roast Rack of Lamb - Menus, 104
Dressed-Up Canned Sauce - Gourmet, 83
Duck Giblet Broth - Menus, 49
Early Giblet Gravy - Adventures, 56
Easy All-Purpose Wine Sauce - Favorite, 80
Easy Mushroom Sauce - Gourmet, 97
Easy Seafood Cocktail Sauce - Adventures, 117
Easy Spaghetti Sauce - Easy, 33
Fiesta Fruit Sauce for Ham - Adventures, 115
Game Sauce - Easy, 34
Giblet Gravy, Roast Turkey - Menus, 119
Ginger-Vermouth Marinade - Favorite, 81
Glaze for Baked Ham - Gourmet, 50
Gold Coast Wine Sauce for Lamb - Adventures, 113
Gravy, Pot Roast - Menus, 17
Gravy, Cornish Game Hens - Menus, 115
Grilled Poultry Baste - Favorite, 120
Grilled Lamb Baste - Favorite, 120
Grilled Fish Baste - Favorite, 120
Ground Beef Gravy - Easy, 34
Ham Sauce - Easy, 33
Hollandaise Sauce - Gourmet, 83
Hunter's Sauce - Menus, 77
Hunter's Wine Sauce - Adventures, 117
Lemon-Butter Sauce - Menus, 107
Lemon-Chablis Fish Sauce - Favorite, 83
Marinade - Easy, 95
Marinating Chicken - Favorite, 120
Mayonnaise-Caper Sauce - Menus, 59
Meat Loaf Sauce - Favorite, 81
Mint Marinade for Lamb - Adventures, 116
Mushroom Sauce, Beef Mousse - Menus, 30
Mushroom Sauce, Chicken and Rice Torta - Menus, 83
Mushroom Sauce, Rolled Chicken Breasts - Menus, 121
Mustard Sauce - Menus, 90
My Favorite Spaghetti Sauce - Favorite, 80
Napa Valley Sauce Piquant - Adventures, 115
Nippy Wine-Cheese Sauce - Favorite, 21

No-Mix Barbecue Sauce - Favorite, 80
Orange Cranberry Sauce - Easy, 34
Pineapple Burgundy Sauce - Gourmet, 98
Port Sauce for Wild Duck - Adventures, 114
Prawn Marinade - Gourmet, 72
Quebec Sauce for Wild Duck - Adventures, 114
Quick Red Wine Sauce - Adventures, 115
Quick Rosé-Cheese Sauce - Favorite, 83
Quick Sherry Cheese Sauce - Gourmet, 97
Ravigote Sauce - Adventures, 117
Red Wine Sauce - Gourmet, 97
Red Wine Sauce - Menus, 26
Roy's Pineapple Glaze - Easy, 34
Santa Rosa Venison Marinade - Adventures, 116
Sauce Bearnaise - Adventures, 116
Sauce Bergère - Menus, 102
Sauce, Cod Auvergne - Easy, 59
Sauce, Copenhagen Meat Balls - Easy, 78
Sauce Diablo - Menus, 26
Sauce, Fisherman's Delight - Easy, 55
Sauce for Chicken - Gourmet, 58
Sauce, Hawaiian Meat Balls - Easy, 79
Sauce, Manicotti Healdsburg - Easy, 31
Sauce, Mexican Beef Pancakes - Menus, 35
Sherried Cream Sauce - Gourmet, 83
Sherried Raisin Sauce - Favorite, 82
Sherried White Sauce - Adventures, 118
Sherry Cherry Sauce - Gourmet, 97
Shrimp Cocktail Sauce - Favorite, 19
Shrimp Cocktail Sauce Davis - Adventures, 117
Simply A Must for Meats Baste - Adventures, 53
Sour Cream Hollandaise - Menus, 59
Spareribs Barbecue Sauce - Favorite, 82
Steak Sauce Bordelaise - Favorite, 82
Sweet-Sour Sauce (Chicken) - Easy, 97
Sweet-Sour Sauce (Quail) - Easy, 61
Turkey Barbecue Sauce - Favorite, 81
Universal B.B.Q. Wine Baste - Favorite, 79
Uncooked Wine Hollandaise - Favorite, 83
Vinaigrette Sauce - Adventures, 114
Vineyard Mushroom Sauce for Broiled Steak or Filet of Beef - Adventures, 113
White Sauce - Easy, 43
Wild Bird Marinade - Easy, 35
Wild Duck Barbecue Sauce - Favorite, 81
Wine and Herb Barbecue Sauce - Gourmet, 96
Wine Barbecue Sauce - Gourmet, 96
Wine Cheese Sauce - Adventures, 96
Wine Currant Basting Sauce - Gourmet, 96
Wine Horseradish Sauce - Gourmet, 95
Wineland Mustard Sauce - Adventures, 115

SOUFFLES

California Orange Soufflé - Adventures, 101
Cheese Soufflé Chablis - Favorite, 87
Chocolate Cloud Soufflé - Menus, 49
Easy Spinach Soufflé - Gourmet, 83
Mushroom Puff - Menus, 103
Potato Soufflé - Easy, 45
Sherry Crab Soufflé - Adventures, 79
Squash Soufflé - Adventures, 95
Spinach Ring - Menus, 45
Zucchini Soufflé Charlotte - Easy, 43

SOUPS
BEAN

Bean Soup Burgundy - Favorite, 31
Black Bean Soup - Easy, 26
Boomba Polivka Spanielska - Favorite, 27
Garbanzo Soup - Easy, 25
Kidney Bean Soup - Favorite, 31
Lentil Soup - Epicurean, 69
Quick Friday Minestrone - Favorite, 21
Sherried Black Bean Onion Soup - Gourmet, 31

CHEESE

Cheese and Bacon Soup - Gourmet, 28
Golden Cheese Soup - Favorite, 28
Sherried Cheese Soup - Gourmet, 32

CHICKEN

Bacchanale Chicken Soup - Favorite, 28
Charbonnet Soup Supreme - Epicurean, 67
Chicken Curry Soup - Gourmet, 30
Chicken in the Pot - Favorite, 56
Chicken Mushroom Soup Supreme - Gourmet, 30
Curried Chicken Soup - Favorite, 28
Hearty Cold Chicken Soup - Gourmet, 29

CONSOMME

Chinese Consommé - Adventures, 31
Consommé with Sherry - Gourmet, 32
Davis Consommé - Easy, 25
Mushroom Consommé Imperial - Menus, 108
Sherried Avocado Consommé - Gourmet, 31
Sherry and Broth - Easy, 26

EGG

Chinese Egg Flower Soup - Adventures, 31
Poached Egg Soup - Adventures, 29
Soup Ticinese - Adventures, 29

FRUIT

Rhubarb Wine Soup - Easy, 113
Another Cherry Soup - Easy, 26
Cherry Soup - Easy, 26
Chilled Cabernet-Cherry Soup - Favorite, 30
Pink Strawberry Soup - Epicurean, 68

GARNISH FOR SOUPS

Garnish for Soups - Adventures, 30
Garnish for Soups - Favorite, 32

MEAT

Fresno Borsch - Favorite, 29
International Minestrone - Favorite, 29
Mock Turtle Soup - Adventures, 29
Oxtail Soup St. Helena - Favorite, 31

SEAFOOD

Bay Cioppino - Adventures, 30
Bayou Seafood Gumbo - Gourmet, 32
Chowder, From Canned Soups - Favorite, 120
Cioppino - Gourmet, 67
Cioppino alla Genovese - Adventures, 30
City Kitchen Chowder - Gourmet, 30
Corn and Seafood Chowder - Gourmet, 30
Corn-Clam Chowder Chablis - Favorite, 27
Crab Bisque - Easy, 24
Easy Lobster Bisque - Favorite, 26
Fisherman's Soup - Epicurean, 56

Fisherman's Wharf Special - Gourmet, 27
Frozen Cream of Clam Soup - Adventures, 118
Golden Gate Shrimp Soup - Favorite, 26
Golden State Seafood Soup - Adventures, 31
Happy Clam Chowder - Menus, 97
Maryland Turtle Soup - Favorite, 27
Napa Oyster Bisque - Favorite, 25
Neapolitan Clam Soup - Adventures, 28
Quick Clam Bisque - Gourmet, 31
Rosy Shrimp Chowder - Gourmet, 27
Sherried Clam Soup - Gourmet, 31
Sherried Crab Soup - Favorite, 26
Shrimp Supper Soup - Menus, 97
Sunday Night Shrimp-Crab Soup - Gourmet, 30
Vintage-of-the-Sea Chowder - Favorite, 27
West Coast Bouillabaisse - Favorite, 26
Willipa Oyster Stew - Menus, 97

VEGETABLE

Avocado Soup - Easy, 25
Black Bean Soup - Easy, 26
Borsch Burgundy - Gourmet, 31
California Green Pea Soup - Gourmet, 28
Celery-Mushroom Bisque - Easy, 24
Classic French Onion - Favorite, 28
Cold Los Gatos Tomato Soup - Adventures, 31
Cream of Fresh Mushroom - Favorite, 25
Cream of Mushroom Soup with Sherry - Epicurean, 70
Creamy Corn Chowder - Favorite, 28
Cuke Soup - Favorite, 30
Fresno Borsch - Favorite, 29
Garbanzo Soup - Easy, 25
Gazpacho - Favorite, 30
Hasty Minestrone - Easy, 25
Hot-Day Cold Soup - Favorite, 30
Iced Borsch - Adventures, 31
International Minestrone - Favorite, 29
Lentil Soup - Epicurean, 69
Mushroom-Asparagus Soup Parmesan - Gourmet, 31
Mushroom Cream Soup - Epicurean, 67
Onion Soup Antonette - Easy, 26
Onion Soup Goorigian - Easy, 26
Onion Soup Sauterne - Gourmet, 29
Potage Boula - Gourmet, 29
Potato Soup with Sauterne - Gourmet, 28
Quick Friday Minestrone - Favorite, 29
Quick Gourmet Soup (Pea) - Favorite, 31
Quick Minestrone with Wine - Gourmet, 29
Quick Onion Soup - Easy, 25
Sherried Black Bean Onion Soup - Gourmet, 31
Spanish Green Pea Soup - Gourmet, 28
Speedy Vegetable Soup - Favorite, 29
Tomato Juice Soup - Favorite, 30
Winemaker's Soup - Adventures, 29
Valley Vegetable Cream Soup - Favorite, 32
Vegetable Soup - Easy, 26
Vichyssoise - Epicurean, 68
Vintage Tomato Bouillon - Adventures, 28

STEWS

Barbara's Beef Stew - Easy, 76
Beef Burgundy - Epicurean, 18
Beef Stew Burgundy - Favorite, 33
Beef Stew Filice - Easy, 80
Bourbonnais Beef Stew - Easy, 80
Burgundy Venison Stew - Adventures, 66
California Beef Stew - Gourmet, 36
Canned Beef Stew - Favorite, 33, 120

Curried Veal Stew - Menus, 18
Easy Baked Stew - Favorite, 34
Easy-Do Beef Stew - Menus, 13
Fisherman's Stew - Adventures, 70
Five Hour Stew - Easy, 81
Giblet Stew - Easy, 106
Golfer's Beef Stew - Easy, 65
Janey's Stew - Easy, 75
Jiffy Beef Stew - Adventures, 118
Lamb Stew Santa Clara - Favorite, 49
Lazy Stew - Menus, 15
Mexican Beef and Bean Stew - Menus, 12
Oxtail Stew with Red Wine - Favorite, 53
Oyster Stew and White Wine - Gourmet, 72
Rump Roast Stew - Easy, 76
Sanger Stew - Easy, 75
Savona Tripe Stew - Adventures, 55
Savory Soup Stew - Gourmet, 36
Savory Stew - Easy, 75
Simple Lamb Stew - Easy, 92
Sonoma Venison Stew - Favorite, 66
Stew à la Grecque - Menus, 14
Stew Rosé - Easy, 74
Stew with Polenta - Favorite, 34
20-Minute Venison Stew - Adventures, 65
Veal Stew - Easy, 86
Venison Stew Kukolsky - Favorite, 65
Vintner's Stew - Favorite, 34
Willipa Oyster Stew - Menus, 97

STUFFINGS AND DRESSINGS

Celery Stuffing, Meat Loaf - Menus, 31
Chestnut Turkey Stuffing - Favorite, 63
Grape Stuffing, Roast Rock Cornish Game Hens - Menus, 115
Hickory Hill Stuffing, Turkey - Menus, 119
Mushroom Stuffing, Rolled Chicken Breasts - Menus, 120
Raisin Turkey Stuffing - Favorite, 64
Rice Dressing for Turkey - Easy, 28
San Francisco Turkey Dressing - Adventures, 62
Turkey Stuffing Muy Bueno - Favorite, 64
Wild Rice Stuffing - Favorite, 62

VEGETABLES

Ada's Zucchini Pudding - Menus, 43
Artichoke & Shrimp Casserole - Epicurean, 48
Artichoke Bottoms Filled with Creamed Spinach - Menus, 105
Artichoke Hearts and Mushrooms - Menus, 29
Artichoke Hearts & Mushrooms Tarragon - Menus, 52
Artichoke Hearts in Wine - Epicurean, 64
Artichokes à l'Italienne - Easy, 48
Artichokes California - Easy, 46
Artichokes in White Wine - Adventures, 90
Artichokes Gourmet - Adventures, 90
Artichokes Sauterne - Easy, 47
Artichoke Shrimp au Gratin - Easy, 48
Asparagus or Broccoli with Lemon-Butter Sauce - Menus, 107
Asparagus with Wine Sauce - Gourmet, 83
Bacchanalian Brussels Sprouts - Favorite, 91
Baclazana - Adventures, 93
Baked Broccoli and Onions - Gourmet, 81
Baked Carrots in Wine - Easy, 42
Baked Celery - Easy, 42
Baked Eggplant Ring - Menus, 61
Baked Kidney Beans - Easy, 45

Baked Mushrooms - Easy, 44
Baked Mushrooms Contra Costa - Favorite, 95
Baked Peaches (garnish) - Menus, 90
Baked Potatoes Caliente - Menus, 17
Baked Spinach-Topped Tomatoes - Menus, 16
Baked Tomatoes au Gratin - Menus, 51
Bartlett Spuds - Adventures, 94
Bear Mountain Zucchini - Epicurean, 61
Beets Burgundian - Favorite, 93
Brandied Carrots - Easy, 47
Brandied Yams - Easy, 44
Broccoli Crown - Epicurean, 63
Broccoli in Sherry-Almond Sauce - Favorite, 96
Broccoli or Spinach Tart - Menus, 42
Broccoli Polonaise - Menus, 10
Broiled Mushroom Caps - Easy, 49
Broiled Sherried Tomatoes - Favorite, 90
Broiled Tomatoes with Sherry - Gourmet, 83
Buffet Baked Beans - Gourmet, 80
Burgundy Beans - Easy, 43
Butter-Baked Mushrooms - Menus, 111
Buttered Carrots with Celery - Menus, 44
California Fried Tomatoes - Favorite, 90
Candied Sweet Potatoes - Easy, 43
Canned Sauerkraut (Chinese) - Favorite, 95
Carrots in Dilled Wine Sauce - Gourmet, 84
Carrots in Sherry - Favorite, 90
Carrots with Sauterne - Favorite, 90
Cauliflower in Wine - Adventures, 90
Cauliflower Santa Rosa - Favorite, 91
Celery Hearts Parmesan - Menus, 109
Celery Root Ring Mold - Adventures, 93
Cheesey Mashed Potatoes - Menus, 27
Chestnuts and Beans Semione - Adventures, 91
Chili Beans Burgundy - Adventures, 89
Chili Beans Diego (main dish) - Menus, 78
Chili Garbanzos - Gourmet, 80
Chinese String Beans - Easy, 44
Company Onions - Favorite, 94
Confetti Carrots - Adventures, 91
Corn-Stuffed Zucchini - Menus, 40
Creamed Chestnuts or Mushrooms - Menus, 119
Creamed Onions and Peas - Gourmet, 82
Creamed Sherry Spinach - Favorite, 92
Creamy Sauterne Cabbage - Gourmet, 84
Creamy Vegetables with Shrimp - Gourmet, 80
Creole Eggplant-Meat Casserole - Adventures, 95
Crumb Crust Potatoes - Menus, 59
Crusty Potato Cheese Casserole - Gourmet, 73
Don's Favorite Beans - Favorite, 93
Easy Gourmet Green Beans - Adventures, 92
Easy Spinach Soufflé - Gourmet, 83
Eggplant Armenian - Menus, 22
Eggplant Parmigiana - Epicurean, 62
Eggplant Tokay - Adventures, 93
Eggplant-Zucchini Casserole - Adventures, 95
Elegant Carrots - Gourmet, 82
Festival Sweet Potatoes - Favorite, 96
French Peas - Menus, 41
Fresh Broccoli with Cream Cheese Sauce - Epicurean, 62
Fricassee of Mushrooms - Favorite, 95
Fried Sherry-Cheese Onions - Adventures, 94
Fruited Yams with Sherry - Gourmet, 81
Garbanzos in White Wine - Favorite, 92
Glazed Celery San Joaquin - Favorite, 91
Glazed Onions - Gourmet, 82
Glorified Zucchini - Favorite, 92
Green Beans Française - Epicurean, 65
Green Bean Fritatta - Adventures, 92

Green Beans in Cheese Sauce - Gourmet, 83
Green Beans Piquant - Menus, 61
Green Beans with A Flourish - Adventures, 91
Green Beans with Bacon - Menus, 39
Green Beans with Pine Nuts - Menus, 11
Green Onion Tart - Menus, 109
Green Peas Gourmet - Favorite, 93
Green Peppers Florentine - Epicurean, 64
Happy Carrots - Easy, 47
Harvard Beets Burgundy - Gourmet, 79
Holiday Cabbage with Red Wine - Adventures, 90
Jerusalem Artichokes - Favorite, 94
Le Celeri à la Eschscholtzia - Epicurean, 63
Leeks Country Style - Favorite, 94
Leeks Poached in Sauterne - Favorite, 94
Lima Bean Casserole - Easy, 45
Lodi Cardoni - Adventures, 92
Madeira Onion Rings - Epicurean, 64
Mimi's Succotash - Menus, 19
Modesto Potatoes - Favorite, 89
Moussaka Tsapralis - Epicurean, 58
Mushroom Puff - Menus, 103
Mushrooms and Artichokes - Easy, 46
Mushrooms Bourguignon - Favorite, 95
Mushrooms Del Bondio - Easy, 47
Mushrooms Delicious - Adventures, 90
Mushrooms Newburg - Favorite, 95
Mushrooms Riddell - Easy, 46
Panned Carrots with Mushrooms - Menus, 34
Parmesan Potato Sticks - Menus, 58
Pattypan Squash with Peas - Menus, 60
Peas Continental - Adventures, 89
Peas with Carrots - Menus, 18
Peas with Mushrooms - Menus, 49
Pickled Artichokes - Easy, 44
Porte Maillot Vegetables - Adventures, 93
Ported Beans - Gourmet, 80
Potato Parmesan - Gourmet, 81
Potatoes in Wine - Easy, 45
Potato Soufflé - Easy, 45
Potatoes Magnifique - Adventures, 94
Quick Green Beans Sauterne - Adventures, 91
Red Cabbage and Rice - Gourmet, 84
Red Cabbage Etiwanda - Favorite, 91
Sauerkraut à la Vermouth - Adventures, 96
Sauerkraut in Wine - Adventures, 96
Scalloped Onions - Epicurean, 61
Sherried Beans with Coffee - Gourmet, 80
Sherried Corn Lucullus - Favorite, 89
Sherried Green Beans - Adventures, 92
Sherried Picnic Beans - Gourmet, 81
Sherried String Beans - Epicurean, 63
Sherried Winter Squash - Favorite, 91
Sherry Sweet Potatoes - Adventures, 94
Special Mashed Potatoes - Menus, 19
Spiced Pineapple - Easy, 43
Spinach Mousse Ring - Menus, 119
Spinach Ring - Menus, 45
Spinach with Mushrooms - Menus, 38
Spinach with Onion Crunch - Menus, 69
Spinach with Sour Cream - Gourmet, 84
Spring Asparagus Rose - Favorite, 96
Spring Squash in Wine - Favorite, 92
Squash Soufflé - Adventures, 95
Squash with Mushrooms - Adventures, 95
Stewed Mushrooms - Easy, 47
Stuffed Potatoes au Gratin - Menus, 57
Stuffed Zucchini Sharon - Easy, 49
Summer Squash Cups with Peas - Menus, 117

Surprise Sweet Potatoes - Adventures, 94
Tomato Pork Kidney Beans - Easy, 46
Vegetables Oriental - Easy, 49
Vegetable Supper Casserole - Gourmet, 81
Vegetables Sunnyvale - Easy, 47
Vintner's Beans - Favorite, 93
Vintner's Brussels Sprouts in White Wine - Gourmet, 79
Vintner's Surprise - Adventures, 93
Wine-Glazed Carrots - Favorite, 90
Wine Marinated Artichokes - Gourmet, 82
Zinfandel Chili Beans - Easy, 44
Zucchini and Corn Sauté - Menus, 58
Zucchini Cucamonga - Easy, 45
Zucchini Montevidean Style - Adventures, 91
Zucchini Pancakes - Easy, 48
Zucchini Parmesan - Menus, 26
Zucchini Sauté - Menus, 12
Zucchini Soufflé Charlotte - Easy, 43
Zucchini with Ground Beef - Easy, 48
Zucchini with Peas - Menus, 81

WILD GAME

BOAR

Wild Boar Barbecue - Easy, 60
Wild Boar, Larkmead - Epicurean, 22

DOVE

Baked Dove Bonanza - Favorite, 68
Smothered Doves - Favorite, 67
Western Dove Dinner - Favorite, 67

DUCK

Barbecued Wild Duck - Adventures, 68
Duck au Vin - Favorite, 64
Duckling with Pineapple - Adventures, 64
Duck with Cherry Sauce - Menus, 49
Grape-Stuffed Wild Duck - Adventures, 67
Oven-Barbecued Duck - Easy, 62
Roast Duck au Naturel - Easy, 62
Roast Duckling Vermouth - Adventures, 63
Roast Duckling with Orange Sauce - Gourmet, 64
Roast Wild Duck - Gourmet, 63
Sacramento Skillet Duck - Gourmet, 63
Stuffed Wild Ducks - Epicurean, 33
Wild Duck Poached in Wine Sauce - Adventures, 67

GOOSE

Breast of Wild Goose - Favorite, 68
Roast Goose - Favorite, 64

GUINEA HEN

Guinea Hen in White Wine - Adventures, 66

PHEASANT

Blossom Hill Pheasant - Epicurean, 41
Braised Pheasant - Easy, 64
Fasan mit Ananas Kraut - Easy, 64
Mandarin Pheasant - Epicurean, 41
Pheasant au Vin - Favorite, 66
Pheasant in Sauce - Gourmet, 64

Pheasant Jubilee - Favorite, 67
Pheasant Katula - Easy, 63
Pheasant Provencal - Easy, 64
Pheasant Surprise - Epicurean, 40
Pheasant with Brandy and Cream - Adventures, 68
Pheasant with Mushrooms - Favorite, 67
Roast Pheasant - Adventures, 66
Roast Pheasant Vermouth - Adventures, 65
Roast Stuffed Pheasant - Epicurean, 42
Sherried Roast Pheasant - Adventures, 68

QUAIL

Quail and Vegetable Sauce - Easy, 60
Quail Carolina - Adventures, 67
Sweet and Sour Quail - Easy, 61
Wild Birds over Rice - Easy, 61

RABBIT

Barbecued Rabbit Selma - Favorite, 68
Burgundy Baked Rabbit - Favorite, 68
Hasenpfeffer - Easy, 61
Rabbit à la Borghese - Epicurean, 28
Rabbit Casserole - Easy, 62
Rabbit in White Wine - Adventures, 69
Rabbit Stew - Easy, 63
Rabbit Sweet and Sour - Adventures, 69
Roast Brace of Rabbit - Adventures, 69
Rosemary Rabbit - Adventures, 69

VENISON

Burgundy Venison Stew - Adventures, 66
Roast Saddle of Venison - Favorite, 65
Roast Venison - Easy, 63
Savory Venison - Adventures, 67
Sonoma Venison Stew - Favorite, 66
20-Minute Venison Stew - Adventures, 65
Venison Casserole - Easy, 64
Venison Chops Cumberland - Easy, 62
Venison Mt. Madonna - Favorite, 66
Venison Spareribs - Adventures, 66
Venison Steaks à la Tedeschi - Favorite, 65
Venison Stew Kukolsky - Favorite, 65
Venison Swiss Steak - Favorite, 66
Wild Game Pot Roast - Adventures, 66

WINE COOKING NOTES

WINE COOKING NOTES

WINE COOKING NOTES

WINE COOKING NOTES

WINE COOKING NOTES

WINE COOKING NOTES

WINE COOKING NOTES

WINE COOKING NOTES

WINE COOKING NOTES

The Wine Advisory Board Cookbooks
"The Classic Series on Cooking With Wine"

This series of six wine cookbooks is the largest collection of cooking with wine recipes available in the World. There is no duplication of features or recipes in the Wine Advisory Board Cookbooks. Specific wine types are recommended as table beverages for all main dishes. The present series represents over 2,800 different recipes of all types using wine. From wine cocktails, hors d'oeuvres, salads, soups, wild game, fish, eggs, many different main dishes to desserts and jellies; the magnitude of this collection of wine recipes is overwhelming. Who could possibly develop and test such a large number of recipes? These books are the result of the cooperation of over 400 people in the wine industry. In 1961 the Wine Advisory Board began collecting the favorite and best recipes of the various winemakers and their families. Most of the recipes are old family favorites, tested with time and then re-tested and proven in Wine Advisory Board test kitchens. We are particularly pleased with the recipes and wine choices from staff members of the Department of Viticulture and Enology and the Department of Food Science and Technology of University of California, Davis and Fresno.

So here is a series of the very best wine recipes; selected and developed by many of the most knowledgeable wine and food lovers of America.

#500 EPICUREAN RECIPES OF CALIFORNIA WINEMAKERS: Did you know that you can buy wild boar, cook it at home with Burgundy and produce a gourmet treat that your guests will rave about for years? Or, that you can make your reputation as an Epicurean cook by preparing and serving Boeuf ala Bourguignonne, according to the recipe of a famous wine authority? This book includes the most elaborate to simple recipes contributed by California Winemakers, their wives and associates; all selected for their unforgetable taste experiences. Another important feature of this book is it includes the comprehensive index of recipes for the entire six cookbook series. 128 pp, 8½" x 11", illustrated, 1978 Edition. $5.95@ ISBN 0-932664-00-8

#501 GOURMET WINE COOKING THE EASY WAY: All new recipes for memorable eating, prepared quickly and simply with wine. Most of the recipes specify convenience foods which can be delightfully flavored with wine, enabling the busy homemaker to set a gourmet table for family and friends with a minimum of time in the kitchen. More than 500 tested and proven recipes; used frequently by the first families of America's wine industry. 128pp, 8½" x 11", illustrated, 1978 edition. $4.95@ ISBN 0-932664-01-6

#502 ADVENTURES IN WINE COOKERY BY CALIFORNIA WINEMAKERS: The life work of the winemaker is to guide nature in the development in wine of beauty, aroma, bouquet and subtle flavors. Wine is part of their daily diet, leading to more flavorful dishes, comfortable living, merriment and goodfellowship. These recipes contributed by Winemakers, their families and colleagues represent this spirit of flavorful good living. A best selling cookbook with 500 exciting recipes including barbecue, wine drinks, salads and sauces. 128pp, illustrated 8½" x 11". $4.95@ ISBN 0-932664-02-4

#503 FAVORITE RECIPES OF CALIFORNIA WINEMAKERS: The original winemakers' cookbook and a best-seller for fifteen years. Over 200 dedicated winemakers, their wives and colleagues have shared with us their love of cooking. They are the authors of this book, which is dedicated to a simple truth known for thousands of years in countless countries: good food is even better with wine. Over 500 authentic recipes, many used for generations, are included in this "cookbook classic". 128pp, 8½" x 11", illustrated. $4.95@ ISBN 0-932664-03-2

#504 WINE COOKBOOK OF DINNER MENUS by Emily Chase and Wine Advisory Board. Over 100 complete dinner menus with recommended complimentary wines. This book will make your dinner planning easy and the results impressive to your family and most sophisticated guests. Emily Chase worked with the winemakers of California a number of years and was also the Home Economics Editor of Sunset Magazine. She tested recipes for six years and is the author of numerous articles and books on cooking. This edition contains 400 different recipes, suggestions for wines to accompany dinners and tips on serving, storing and enjoying wine. 128pp, illustrated, 8½" x 11", 1978 edition $4.95@ ISBN 0-932664-04-0

#505 EASY RECIPES OF CALIFORNIA WINE-MAKERS: "I wonder often what vintners buy one-half so precious as the stuff they sell" questioned Omar Khayyam 1100 A.D. We wonder what the vintners could possibly eat one-half so delicious as the food they prepare. This is a collection of "precious" recipes that are easy to prepare and each includes the vintners favorite beverage. Many are recipes concocted in the vintners kitchens and some are family favorites proven for their flavor and ease of preparation. No duplication with the other cookbooks. 128pp, Illustrated 8½" x 11" $4.95@ ISBN 0-932664-05-9

Each book includes its own index; however, **EPICUREAN RECIPES** includes a comprehensive index for the entire series, as well. These books are available at bookstores, wine shops and wineries. If you have trouble finding them, they may be ordered direct from The Wine Appreciation Guild. Also, most other wine books and wine related items are available.

HOW TO ORDER BY MAIL: Indicate the number of copies and titles you wish on the order form below and include your check, money order, or MasterCharge, or VISA card number. California residents include 6% sales tax. There is a $1.00 shipping and handling charge per order, regardless of how many books you order. (If no order form—any paper will do.) Orders shipped promptly via U.S. Mail—U.S. & Canada shipments ONLY.

ORDER FORM
WINE APPRECIATION GUILD
1377 Ninth Avenue
San Francisco, California 94122

SHIP TO: _____

Address _____ City _____ State _____ Zip _____

Please send the following:

_____ Copies, #500 EPICUREAN RECIPES OF CALIFORNIA WINEMAKERS, $5.95@ _____
_____ Copies, #501 GOURMET WINE COOKING THE EASY WAY, $4.95@ _____
_____ Copies, #502 ADVENTURES IN WINE COOKERY, $4.95@ _____
_____ Copies, #503 FAVORITE RECIPES OF CALIFORNIA WINEMAKERS, $4.95@ _____
_____ Copies, #504 WINE COOKBOOK OF DINNER MENUS, $4.95@ _____
_____ Copies, #505 EASY RECIPES OF CALIFORNIA WINEMAKERS, $4.95@ _____
Subtotal _____
California Residents 6% sales tax _____
Plus $1.00 Shipping and handling (per order) $1.00
TOTAL enclosed or charged to credit card _____

Please charge to my Mastercharge ____ or VISA card # _____

Expiration Date _____ Signature _____